D1091080

5

STATE PAPERS ON NULLIFICATION

Da Capo Press Reprints in

AMERICAN CONSTITUTIONAL AND LEGAL HISTORY

GENERAL EDITOR: LEONARD W. LEVY
Brandeis University

STATE PAPERS ON
NULLIFICATION

Including

The Public Acts of the Convention of the
People of South Carolina (1832-33)

The Proclamation of the President
of the United States

The Proceedings of the Several State
Legislatures Which Have Acted on the Subject

DA CAPO PRESS • NEW YORK • 1970

A Da Capo Press Reprint Edition

This Da Capo Press edition of
State Papers on Nullification
is an unabridged republication of the
first edition published in Boston in 1834.

Library of Congress Catalog Card Number 69-16649

SBN 306-71126-5

Published by Da Capo Press
A Division of Plenum Publishing Corporation
227 West 17th Street
New York, N. Y. 10011
All Rights Reserved

Manufactured in the United States of America

STATE PAPERS

ON

NULLIFICATION:

INCLUDING THE PUBLIC ACTS OF THE

CONVENTION OF THE PEOPLE

OF

SOUTH CAROLINA,

ASSEMBLED AT

COLUMBIA, NOVEMBER 19, 1832 AND MARCH 11, 1833;

THE

PROCLAMATION

OF THE

President of the United States,

AND THE

PROCEEDINGS OF THE SEVERAL STATE LEGISLATURES

WHICH HAVE ACTED ON THE SUBJECT.

———

BY ORDER OF THE GENERAL COURT OF MASSACHUSETTS,

Under the direction of the Committee on the Library.

———

Boston:

DUTTON AND WENTWORTH, PRINTERS TO THE STATE.

1834.

Commonwealth of Massachusetts.

HOUSE OF REPRESENTATIVES, MARCH 26, 1833.

Ordered, That the Joint Committee on the Library be instructed to collect the documents received from the State of South
Carolina on the subject of Nullification, the Proclamation of the
President of the United States, and the communications from
the several States in relation thereto, and to cause the same to
be printed and bound, for the use of the members of this Legislature.

Sent up for concurrence.

L. S. CUSHING, *Clerk.*

IN SENATE, MARCH 26, 1833

Concurred.

CHA'S. CALHOUN, *Clerk.*

TABLE OF CONTENTS.

In the following table, the titles of all the papers comprehended in the volume, a few of which were received too late to be inserted in their proper places, are arranged in the natural order of the subjects, with references to the pages at which they respectively appear.

---

vii

REPORT.

The Committee to whom was referred "the Act to provide for the calling of a Convention of the people of this State," with instructions "to consider and report thereon, and especially as to the measures proper to be adopted by the Convention, in reference to the violations of the Constitution of the United States, in the enactment by Congress on divers occasions of laws laying duties and imposts for the purpose of encouraging and protecting domestic manufactures, and for other unwarrantable purposes," beg leave respectfully to submit the following

REPORT :

The Committee deeply impressed with the importance of the questions submitted to them, and the weight of responsibility involved in their decision, have given to the subject their most deliberate and anxious consideration. In stating the conclusions to which they have arrived, they feel that it is due to themselves, to this Convention, and to the public at large, briefly to review the history of the Protecting system in this country, to show its origin, to trace its progress, to examine its character, point out ts evils, and suggest the appropriate remedy. They propose to execute this task with all possible brevity and simplicity, sensible that the subject is too well understood in all its bearings to require at this time a very elaborate investigation.

In the natural course of human affairs, the period would have been very remote when the people of the United States would have engaged in manufactures, but for the restrictions upon our commerce, which grew out of the war between Great Britain and France, and which led to the non-intercourse act, the embargo, and finally our own war of 1812. Cut off by these events from a free commercial intercourse with the rest of the world, the people of the United States turned their attention to manufactures, and on the restoration of peace in 1815, an amount of capital had been already invested in these establishments, which made a strong appeal to the liberality, we might almost say to the justice of the country, for protection, at least against that sudden influx of foreign goods, which it was feared would entirely overwhelm these domestic establishments. When therefore in 1816 it became necessary that the Revenue should be brought down to the peace establishment, by a reduction of the duties upon imports, it was almost by common consent conceded to the claims of the manufacturers, that this reduction should be gradual, and three years were accordingly allowed for bringing down the duties to the permanent revenue standard, which (embracing all the ordinary expenses of the government, with liberal appropriations for the Navy and the Army, an extensive system of fortifications, and the gradual extinction of the public debt, then amounting to $130,000,000,) was fixed at 20 per cent. If the manufacturers had at that time even hinted that permanent protection was deemed indispensable to their success,—if the slightest suspicion had been entertained that instead of the gradual reduction expressly provided for by the act of 1816, there would be claimed a gradual increase of the protecting duties, and that instead of being brought down in three years to 20 per cent., the duties were to be carried up to 50 or 100 per cent., and in many cases to prohibition,—the painful contest in which the country has been engaged for the last ten years on this subject would have commenced immediately, and it is confidently believed that in the temper of the public mind at that time, ample security would have been found against the introduction of such a system. But in defiance of the clear understanding of the whole country, and in violation of the principles of justice and of good faith, that part of the act above-mentioned which required that the duties should be reduced in three years to 20 per cent., was repealed, and a broad foundation thus laid for the permanent establishment of the protecting system. This system has been still further extended and fortified by the several successive acts of 1820, 1824, and 1828, until by the passing of the act of 1832, (to take effect after the discharge of the public debt,) it has become incorporated into our political system, as the "SETTLED POLICY OF THE COUNTRY." We have not deemed it necessary, in tracing the origin and progress of this system, to go further back than the commercial restrictions which preceded the late war ;—for whatever theoretical opinions may have been expressed by Alexander Hamilton and others in relation to it, at an earlier period, it cannot be denied that no duties were actually imposed beyond those deemed indispensable for the public exigencies, and that prior to the year 1816, no protection whatever was actually extended to manufactures, beyond what was strictly incidental to a system for revenue. The discrimination between the protected and unprotected articles now contended for as the very corner stone of the protecting system, was so far from being established by that act, that the highest duties were actually imposed on the very articles now admitted duty free, while the foreign manufactures which came into competition with our domestic fabrics were subjected to a lower rate of duty. The truth then unquestionably is, that the protecting policy, according to the principles now contended for, was never introduced into this country until the period we have mentioned, when it crept insidiously into the legislation of Congress in the manner above described. This will be made abundantly manifest to every one who will take the pains to trace the progress of the duties from $7\frac{1}{2}$ per cent., in 1790, up to 25 per cent., in 1816, 40 per cent., in 1824, and 50, 60, and even 100 per cent., in 1828 and 1832, and who will merely examine the manner in which these duties were adjusted in the various acts here referred to. As early as 1820, so soon indeed as the capitalists who had relied upon the powers of the Federal Government to enhance the profits of their investments by legislation, began to look forward to its eventful establishment as the settled policy of the country, they clearly perceived that an extension of the appropriations to objects not embraced in the specific grants of the Federal constitution, was the necessary appendage of their system. They well knew that the people would not long submit to the levying of a large surplus revenue merely for the protection of manufactures, carried on almost exclusively in one quarter of the Union; and they therefore sought in the extension of the appropriations to new objects, for a plausible and popular excuse for the continuance of a system of high duties. With that instinctive sagacity, which belongs to men who convert the Legislature of a country into an instrument for the promotion of their own private ends, they clearly saw that the distribution of an enormous surplus treasure, would afford the surest means of bringing over the enemies of the American System to its support, and of enlisting in their cause not only large masses of the people, but entire States who had no direct interest in maintaining the protecting system, or who were even, in some respects, its victims. No scheme that the wit of man could possibly have devised, was better calculated for the accomplishment of this object. It proposed simply to reconcile men to an unjust system of national policy, by admitting them to a large share of the spoils;—in a word, to levy contributions by the aid of those who were to divide the plunder. If the United States had constituted one great nation, with a consolidated Government, occupying a territory of limited extent, inhabited by a people engaged in similar pursuits, and having homogeneous interests, such a system would only have operated as a tax upon all the other great interests of the State, for the benefit of that which was favored by the laws, and when time had been allowed for the adjustment of society to this new condition of its affairs, the final result must have been an aggregate diminution of the profits of the whole community, by diverting a portion of the people from their accustomed employments to less profitable pursuits. In such a case, the hope might perhaps have been indulged that experience would demonstrate the egregious folly of enacting laws, the only effect of which would be, to supply the wants of the community at an increased expense of labor and capital. But it is the distinguishing feature of the American System, and one which stamps upon it the character of peculiar and aggravated oppression, that it is made applicable to a Confederacy of twenty-four Sovereign and Independent States,—occupying a territory upwards of 2000 miles in extent,—embracing every variety of soil, climate, and productions,—inhabited by a people whose institutions and interests are in many respects diametrically opposed to each other,—with habits and pursuits infinitely diversified,—and in the great Southern section of the Union, rendered by local circumstances altogether incapable of change. Under such circumstances, a system, which under a consolidated Government would be merely impolitic, and so far, an act of injustice to the whole community, becomes in this country a scheme of the most intolerable oppression, because it may be, and has in fact been, so adjusted as to operate exclusively to the benefit of a particular interest, and of particular sections of country, rendering in effect the industry of one portion of the confederacy tributary to the rest. The laws have accordingly been so framed as to give a direct pecuniary interest to a sectional majority, in maintaining a grand system, by which taxes are in effect imposed upon the few, for the benefit of the many;—and imposed too, by a system of indirect taxation, so artfully contrived, as to escape the vigilance of the common eye, and masked under such ingenious devices as to make it extremely difficult to expose their true character. Thus under the pretext of imposing duties for the payment of the public debt, and providing for the common defence and general welfare, (powers expressly conferred on the Federal Government by the Constitution,) acts are passed containing provisions designed exclusively and avowedly for the purpose of securing to the American Manufacturers, a monopoly in our own markets, to the great and manifest prejudice of those who furnish the agricultural productions which are exchanged in foreign markets for the very articles which it is the avowed object of these laws to exclude. It so happens, that six of the Southern States, whose industry is almost exclusively agricultural, though embracing a population equal to only one third part of the whole Union, actually produce for exportation near 40,000,000 annually, being about two-thirds of the whole domestic exports of the United States. As it is their interest, so it is, unquestionably, their right, to carry these fruits of their own honest industry, to the best market, without any molestation, hindrance, or restraint, whatsoever, and

subject to no taxes, or other charges, but such as may be necessary for the payment of the reasonable expenses of the government. But how does this system operate upon our industry?
While imposts to the amount of 10 or 12 per cent., (if arranged
on just and equal principles) must be admitted to be fully adequate to all the legitimate purposes of Government, duties are
actually imposed (with a few inconsiderable exceptions) upon
all the Woollens, Cottons, Iron and Manufactures of Iron, Sugar,
and Salt, and almost every other article received in exchange for
the Cotton, Rice, and Tobacco of the South, equal on an average to about 50 per cent., whereby (in addition to the injurious
effects of this system in prohibiting some articles, and discouraging the introduction of others,) a tax equal to one-half of the
first cost is imposed upon the Cottons, Woollens, and Iron,
which are the fruits of Southern industry, in order to secure an
advantage in the home market, to their rivals the American
Manufacturers of similar articles, equivalent to one-half of their
value, thereby stimulating the industry of the North, and discouraging that of the South, by granting bounties to the one,
and imposing taxes upon the other.

The Committee deem it unnecessary to go into an elaborate
examination of the true character and sectional operation of the
protecting system. The subject has of late been so frequently
and thoroughly examined, and the bearing of the System been
so completely exposed, that the argument is exhausted. To the
people of the Southern States, there cannot be presented a more
touching or irresistible appeal, either to their understandings or
their hearts, than is found in the melancholy memorials of ruin
and decay which are every where visible around us,—memorials
proclaiming the fatal character of that system, which has brought
upon one of the finest portions of the globe, in the full vigor of
its early manhood, the poverty and desolation, which belong
only to the most sterile regions, or to the old age and decrepi-
tude of nations. The moral blight and pestilence of unwise
and partial legislation, has swept over our fields, with "the
besom of destruction." The proofs are every where around us.

It is in vain for any one to contend that this is a just and
equal system, or that the Northern States pay a full proportion
of the tax. If this were so, how is it to be accounted for, that

high duties are regarded in that quarter of the Union, not as a burden, but as a blessing?

How comes it that a people, certainly not unmindful of their interests, are seen courting the imposition of taxes, and crying out against any material reduction of the public burdens? Does not this extraordinary fact afford conclusive evidence that high duties operate as a bounty to Northern industry; and that whatever taxes the manufacturers may pay, as consumers, they are more than remunerated by the advantages they enjoy as producers?—or, in other words, that they actually receive more than they pay, and therefore cannot be justly said to be taxed at all? When, in addition to all this, we take into consideration that the amount of duties annually levied for the protection of manufactures, beyond the necessary wants of the Government, (which cannot be estimated at less than 10 or 12,000,000) is expended almost exclusively in the Northern portion of the Union, can it excite any surprise, that under the operation of the Protecting System, the manufacturing States should be constantly increasing in riches, and growing in strength, with an inhospitable climate and barren soil, while the Southern States, the natural garden of America, should be rapidly falling into decay? It is contrary to the general order of Providence, that any country should long bear up against a system, by which enormous contributions, raised in one quarter, are systematically expended in another. If the sixteen millions of dollars now annually levied in duties on the foreign goods received in exchange for Southern productions were allowed to remain in the pockets of the people, or by some just and equal system of appropriation could be restored to them, the condition of the plantation States would unquestionably be one of unexampled prosperity and happiness. Such was our condition under a system of free trade, and such would soon again be our enviable lot. Of the results which would thereby be produced, some faint conception may be formed by imagining what would be the effect upon the industry of the people of our own State, if the $8,000,000 of foreign goods now annually received in exchange for our productions, and paying duties to the amount of upwards of $3,000,000, could be obtained by us duty free, or the duties thus levied, were expended within our own limits. Is it not obvious that several millions per annum would thereby be added to the available industry of South Carolina? the effect of which would assuredly be, to change the entire face of affairs in this State, by enhancing the profits of the agriculturists, accumulating capital, giving a fresh impulse to commerce, and producing a vivifying influence upon every department of industry, the happy consequences of which would be experienced by every inhabitant of the State. We present this strong view of the subject, to shew the manifest justice of the claim which South Carolina now sets up to have this system of raising revenue by duties upon imports restricted within the narrowest limits, and to shew how utterly impossible it is for us to consent to have it extended beyond the indispensable wants of the government, either for the purpose of affording protection to the industry of others, or of distributing the proceeds among individuals or States.

Grievous, however, as the oppression unquestionably is, and calculated in the strong language of our own Legislature, "to reduce the Plantation States to POVERTY and UTTER DESOLATION," it is not in this aspect that the question is presented in its most dangerous and alarming form. It is not merely that Congress have resorted for unwarrantable purposes to an oppressive exercise of powers granted to them by the Constitution; but that they have usurped a power not granted, and have justified that usurpation on principles, which, if sanctioned or submitted to, must entirely change the character of the Government, reduce the Constitution to a dead letter, and on the ruins of our confederated republic, erect a consolidated despotism, " without limitation of powers." If this be so, there is no man who is worthy of the precious heritage of liberty derived from our ancestors, or who values the free institutions of his country, who must not tremble for the cause of freedom, not only in this country, but throughout the world, unless the most prompt and efficient measures are at once adopted, to arrest the downward course of our political affairs, to stay the hand of oppression, to restore the Constitution to its original principles, and thereby to perpetuate the Union.

It cannot be denied that the Government of the United States possesses no inherent powers. It was called into being by the

States. The States not only created it, but conferred upon it all its powers, and prescribed its limits by a written charter called the Constitution of the United States. Before the Federal Government had thus been called into being, the several States unquestionably possessed as full sovereignty, and were as independent of each other as the most powerful nations of the world; and in the free and undisputed exercise of that sovereignty, they entered into a solemn compact with each other, by which it was provided, that for certain specified objects, a General Government should be established with strictly limited powers;—the several States retaining their sovereignty unimpaired, and continuing to exercise all powers not expressly granted to the Federal Government.

In the clear and emphatic language of Mr. Jefferson, "the several States composing the United States of America, are not united on the principle of unlimited submission to the General Government, but by a compact under the style and title of the Constitution of the United States, they constituted a General Government for special purposes, delegated to that Government certain definite powers, reserving each State to itself the residuary mass of right to their own self-government, and whensoever the General Government assumes undelegated powers, its acts are unauthoritative, void, and of no force."* That such is the true nature of the Federal compact, cannot admit of a reasonable doubt, and it follows of necessity, that the Federal Government is merely a joint agency, created by the States,— that it can exert no power not expressly granted by them, and that when it claims any power, it must be able to refer to the clause in the charter which confers it. This view of the Constitution of the United States, brings the question of the constitutionality of the Tariff within the narrowest limits.

The regulation of domestic industry, so far as Government may rightfully interfere therewith, belonged to the several States before the Constitution was adopted, or the Union sprang into existence; and it still remains exclusively with them, unless it has has been expressly granted to the Federal Government. If such a grant has been made, it is incumbent on those claiming,

*See Kentucky Resolutions of 1778.

under it, to point out the provision in the Constitution which embraces it. It must be admitted that there is not a clause or article in that instrument, which has the slightest allusion either to manufactures or to agriculture : while, therefore, the "regulation of commerce" is expressly conferred on the General Government, the regulation of every branch of domestic industry is reserved to the several States, exclusively, who may afford them encouragement, by pecuniary bounties, and by all the other means, not inconsistent with the Constitution of the United States. To say that the power to regulate commerce embraces the regulation of agriculture, and manufactures, and all other pursuits of industry, (for they all stand upon the same footing,) is to confound the plainest distinctions, and to lose sight of the true meaning and intent of the grant in question. Commerce is, in general, regulated by treaties with foreign nations ; and, therefore, it was deemed necessary that this power should be confided to the General Government : but agriculture, manufactures, and the mechanic arts, can only be wisely ordered by municipal regulation. Commerce is one object of legislation, manufactures another, agriculture a third ; and if the regulation of commerce implies an unlimited control over every thing which constitutes the object of commerce, it would follow, as a matter of course, that the Federal Government may exert a supreme dominion over the whole labor and capital of the country. This would transform our confederated Government, with strictly limited powers, into an absolute despotism, and of the worst sort, where, under the forms of a free Government, we should have the spirit of a despotic one. This view of the subject, we should deem perfectly conclusive, even if it could not be shewn that the power in question, so far from being granted, was purposely withheld from the Federal Government, by the framers of the Constitution ; and that there are provisions of the Constitution, from which it may be fairly inferred, that it was intended to be reserved to the States respectively. It appears from the history of the proceedings of the Convention which framed the Constitution, that the subject of the protection of manufactures, was several times brought distinctly to the view of that body, and that they did not see fit to grant to the Federal Government the power in question. In the original proposition, to confer on Congress the power to impose "duties, imposts, and excises," was embraced "prohibitions and restraints," which may well be supposed to be intended to embrace the protection of manufactures; but it is is remarkable, that these words were omitted in the Report of the Committee, on that clause. On the 18th of August, a motion was made, "to establish rewards and immunities, for the promotion of agriculture, commerce, trades, and manufactures;" but this proposition also failed. On a subsequent day, it was moved, that there should be " a Secretary of Domestic Affairs, &c., whose duty it should be to attend to matters of general police, the state of agriculture and manufactures, the opening of roads and navigation, and facilitating of intercourse through the United States; and that he shall, from time to time, recommend such measures and establishments as may tend to promote these objects." This proposition likewise failed, the Constitution containing no provision in conformity therewith.

Now, as it is utterly impossible, that these several propositions, embracing imposts, duties, prohibitions and restraints, and the encouragement of manufactures, could have been disposed of, without bringing the whole question of domestic manufactures fully into view, it must follow, that, as no power was given to Congress over manufactures, while the power to regulate commerce is expressly conferred, it was not the intention of the framers of the Constitution, to entrust this power to Congress. Although repeatedly urged to confer such a power, they constantly refused it; and the Constitution, as finally ratified, contains no provision, whatever, upon the subject. In the Report of Luther Martin, a delegate from Maryland, made to the Legislature of his State, an explanation is given of the proceedings of the Convention, in relation to this matter, which removes every shadow of doubt, with regard to the true meaning and intent of the framers of the Constitution, in relation to the protection of manufactures. It appears from this statement, that, as the encouragement of manufactures had been refused to be conferred upon the Federal Government, it was the desire of Mr. Martin and others, to reserve to the states all the means which they supposed to be necessary for affording effectual encouragement to manufactures within their own limits. Among those it was presumed "that there might be cases in which it would be proper for the purpose of encouraging manufactures to lay duties to prohibit the exportation of raw materials, and even in addition to the duties laid by Congress on imports for the sake of revenue, to lay a duty to discourage the importation of particular articles into a State, or to enable the manufacturer here to supply us on as good terms as could be obtained from a foreign market."* Here it will be seen that it is positively stated by Mr. Martin that the power given to Congress to impose duties upon imports, was given expressly "for the sake of revenue," and was not considered as extending to any duty "to discourage the importation of particular articles, for the purpose of encouraging manufactures," and that it was considered that unless the several States should possess this power as well as that of prohibiting the exportation of certain raw materials, they would not be enabled to extend that complete protection to their own manufacturers which might be deemed indispensable to their success. "The most, however," says Mr. Martin, "which we could obtain, was, that this power might be exercised by the States, by and with the consent of Congress, and subject to its control." Thus, then, it manifestly appears, that in relation to manufactures, the framers of the Constitution positively refused to confer upon the Federal Government, any power whatever;—that the power to lay duties, &c., was conferred for the sake of revenue alone, and was not intended to embrace the power to lay duties "to discourage the importation of particular articles, to enable the manufacturers here to supply us on as good terms as could be obtained from a foreign market;" and finally, that the whole subject was left in the hands of the several States, with the restriction, "that no State shall, without the consent of Congress, lay any impost or duties on imports or exports, except what may be absolutely necessary for executing their inspection laws." This power, it appears, was expressly inserted for the purpose of enabling the States to protect their own manufactures ; and this, it seems, was the only provision which friends of domestic industry could obtain. It is vain to allege that the powers retained by the States on this subject, are inadequate to the effectual accom-

*Yates's Secret Debates in the Convention, p. 71.

plishment of the object.   If this were so it would only shew the necessity of some further provision on this subject,—but surely it will not be pretended that it would justify the usurpation by Congress of a power, not only not granted by the Constitution, but purposely withheld.

We think, however, that this exposition of the Constitution places the protection of manufactures on the true foundation, on which it should stand in such a Government as ours.   Nothing can be more monstrous than that the industry of one or more States in this confederacy, should be made profitable at the expense of others, and this must be the inevitable result of any scheme of legislation by the General Government, calculated to promote Manufactures by restrictions upon Commerce or Agriculture.   But leave manufactures where agriculture and other domestic pursuits have been wisely left by the Constitution— with the several States ; and ample security is furnished that no preference will be given to one pursuit over another, and if it should be deemed adviseable in any particular State, to extend encouragement to manufactures, either by direct appropriations of money, or in the way pointed out in the Article of the Constitution above quoted, that this will be done not at the expense of the rest of the Union, but of the particular State whose citizens are to derive the advantages of those pursuits.   Should Massachusetts, for instance, find it to her advantage to engage in the Manufacture of Woollens or Cottons, or Pennsylvania be desirous of encouraging the working of her Iron Mines, let those States grant bounties out of their own Treasuries, to the persons engaged in these pursuits ; and should it be deemed adviseable to encourage their manufactures by duties, "discouraging the importation of similar articles," in these respective States, let them make an application to Congress, whose consent would doubtless be readily given to any acts of those States, having these objects in view.   The Manufacturers of Massachusetts and Pennsylvania would thus be encouraged at the expense of the people of these States respectively.   But when they claim to do more than this,—to encourage their industry, at the expense of the industry of the people of the other States, to promote the Manufactures of the North, at the expense of the Agriculture of the South, by restrictions upon Commerce,—in a word, to secure a monopoly for their manufactures, not only in their own market, but throughout the United States, then we say, that the claim is unjust, and cannot be granted consistently with the principles of the Constitution, or the great ends of a Confederated Government. We shall not stop to inquire whether, as has been urged with great force, that provision of the Constitution, which confers the power upon Congress "to promote the progress of science and the useful arts, by securing, for limited times, to authors and inventors, the exclusive right to their respective writings and discoveries," does not, by a necessary implication, deny to Congress the power of promoting the useful arts (which include both agriculture and manufactures) by any other means than those here specified. It is sufficient for our purpose to shew that the power of promoting manufactures as a distinct substantive object of legislation, has no where been granted to Congress. As to the incidental protection that may be derived from the rightful exercise of the power, either of regulating commerce, or of imposing taxes, duties and imposts, for the legitimate purposes of government,—this certainly, may be as freely enjoyed by manufactures as it must be by every other branch of domestic industry. But as the power to regulate commerce, conferred expressly for its security, cannot be fairly exerted for its destruction, so neither can it be perverted to the purpose of building up manufacturing establishments,—an object entirely beyond the jurisdiction of the Federal Government,—so also, the power to levy taxes, duties, imposts and excises, expressly given for the purpose of raising revenue, cannot be used for the discouragement of importations, for the purpose of promoting manufactures, without a gross and palpable violation of the plain meaning and intent of the federal compact. Acts may be passed on these subjects, falsely purporting, on their face, to have been enacted for the purpose of raising revenue and regulating commerce,—but if in truth, they are designed (as the Acts of 1824, 1828, and 1832, confessedly and avowedly have been) for an entirely different purpose, viz : for the encouragement and promotion of manufactures—the violation of the Constitution is not less gross, deliberate and palpable, because it assumes the most dangerous of all forms, a violation by perversion, the use of a power granted for one purpose, for another and a different purpose, in relation to which, Congress has no power to act at all. On the whole, even from the very brief and imperfect view which we have here taken of this subject, we think we have demonstrated that the protecting system is as gross and palpable a violation of the Constitution, according to its true spirit, intent and meaning, as it is unquestionably unequal, oppressive and unjust in its bearing upon the great interests of the country, and the several sections of the Union.

But great as are the evils of the American System, fatal as it assuredly must be to the prosperity of a large portion of the Union, and gross as is the violation of the letter and spirit of the Constitution which it perpetrates, the consequences which must inevitably result from the establishment of the pernicious principles on which it is founded, are evils of still greater magnitude. An entire change in the character of the Government is the natural and necessary consequence of the application to the Constitution of those latitudinous rules of construction, from which this system derives its existence, and which must "consolidate the States by degrees into one sovereignty ; the obvious tendency and inevitable result of which would be to transform the present representative system of the United States into a Monarchy."*

We fearlessly appeal to all considerate men, whether it be in the nature of things possible, to hold together such a Confederacy as ours, by any means short of a military despotism, after it has degenerated into a Consolidated Government ;—that is to say, after it shall come to be its established policy to exercise a general legislative control over the interests and pursuits of the whole American People.

Can any man be so infatuated as to believe, that Congress could regulate wisely the whole labor and capital of this vast Confederacy? Would it not be a burden too grievous to be borne, that a great central Government, necessarily ignorant of the condition of the remote parts of the country, and regardless perhaps of their prosperity, should undertake to interfere with their domestic pursuits, to control their labor, to regulate their property, and to treat them in all respects as dependent Colonies, governed not with reference to their own interests but the inter-

*Madison's Report.

ests of others? If such a state of things must be admitted to be altogether intolerable, we confidently appeal to the sober judgment and patriotic feelings of every man who values our free institutions and desires to preserve them whether the progress of the Government towards this result has not, of late years, been rapid and alarming? and whether, if the downward course of our affairs cannot be at once arrested, the consummation of this system is not at hand? No sooner had Congress assumed the power of building up manufactures, by successive tariffs, calculated and intended to drive men from agriculture and commerce into more favored pursuits, than internal improvements sprung at once into vigorous existence. Pensions have been enlarged to an extent not only before unknown in any civilized country, but they have been established on such principles, as manifest the settled purpose of bestowing the public treasure in gratuities to particular classes of persons, and particular sections of country. Roads and canals have been commenced, and surveys made in certain quarters of the Union, on a scale of magnificence, which evinces a like determination to distribute the public wealth into new and favored channels; and it is in entire accordance both with the theory and practice of this new system, that the General Government should absorb all the authority of the States, and eventually become the grand depository of the powers, and the general guardian and distributor of the wealth of the whole Union. It is known to all who have marked the course of our national affairs, that Congress has undertaken to create a Bank, and have already assumed jurisdiction over science and the arts, over education and charities, over roads and canals, and almost every other subject, formerly considered as appertaining exclusively to the States; and that they claim and exercise an unlimited control over the appropriation of the public lands as well as of the public money. On looking, indeed, to the legislation of the last ten years, it is impossible to resist the conviction, that a fatal change has taken place in the whole policy and entire operation of the Federal Government; that in every one of its departments, it is, both in theory and practice, rapidly verging towards Consolidation; asserting judicial supremacy over the sovereign States, extending Executive Patronage and influence to the remotest ramifications of society, and assuming legislative control over every object of local concernment; thereby reducing the States to petty corporations, shorn of their sovereignty, mere parts of one great whole, standing in the same relation to the Union as a county or parish to the State of which it is a subordinate part.

Such is the true character, and such the inevitable tendencies of the American System. And when the case, thus plainly stated, is brought home to the bosoms of patriotic men, surely it is not possible to avoid the conclusion, that a political system, founded on such principles, must bear within it the seeds of premature dissolution, and that though it may for a season be extended, enlarged and strengthened, through the corrupting influence of patronage and power, until it shall have embraced in its serpent folds all the great interests of the State, still the time must come when the people, deprived of all other means of escape. will rise up in their might and release themselves from this thraldom, by one of those violent convulsions, whereby society is uprooted from its foundations, and the edict of Reform is written in blood.

Against this system, South Carolina has remonstrated in the most earnest terms. As early as 1820, there was hardly a district or parish in the whole State, from which memorials were not forwarded to Congress, the general language of which was, that the protecting system was "utterly subversive of their rights and interests." Again, in 1823 and 1827, the people of this State rose up almost as one man, and declared to Congress and the world, "that the protecting system was unconstitutional, oppressive and unjust." But these repeated remonstrances were answered only by repeated injuries and insults, by the enacting of the tariffs of 1824 and 1828. To give greater dignity, and if possible more effect to these appeals, the Legislature, in Dec. 1825, solemnly declared, "that it was an unconstitutional exercise of power on the part of Congress, to lay duties to protect domestic manufactures," and in 1828, they caused to be presented to the Senate of the U. States, and claimed to have recorded on its Journals the solemn Protest of the State of South Carolina, denouncing this system as "utterly unconstitutional, grossly unequal and oppressive, and such an abuse of power as was incompatible with the principles of a free government, and the great ends of civil society," and that they were "then only restrained from the assertion of the sovereign rights of the State, by the hope that the magnanimity and justice of the good people of the Union would effect an abandonment of a system partial in its nature, unjust in its operation, and not within the powers delegated to Congress." And finally, in Dec. 1830, it was Resolved, "That the several Acts of Congress, imposing duties on imports, for the protection of domestic manufactures are highly dangerous, and oppressive violations of the constitutional compact; and that whenever the States which are suffering under the oppression, shall lose all reasonable hope of redress from the wisdom and justice of the Federal Government, it will be their right and duty to interpose, in their sovereign capacity, for the purpose of arresting the progress of the evil occasioned by the said unconstitutional acts."

Nor has South Carolina stood alone in the expression of these sentiments: Georgia and Virginia, Alabama and Mississippi, and North Carolina, have raised their voices in earnest remonstrances and repeated warnings. Virginia, in 1828, in responding to South Carolina, declared "that the Constitution of the United States, being a Federative compact between sovereign States, in construing which no common arbiter is known, each State has a right to construe the compact for itself; and that Virginia as one of the high contracting parties, feels itself bound to declare, and does hereby, most solemnly declare its deliberate conviction, that the acts of Congress usually denominated the Tariff Laws, passed avowedly for the protection of domestic manufactures, are not authorized by the plain construction, true intent and meaning of the Constitution."

Georgia, through her Legislature, pronounced this system to be one "which was grinding down the resources of one class of the States to build up and advance the prosperity of another of the same confederacy—and which they solemnly believed to be contrary to the letter and spirit of the Federal Constitution," and declared it to be the right of the several States, in case of any infraction of the general compact, "to complain, remonstrate, and even refuse obedience to any measure of the General Government manifestly against and in violation of the Constitution, that otherwise the law might be violated with impunity,

remain any means, within the power of the State by which these evils may be redressed.

It is useless to disguise the fact, or to attempt to delude ourselves on this subject ; the time has come when the State must either adopt a decisive course of action, or we must at once abandon the contest. We cannot again petition, it would be idle to remonstrate, and degrading to protest. In our estimation it is now a question of Liberty or Slavery. It is now to be decided, whether we shall maintain the rights purchased by the precious blood of our fathers, and transmit them unimpaired to our posterity, or tamely surrender them without a struggle. We are constrained to express our solemn conviction, that, under the protecting system, we have been reduced to a state of "colonial dependence, suffering and disgrace," and that unless we now fly with the spirit which becomes freemen, to the rescue of our liberties, they are lost forever. Brought up in an ardent devotion to the Union of the States, the people of South Carolina have long struggled against the conviction, that the powers of the Federal Government have been shamefully perverted to the purposes of injustice and oppression. Bound to their brethren by the proud recollections of the past, and fond hopes of the future, by common struggles for liberty and common glories, acquired in its defence, they have been brought slowly, and with the utmost reluctance, to the conclusion, that they are shut out from their sympathies, and made the unpitied victims of an inexorable system of tyranny, which is without example in any country claiming to be free. Experience has at length taught us the lamentable truth, that administered as the government now is, and has been for several years past, in open disregard of all the limitations prescribed by the Constitution, the Union itself, instead of being a blessing must soon become a curse. Liberty, we are thoroughly persuaded, cannot be preserved under our system without a sacred and inviolable regard not merely to the letter, but to the true spirit of the Constitution ; and without liberty the Union would not be worth preserving. If then there were no alternative but to submit to these evils, or to seek a remedy even in Revolution itself, we could not, without proving ourselves recreant to the principles hallowed by the example of our ancestors, hesitate a moment as to our choice. We should say,

in the spirit of our fathers, "we have counted the cost, and find nothing so intolerable as voluntary slavery." But we cannot bring ourselves for one moment to believe that the alternative presented to us is revolution or slavery. We confidently believe that there is a redeeming spirit in our institutions, which may, on great occasions, be brought to our aid for the purpose of preserving the public liberty, restoring the Constitution, and effecting a regeneration of the Government; and thereby producing a redress of intolerable grievances, without war, revolution, or a dissolution of the Union. These great objects, we feel assured, may even now be effected, unless those who are in possion of the powers of the government, and charged with the administration of our national affairs, shall resolve to persevere in a course of injustice, and prove by their conduct that they love the usurpation (to which the people of this State are unalterably determined not to submit) better than the Union. We believe that the redeeming spirit of our system is State Sovereignty and that it results from the very form and structure of the Federal Government; that when the rights reserved to the several States are deliberately invaded, it is their right and their duty to "interpose for the purpose of arresting the progress of the evil of usurpation, and to maintain within their respective limits the authorities and privileges belonging to them as independent sovereignties."* If the several States do not possess this right, it is in vain that they claim to be sovereign. They are at once reduced to the degrading condition of humble dependants on the will of the Federal Government. South Carolina claims to be a sovereign State. She recognizes no tribunal upon earth as above her authority. It is true she has entered into a solemn compact of Union with other sovereign States; but she claims, and will exercise the right to determine the extent of her obligations under that compact, nor will she consent that any other power shall exercise the right of judgment for her. And when that compact is violated by her co-States, or by the Government which they have created, she asserts her unquestionable right, " to judge of the infractions, as well as of the mode and measure of redress."†
South Carolina claims no right to judge for others. The States

*Virginia Resolutions of '98.   †Kentucky Resolutions of 1798.

who are parties to the compact, must judge each for itself, whether that compact has been pursued or violated; and should they differ irreconcileably in opinion, there is no earthly tribunal that can authoritatively decide between them. It was in the contemplation of a similar case, that Mr. Jefferson declared that if the difference could neither be compromised, nor avoided, it was the peculiar felicity of our system, to have provided a remedy in a Convention of all the States, by whom the Constitution might be so altered or amended, as to remove the difficulty.— To this tribunal, South Carolina is willing that an appeal should now be made, and that the constitutional compact should be so modified as to accomplish all the great ends for which the Union was formed, and the Federal Government constituted, and, at the same time, restore the rights of the States, and preserve them from violation hereafter. Your Committee purposely avoid entering here into an examination of the nature and character of this claim, which South Carolina asserts, to interpose her sovereignty, for the protection of her citizens from the operation of unconstitutional Laws, and the preservation of her own reserved rights. In an Address, which will be submitted to the Convention, this subject will be fully examined, and they trust that it will be made to appear, to the entire satisfaction of every dispassionate mind, that in adopting the Ordinance which the Committee herewith report, declaring the Tariff Laws passed for the protection of Domestic Manufacturers, null and void, and not Law, and directing the Legislature to provide, that the same shall not be enforced within the limits of this State,— South Carolina will be asserting her unquestionable rights, and in no way violating her obligations under the Federal Compact.

The Committee cannot dismiss this point, however, even for the present, without remarking, that in asserting the principles, and adopting the course, which they are about to recommend, South Carolina will only be carrying out the doctrines which were asserted by Virginia and Kentucky in 1798, and which have been sanctified by the high authority of Thomas Jefferson. It is from the pen of this great apostle of liberty, that we have been instructed that to the Constitutional compact, " each State acceded as a State, and is an integral party, its co-states forming as to itself the other party," that " they alone being parties to the compact, are solely authorized to judge in the last resort of the powers exercised under it; Congress being not a party, but merely the creature of the compact," that it becomes a sovereign State, " to submit to undelegated, and, consequently, unlimited power in no man or body of men on earth; that in cases of abuse of the delegated powers, the members of the General Government being chosen by the people, a change by the people would be the Constitutional remedy; but where powers are assumed which have not been delegated, [the very case now before us] a, nullification of the act is the rightful remedy; that every State has a natural right, in cases not within the compact, [*casus non foederis*] to nullify, of their own authority, all assumption of power by others within their limits, and that without this right they would be under the dominion absolute and unlimited, of whomsoever might exercise the right of judgment for them;" and that in case of acts being passed by Congress, " so palpably against the Constitution as to amount to an undisguised declaration, that the compact is not meant to be the measure of the powers of the General Government, but that it will proceed to exercise over the States all powers whatsoever, by seizing the rights of the States, and consolidating them in the hands of the General Government, with a power assumed of binding the States, not merely in cases made federal, but in all cases whatsoever, by laws made, not with their consent, but by others against their consent, it would be the duty of the States to declare the Acts void and of no force, and that each should take measures of its own for providing that neither such acts, nor any other of the General Government, not plainly and intentionally authorized by the Constitution, shall be exercised within their respective territories."

In acting on these great and essential truths, South Carolina surely cannot err. She is convinced, and has so declared to Congress and the World, that the protecting system is in all its branches a "gross, deliberate, and palpable violation of the Constitution." She believes that after having exhausted every other means of redress in vain, it is her right, and that it has now become her solemn duty, to interpose for arresting the evil within her own limits, by declaring said Acts " to be null and void, and no law, and taking measures of her own that they shall not be enforced within her territory." That duty she means to perform, and to leave the consequences in the hands of Him, with whom are the issues of life and the destinies of nations.

South Carolina will continue to cherish a sincere attachment to the UNION of the States, and will to the utmost of her power endeavor to preserve it, " and believes that for this end, it is her duty to watch over and oppose any infraction of those principles which constitute the only basis of that union, because a faithful observance of them can alone secure its existence." She venerates the Constitution, and will protect and defend it " against every aggression, either foreign or domestic;" but, above all, she estimates as beyond all price her liberty, which she is unalterably determined never to surrender while she has the power to maintain it. Influenced by these views, your Committee report herewith, for the adoption of the Convention, a solemn Declaration and Ordinance.

AN ORDINANCE,

To Nullify certain Acts of the Congress of the United States, purporting to be Laws laying Duties and Imposts on the Importation of Foreign Commodities.

WHEREAS, the Congress of the United States, by various acts, purporting to be acts laying duties and imposts on foreign imports, but in reality intended for the protection of domestic manufactures, and the giving of bounties to classes and individuals engaged in particular employments, at the expense and to the injury and oppression of other classes and individuals, and by wholly exempting from taxation, certain foreign commodities, such as are not produced or manufactured in the United States, to afford a pretext for imposing higher and excessive duties on articles similar to those intended to be protected, hath exceeded its just powers under the Constitution, which confers on it no authority to afford such protection, and hath violated the true meaning and intent of the Constitution, which provides for equality in imposing the burdens of taxation upon the several States and portions of the Confederacy;—And, whereas, the said Congress, exceeding its just power to impose taxes and collect revenue for the purpose of effecting and accomplishing the specific objects and purposes which the Constitution of the United States authorizes it to effect and accomplish, hath raised and collected unnecessary revenue, for objects unauthorized by the Constitution;

We, therefore, the people of the State of South Carolina, in Convention assembled, do declare and ordain, and it is hereby declared and ordained, that the several acts and parts of acts of the Congress of the United States, purporting to be laws for the imposing of duties and imposts on the importation of foreign commodities, and now having actual operation and effect within the United States, and more especially an act entitled "an act in alteration of the several acts imposing duties on imports," approved on the nineteenth day of May, one thousand eight hundred and twenty-eight, and also an act entitled " an act to alter and amend the several acts imposing duties on imports," approved on the fourteenth day of July, one thousand eight hundred and thirty-two, are unauthorized by the Constitution of the United States, and violate the true meaning and intent thereof, and are null, void, and no law, nor binding upon this State, its officers or citizens ; and all promises, contracts, and obligations made or entered into, or to be made or entered into with purpose to secure the duties imposed by the said acts, and all judicial proceedings which shall be hereafter had in affirmance thereof, are and shall be held utterly null and void.

And it is further ordained, That it shall not be lawful for any of the constituted authorities, whether of this State, or of the United States, to enforce the payment of duties imposed by the said acts within the limits of this State ; but it shall be the duty of the Legislature to adopt such measures, and pass such acts as may be necessary to give full effect to this ordinance, and to prevent the enforcement and arrest the operation of the said acts and parts of acts of the Congress of the United States, within the limits of this State, from and after the first day of February next, and the duty of all other constituted authorities, and all persons residing or being within the limits of this State, and they are hereby required and enjoined to obey and give effect to this Ordinance, and such acts and measures of the Legislature as may be passed or adopted in obedience thereto.

And it is further ordained, That in no case of law or equity, decided in the Courts of this State, wherein shall be drawn in question the authority of this Ordinance, or the validity of such act or acts of the Legislature as may be passed for the purpose of giving effect thereto, or the validity of the aforesaid acts of Congress, imposing duties, shall any appeal be taken or allowed to the Supreme Court of the United States, nor shall any copy of the record be permitted or allowed for that purpose ; and if any such appeal shall be attempted to be taken, the Courts of this State, shall proceed to execute and enforce their judgments, according to the laws and usages of the State, without reference to such attempted appeal, and the person or persons attempting to take such appeal may be dealt with as for a contempt of the Court.

And it is further ordained, That all persons now holding any office of honor, profit or trust, civil or military, under this State, (members of the Legislature excepted) shall, within such time, and in such manner as the Legislature shall prescribe, take an oath, well and truly to obey, execute and enforce this Ordinance, and such act or acts of the Legislature as may be passed in pursuance thereof, according to the true intent and meaning of the same; and, on the neglect or omission of any such person or persons so to do, his or their office or offices shall be forthwith vacated, and shall be filled up, as if such person or persons were dead, or had resigned; and no person hereafter elected to any office of honor, profit or trust, civil or military, (members of the Legislature excepted) shall, until the Legislature shall otherwise provide and direct, enter on the execution of his office, or be in any respect competent to discharge the duties thereof, until he shall, in like manner, have taken a similar oath; and no juror shall be impannelled in any of the Courts of this State, in any cause in which shall be in question this Ordinance, or any act of the Legislature passed in pursuance thereof, unless he shall first, in addition to the usual oath, have taken an oath that he will well and truly obey, execute, and enforce this Ordinance, and such act or acts of the Legislature, as may be passed to carry the same into operation and effect, according to the true intent and meaning thereof.

And we, the people of South Carolina, to the end that it may be fully understood by the Government of the United States, and the people of the co-States, that we are determined to maintain this, our Ordinance and declaration, at every hazard, do further declare that we will not submit to the application of force, on the part of the Federal Government, to reduce this State to obedience; but that we will consider the passage by Congress, of any act authorizing the employment of a military or naval force against the State of South Carolina, her constituted authorities or citizens,—or any act, abolishing or closing the ports of this State, or any of them, or otherwise obstructing the free ingress and egress of vessels to and from the said ports,—or any other act on the part of the Federal Government, to coerce the State, shut up her ports, destroy or harrass her commerce, or to enforce the acts hereby declared to be null and void, otherwise than through the civil tribunals of the country, as inconsistent with the longer continuance of South Carolina in the Union ; and that the people of this State will thenceforth hold themselves absolved from all further obligation to maintain or preserve their political connexion with the people of the other States, and will forthwith proceed to organize a separate Government, and do all other acts and things which sovereign and independent States may of right do.

Done in Convention, at Columbia, the twenty-fourth day of November, in the year of our Lord, one thousand eight hundred and thirty-two, and in the fifty-seventh year of the Declaration of the Independence of the United States of America.

JAMES HAMILTON, Jun., *President of the Convention,*
and Delegate from St. Peters.

James Hamilton, sen.
Richard Bohun Baker, sen.
Samuel Warren.
Nathaniel Heyward.
Robert Long.
J. B. Earle.
L. M. Ayer.
Benjamin Adams.
James Adams.
James Anderson.
Robert Anderson.
William Arnold.
John Ball.
Barnard E. Bee.
Thomas W. Boone.
James Lynah.
Francis Y. Legare.
Alex. J. Lawton.
John Lipscomb.
John Logan.
J. Littlejohn.
A. Lancastar.
John Magrath.

Wm. M. Murray.
R. G. Mills.
John B. McCall.
D. H. Means.
R. G. Mays.
R. W. Barnwell.
Isaac Bradwell jr.
Thomas G. Blewett.
P. M. Butler.
John G. Brown.
J. G. Brown.
John Bauskett.
A. Burt.
Francis Burt, jr.
Bailey Barton.
A. Bowie.
James A. Black.
A. H. Belin.
Philip Cohen.
Samuel Cordes.
Thomas H. Colcock.
C. J. Colcock.
Charles G. Capers.

Benj. A. Markley.
John S. Maner.
John Counts.
Benjamin Chambers.
I. A. Campbell.
Wm. Dubose.
John H. Dawson.
John Douglas.
George Douglas.
F. H. Elmore.
Wm. Evans.
Edmund J. Felder.
A. Fuller.
Theo. L. Gourdin.
Peter G. Gourdin.
T. J. Goodwyn.
Peter Gaillard, jr.
John K. Griffin.
George W. Gleen.
Alex. L. Gregg.
Robert Y. Hayne.
William Harper.
Thomas Harrison.
John Hatton.
Thomas Harllee.
Abm. Huguenin.
Jacob Bond I'On.
John S. Jeter.
Job Johnston.
John S. James.
M. Jacobs.
J. A. Keith.
John Key.
Jacob H. King.
Stephen Lacoste.
George McDuffie.
James Moore.
John L. Miller.
Stephen D. Miller.

Wm. C. Clifton.
West Caughman.
Wm. Porcher.
Edward G. Palmer.
Chs. C. Pinckney.
Wm. C. Pinckney.
Thomas Pinckney.
Francis D. Quash.
John Rivers.
Donald Rowe.
Benjamin Rogers.
Thomas Ray.
James G. Spann.
James Spann.
S. L. Simons.
Peter J. Shand.
James Mongin Smith.
G. H. Smith.
Wm. Smith.
Stepen Smith.
Wm. Stringfellow.
Edwin J. Scott.
F. W. Symmes.
J. S. Sims.
T. D. Singleton.
Joseph L. Stevens.
T. E. Screven.
Robt. J. Turnbull.
Elisha Tyler.
Philip Tidyman.
Isaac B. Ulmer.
Peter Vaught.
Elias Vanderhorst.
John L. Wilson.
Isham Walker.
Wm. Williams.
Thos. B. Woodward.
Sterlin C. Williamson.
F. H. Wardlaw.

John B. Miller.
R. P. McCord.
John L. Nowell.
Jennings O'Bannon.
J. Walter Phillips.
Charles Parker.

Abner Whatley.
J. T. Whitefield.
Saml. L. Watt.
Nicholas Ware.
Wm. Waties.
Archibald Young.

[Attest.]

ISAAC W. HAYNE,
Clerk of the Convention.

ADDRESS

TO THE

PEOPLE OF SOUTH CAROLINA,

BY THEIR

DELEGATES IN CONVENTION.

ADDRESS.

FELLOW CITIZENS:

THE situation in which you have been placed by the usurpations of the Federal Government, is one which you so peculiarly
feel, as to render all reference to it at this moment unnecessary.
For the last ten years the subject of your grievances has been
presented to you. This subject you have well considered You
have viewed it in all its aspects, bearings, and tendencies, and
you seem more and more confirmed in the opinion, expressed by
both branches of the Legislature, that the Tariff, in its operation,
is not only "grossly unequal and unjust, but is such an abuse of
power as is incompatible with the principles of a Free Government, and the great ends of civil society;" and that, if persisted
in, "the fate of this State would be poverty and utter desolation."
Correspondent with this conviction, a disposition is manifested
in every section of the Country, to arrest, by some means or
other, the progress of this intolerable evil. This disposition
having arisen, from no sudden excitement, but having been gradually formed by the free and temperate discussions of the Press,
there is no reason to believe that it can ever subside, by any
means short of the removal of the urgent abuse ; and it is under
this general conviction, that we have been convened to take into
consideration, not only the character and extent of your grievances, but also the mode and measure of redress.

This duty, Fellow Citizens, we have discharged to the best of
our judgments, and the result of our deliberations will be found
in the Declaration and Ordinance, just passed by us—founded
on the great and undeniable truth, that in all cases of a palpa-

ble, oppressive, and dangerous infraction of the Federal compact, each State has a right to annul, and to render inoperative within its limits, all such unauthorized acts. After the luminous expositions which have been already furnished by so many great minds, that the exercise of this right is compatible with the first principles of our anomalous scheme of Government, it would be superfluous here to state at length, the reasons by which this mode of redress is to be sustained. A deference however, for the opinions of those of our fellow citizens who have hitherto dissented from us, demands, that we should briefly state the principal ground upon which we place the right, and the expediency of Nullification.

The Constitution of the United States, as is admitted by cotemporaneous writers, is a compact between Sovereign States. Though the subject matter of that compact, was a Government, the powers of which Government were to operate, to a certain extent, upon the People of those Sovereign States, aggregately, and not upon the State Authorities, as is usual in Confederacies, still the Constitution is a Confederacy. First : It is a Confederacy, because in its foundations, it possesses not one single feature of nationality. The people of the separate States, as distinct political communities, ratified the Constitution, each State acting for itself, and binding its own citizens, and not those of any other State. The act of ratification declares it "to be binding on the States, so ratifying. The States are its authors —their power created it—their voice clothed it with authority— the Government it formed is in reality their Government, and the Union of which it is the bond, is a Union of States, and not of individuals." Secondly : It is a Confederacy, because the extent of the powers of the Government, depends, not upon the People of the United States, collectively, but upon the State Legislatures, or on the people of the separate States, acting in their State Conventions, each State being represented by a single vote.

It must never be forgotten, that it is to the creating and to the controlling power, that we are to look for the true character of the Federal Government ; for the present controversy is, not as to the sources from which the ordinary powers of the Government are drawn ; these are partly federal, and partly national.

Nor is it relevant, to consider upon whom those powers operate. In this last view, the Government, for limited purposes, is entirely national. The true question is, who are the parties to the compact? Who created, and who can alter and destroy it. Is it the States, or the People? This question has been already answered. The States, as States, ratified the compact. The People of the United States, collectively, had no agency in its formation. There did not exist then, nor has there existed at any time since, such a political body as the People of the United States. There is not now, nor has there ever been such a relation existing, as that of a citizen of New Hampshire, and a citizen of South Carolina, bound together in the same Social Compact. It would be a waste of time to dwell longer on this part of our subject. We repeat, that as regards the foundation, and the extent of its powers, the Government of the United States is strictly, what its name implies, a Federal Government, —a league between several Sovereigns ; and in these views, a more perfect Confederacy has never existed in ancient or modern times.

On looking into this Constitution, we find that the most important sovereign powers are delegated to the central Government, and all other powers are reserved to the States. A foreign, or an inattentive reader, unacquainted with the origin, progress, and history of the Constitution, would be very apt, from the phraseology of the instrument, to regard the States, as having divested themselves of their Sovereignty, and to have become great corporations, subordinate to one Supreme Government.— But this is an error. The States are as Sovereign now, as they were prior to their entering into the compact. In common parlance, and to avoid circumlocution, it may be admissible enough, to speak of delegated and reserved Sovereignty. But, correctly speaking, Sovereignty is an unit. It is "one, indivisible and unalienable." It is, therefore, an absurdity to imagine, that the Sovereignty of the States, is surrendered in part, and retained in part. The Federal Constitution, is a treaty, a confederation, an alliance by which so many Sovereign States, agree to exercise their sovereign powers conjointly, upon certain objects of external concern, in which they are equally interested, such as War, Peace, Commerce, Foreign Negotiation, and Indian Trade ; and upon all other subjects of civil Government, they were to exercise their Sovereignty separately. This is the true nature of the compact.

For the convenient conjoint exercise of the Sovereignty of the States, there must of necessity be some common agency or functionary. This agency is the Federal Government. It represents the confederated States, and executes their joint will, as expressed in the compact. The powers of this government are wholly derivative. It possesses no more inherent sovereignty, than an incorporated town, or any other corporate body;—it is a political corporation, and like all corporations, it looks for its powers to an exterior source. That source is the States. It wants that "irresistible, absolute, uncontrolled authority," without which, according to jurists, there can be no sovereignty. As the States conferred, so the States can take away its powers. All inherent sovereignty, is therefore in the States. It is the moral obligation alone, which each State has chosen to impose upon herself, and not the want of sovereignty, which restrains her from exercising all those powers, which (as we are accustomed to express ourselves) she has surrendered to the Federal Government.— The present organization of our Government, as far as regards the terms in which the powers of Congress are delegated, in no wise differs from the old Confederation. The powers of the Old Congress were delegated rather in stronger language, than we find them written down in the new charter, and yet he would hazard a bold assertion, who would say, that the States of the old Confederacy were not as Sovereign as Great Britain, France and Russia would be in an alliance offensive and defensive. It was not the reservation, in express terms, of the "Sovereignty, Freedom, and Independence of each State" which made them Sovereign. They would have been equally Sovereign, as is universally admitted, without such a reservation.

We have said thus much upon the subject of Sovereignty, because the only foundation upon which we can safely erect the right of a State to protect its citizens, is, that South Carolina, by the Declaration of Independence, became, and has since continued a Free, Sovereign, and Independent State. That as a Sovereign State, she has the inherent power, to do all those acts, which by the law of nations, any Prince or Potentate may of right do. That, like all independent States, she neither has, nor ought she to suffer any other restraint upon her sovereign will and pleasure, than those high, moral obligations, under which all Princes and States are bound, before God and man, to perform their solemn pledges. The inevitable conclusion from what has been said, therefore is, that as in all cases of compact between Independent Sovereigns, where, from the very nature of things, there can be no common judge or umpire, each sovereign has a right "to judge as well of infractions, as of the mode and measure of redress," so in the present controversy between South Carolina and the Federal Government, it belongs solely to her, by her delegates in solemn Convention assembled, to decide whether the federal compact be violated, and what remedy the State ought to pursue. South Carolina therefore cannot, and will not yield to any department of the Federal Government, and still less to the Supreme Court of the United States, the creature of a Government, which itself is a creature of the States, a right which enters into the essence of all sovereignty, and without which it would become a bauble and a name.

It is fortunate for the view which we have just taken, that the history of the Constitution, as traced through the Journals of the Convention which framed that instrument, places the right contended for upon the same sure foundation. These journals furnish abundant proof, that "no line of jurisdiction between the States and Federal Government, in doubtful cases," could be agreed on. It was conceded by Mr. Madison and Mr. Randolph, the most prominent advocates for a Supreme Government, that it was impossible to draw this line, because no tribunal sufficiently impartial, as they conceived, could be found, and that there was no alternative, but to make the Federal Government supreme, by giving it, in all such cases, a negative on the acts of the State Legislatures. The pertinacity with which this negative power was insisted on by the advocates of a national Government, even after all the important provisions of the judiciary or third article of the Constitution were arranged and agreed to, proves beyond doubt, that the Supreme Court was never contemplated by either party, in that Convention, as an arbiter, to decide conflicting claims of sovereignty between the States and Congress; and the repeated rejection of all proposals to take from the States the power of placing their own construction upon the articles of Union, evinces that the States were resolved never to part with the right to judge, whether the acts of the Federal Legislature were, or were not, an infringement of those articles.

Correspondent with the right of a Sovereign State to judge of the infractions of the Federal Compact, is the duty of this Convention to declare the extent of the grievance, and the mode and measure of redress. On both these points, public opinion has already anticipated us, in much that we could urge. It is doubted, whether in any country, any subject has undergone, before the people, a more thorough examination than the constitutionality of the several acts of Congress for the protection of Domestic Manufactures. Independent of the present embarrassments, they throw in the way of our commerce, and the plain indications, that certain articles, which are the natural exchange for our valuable staple products, are sooner or later to be virtually prohibited—independent of the diminution which these impost duties cause in our incomes, and the severity of the Tax upon all articles of consumption needed by the poor, they recognize a principle, not less at war with the ends for which this great confederacy was formed, than it is with that spirit of justice, and [those feelings of concord which ought to prevail amongst States, united by so many common interests and exalted triumphs. The people surely need not be told, in this advanced period of intellect and of freedom, that no government can be free, which can rightfully impose a tax, for the encouragement of one branch of industry at the expense of all others, unless such a tax be justified by some great and unavoidable public necessity. Still less can the people believe, that in a confederacy of States, designed principally, as an alliance offensive and defensive, its authors could ever have contemplated, that the federal head should regulate the domestic industry of a widely extended country ; distinguished, above all others, for the diversity of interests, pursuits and resources, in its various sections. It was this acknowledged diversity, that caused the arrangement of a conjoint and separate exercise of the sovereign authority ; the one to regulate external concerns, and the other to have absolute control "over the lives, liberties, and properties of the people, and the internal order, improvement, and prosperity of the States."

It is the striking characteristic in the operation of a simple and consolidated government, that it protects Manufactures, Agriculture, or any other branch of the public industry—that it can establish corporations or make Roads and Canals, and patronize learning and the arts. But it would be difficult to shew, that such was the government which the sages of the Convention designed for the States. All these powers were proposed to be given to Congress, and they were proposed by that party in the Convention who desired a firm National Government. The Convention having decided on the federal form, in exclusion of the national, all these propositions were rejected ; and yet we have lived to see an American Congress, who can hold no power except by express grant, as fully in the exercise of these powers, as if they were part and parcel of their expressly delegated authority. Under a pretence of regulating Commerce; they would virtually prohibit it. Were this regulation of Commerce resorted to, as a means of coercing foreign nations to a fair reciprocity in their intercourse with us, or for some other bona fide commercial purpose, as has been justly said by our Legislature, the Tariff acts would be constitutional. But none of these acts have been passed as countervailing or retaliatory measures, for restrictions placed on our Commerce by foreign nations. Whilst other nations seem disposed to relax in their restraints upon trade, our Congress seems absolutely bent upon the interdiction of those articles of Merchandize, which are exchangeable for the products of Southern labor, thus causing the principal burthen of taxation to fall upon this portion of the Union, and by depriving us of our accustomed Markets, to impoverish our whole Southern country. In the same manner, and under the pretence of promoting the Internal Improvement of the States, and for other equally unjustifiable and unconstitutional purposes, Congress is in the constant habit of violating those fundamental principles of the Constitution, on which alone can rest the prosperity of the States, and the durability of the Union.

It is in vain to imagine, that with a people who have struggled for freedom, and know its inestimable value, such a state of affairs can be endured longer than there is a well founded hope, that reason and justice will resume their empire in the common council of the confederacy. That hope having expired with the last session of Congress, by the present Tariff act, distinctly and fully recognizing as the permanent policy of the country, the odious principle of protection, it occurs to us, that there is but one course for the State to pursue. That course fellow-citizens is resistance. Not physical, but moral resistance—not resistance in an angry or irritated feeling, but resistance by such counter-legislation, which, whilst it shall evince to the world that our measures are built upon the necessity of tendering to Congress an amicable issue, to try a doubtful question between friends and neighbors, shall at the same time secure us in the enjoyment of our rights and privileges. It matters not, fellow citizens, by what name this counter-legislation shall be designated ; call it Nullification, State interposition, State veto, or by whatever other name you please, still if it be but resistance to an oppressive measure, it is the course which duty, patriotism, and self-preservation prescribes. If we are asked, upon what ground we place the right to resist a particular law of Congress, and yet regard ourselves as a constituent member of the Union, we answer—the ground of the Compact. We do not choose, in a case of this kind, to recur to what are called our natural rights, or the right of revolution. We claim to nullify by a more imposing title. We claim it as a constitutional right, not meaning as some have imagined, that we derive the right from the Constitution, for derivative rights can only belong to the functionaries of the high contracting parties to the Constitution, but we claim to exercise it as one of the parties to the compact, and as consistent with its letter, its genius, and its spirit, it being distinctly understood at the time of ratifying the Constitution, that the exercise of all sovereign rights not agreed to be had conjointly, were to be exerted separately by the States. Though it be true, that the provision in favor of what we call the reserved rights of the States, was not necessary to to secure to the States such reserved rights, yet the mere circumstance, of its insertion in the instrument, makes it as clear a constitutional provision, as that of the power of Congress to raise armies, or to declare war. Any exercise of a right in conformity with a constitutional provision, we conceive to be a constitutional right, whether it be founded on an express grant of the right, or be included in a general reservation of undefined powers. The Constitution being the supreme law, and an instrument in which a distribution of powers is made between the Federal Government and the States, it is incumbent on the authorities of each Government, so to shape their legislation, as not to overstep the boundaries assigned to them. No act can therefore be done by either Government, which for its validity can be referred to any other test, than the standard of the Constitution. If a State Government passes an act, defining and punishing a burglary, or a law abolishing the rights of primogeniture, it is more correct to say, that she is in the exercise of her constitutional, than of her natural rights, because it is an express constitutional provision, that she should exercise all her sovereign rights, not already entrusted to the common functionary of the parties. As it is impossible then that any act can be passed by either Government, which, if disputed, must not be referred to the Constitution as the supreme law of the parties, so a right is constitutional or unconstitutional, as it shall be found to comport with, or to be repugnant to, the terms or the spirit of that instrument. There is not, therefore, a sovereign, or a natural right, which South Carolina can lawfully exercise in conformity with her engagements, which is not stipulated for in the tenth amendment to the Constitution. All such rights stipulated for, must be constitutional; to regard them otherwise, would be a perversion of terms.

That Nullification under our reserved rights was regarded as constitutional by the Virginia Resolutions of 1798, is clear from the exposition of them by the celebrated Report, drawn by Mr. Madison. In defending the third of these Resolutions, which asserts the doctrine of State interposition and protection, the Committee say "that they have scanned it not merely with a strict, but with a severe eye, and they feel confidence in pronouncing, that in its just and fair construction, it is unexceptionably true in its several positions, as well as constitutional and conclusive in its inferences." What were the positions of the third Resolution. 1. That the powers of the Federal Government were limited to the plain sense of the instrument constituting the compact. 2. That in case of a deliberate, palpable and dangerous infraction of the compact, the State has the right to interpose, &c. Now what is the inference? It is, that " they are in duty bound to arrest the progress of the evil, by maintaining within their respective limits, the authorities, rights, and liberties appertaining to them." This inference, says the Report, is " constitutional and conclusive." The same doctrine was as distinctly affirmed by the Virginia Assembly, in their Resolutions adopting the Report. They say, " that having fully and accurately re-examined and reconsidered these Resolutions, they find it to be their indispensable duty to adhere to the same as founded in truth, as consonant with the Constitution, and as conducive to its preservation."

We are aware that it has been recently maintained, that by the State interposition referred to in this third Resolution, the Virginia Assembly had allusion to the natural right, and Mr. Madison himself has been brought forward to give a construction to this Resolution contrary to the most obvious import of the terms. Be it so. Then, if the State interposition here spoken of, be a natural right, it is a right which the Virginia Assembly have pronounced " consonant with the Constitution, and as conducive to its preservation,"—or, in other words, that without the exercise of this natural sovereign right of interposition, the Constitution cannot be preserved. There is no incongruity in this. It is quite competent for two monarchs to stipulate in a treaty for that right, which, independent of the treaty, would be a natural right, as if a power were conferred by the treaty on the citizens of either prince, to capture, adjudge, and execute all subjects of the other, engaged in piracy on the high seas. It certainly would be more proper to call such a right a Conventional right, than a natural right, though it be both. Several of the State Constitutions furnish instances of natural rights being secured by a constitutional provision. Even in the instrument we are now considering, there is a distinct affirmation in terms of a natural right of sovereignty—such as the sovereign right of a State to keep troops and ships of war in a certain emergency, or the sovereign right of a State to lay import and export duties, for the purpose of executing its inspection laws. In these cases, a natural right is also a constitutional right, contrary to the definition of those who maintain that no right is properly constitutional which is a sovereign right, because constitutional rights are derivative rights exercised by functionaries. That reasoning would be indeed strange, which would place a natural reserved sovereign right, expressed in terms upon a better footing, than all that mass of residuary power included in the general reservation of the tenth amendment. It would be to create a distinction without a difference. The reserved rights, though undefined, are easily ascertained. Any particular right not found in the enumerated powers of Congress, of course belongs to the States.

The right to nullify is universally admitted to be a natural or sovereign right. The natural rights of the States are also admitted to be their reserved rights. If they are reserved, they must be constitutional, because the Constitution being an agreement to arrange the mode by which the States shall exercise their sovereignty, expressly stipulates for the exercise of these powers in all cases not enumerated. To some it may be unimportant upon what basis we place the right of a State to protect its citizens, as counter-legislation would be the beginning of resistance in either case; others may, perhaps, justly say, that the whole controversy is resolvable into a dispute as to what is, or is not, the proper definition of a constitutional right. We, however, think it of infinite importance, in urging the right of nullification, to regard it as a constitutional, rather than as a natural remedy, because a constitutional proceeding is calculated to give it a pacific course and a higher recommendation. The characteristic, in fact, of the American Constitutions in general, is, that they sanctify the fundamental principles of the American Revolution. Whilst other nations have to resort to the law of nature, and by force to drive despots from their thrones, thus incurring what amongst them is odiously termed the guilt of rebellion; we here have the incalculable advantage of a thorough understanding amongst all classes, that it is the right, as well as the duty, of a free people, to recur when necessary to their sovereign rights, to resist oppression. Such a sentiment as this becoming familiar to the public mind, acquires prodigious strength, when its spirit is seen to pervade a written Constitution, and prevents rather than accelerates opportunities for an unnecessary recurrence to revolutionary movements. Under such a structure of the public sentiment, when the voice of a sovereign State shall be spoken, "it will be heard in a tone which virtuous governors will obey, and tyrannical ones shall dread." Nothing can more reconcile nullification to our citizens, than to know, that if we are not proceeding according to the forms of the Constitution, we are, nevertheless, adhering to its spirit. The convention which framed the Constitution, could not agree upon any mode of settling a dispute, like the present. The case was therefore left unprovided for, under the conviction no doubt, as is admitted by Mr. Hamilton in "The Federalist," that if the Federal Government should oppress the States, the State governments would be ready to check it, by virtue of their own inherent sovereign powers. "It may safely be received as an axiom in our political system, (says Mr. Hamilton,) that the State Governments will, in all possible contingencies, afford complete security against invasion of the public liberty by the national authority. Projects of usurpation cannot be masked under pretences so likely to escape the penetration of select bodies of men, as of the people at large,—the Legislatures will have better means of information,—they can discover the danger at a distance ; and, possessing all the organs of civil power, and the confidence of the people, they can at once adopt a regular plan of opposition, in which they can combine all the resources of the community."

That measure cannot be revolutionary, which is adopted, not with a view to resort to force, but by some decisive measures, to call the attention of the co-States to a disputed question, in such a form, as to compel them to decide what are or are not the rights of the States, in a case of a palpable and dangerous infraction of those fundamental principles of liberty in which they all have an interest.

In the exercise of the right of nullification, we are not unmindful of the many objections which have been urged against it. That it may embarrass the present majority in Congress, who are fatally bent upon building up the sectional interests of their constituents, upon the ruin of our commerce, we can readily imagine : but these embarrassments, on examination, will be found to proceed rather from an unwillingness, on their part, to adjust the controversy on principles of reason and justice, than from any real difficulty existing in the Constitution. The provisions of the Constitution are ample for taking the sense of the States on a question more important than any which has occurred since the formation of the Government. But if the spirit of justice departs from the councils, to which we have a right to look up as the guardians of the public liberty and the public peace, no provisions of human wisdom can avail. We have heard much of the danger of suffering one State to impede the operations of twenty-three States : but it must be obvious to every considerate. man, that the danger can only exist where a State is wrong. If the people of any one State are right in the principles for which they contend, it is desirable that they should impede the operations of Congress, until the sentiments of its co-States shall be had. A higher eulogy could not be bestowed upon our system, than the power of resorting to some conservative principle, that shall stay a disruption of the league. It is no argument to say that a State may have no grounds on which to place herself upon her sovereign rights. This is a possible, but by no means a probable case. Experience has given us a most instructive lesson on this very subject—it has taught us that, the danger is not that a State may resort to her sovereign rights too often, but that it will not avail herself of them when necessary. Look, fellow citizens, to our State : for ten years we have petitioned and remonstrated against the unconstitutionality of the Tariff Acts, and though the conviction has been universal, that the effects of the system would be ruinous to our interests, yet the difficulty has been great, to bring the people to the resisting point.

And so with other objections. It has been maintained by us, that, according to the philosophy of the government, and the true spirit of the compact, it becomes Congress in all emergencies like the present, to solicit from the States, the call of a Convention. That, upon such a convocation, it should be incumbent on the States claiming the doubtful power, to propose an amendment to the Constitution, giving the doubtful power ; and on failue to obtain it by a consent of three fourths of all the States, to regard the power as never having been intended to be given. We must not be understood to say, that this was matter even of implied stipulation, at the formation of the compact.— The Constitution is designedly silent on the subject, on account of the extreme difficulty in the minds of its framers of appointing a mode of adjusting these differences. This difficulty we now discover was imaginary. It had its source in apprehensions, which an experience of upwards of forty years has proved to be without the shadow of a foundation. Many of the sages of that day, were dissatisfied with their work, for a reason which is the very opposite of the truth. They feared, not that the General Government would encroach upon the rights of the States, but that the States would perpetually be disposed to pass their boundaries of power, and finally destroy the confederation. Had they been blessed with the experience which we have acquired, there could have been no objection to trusting the States,—who created the Government, and who would not wilfully embarrass it,—with a veto under certain modifications. It seems but reasonable, that a disputed power, which it would have required three fourths of the States to add to the Constitution, ought not to be insisted on by a majority in Congress, as impliedly conferred, if more than one fourth should object to it. To deny this, would be to decide finally the validity of a power, by a positive majority of the people at large, instead of a concurring majority of the States. There is, it is true, one objection, and only one to this view : and that is, that under this theory, a majority little beyond the three fourths, as for instance, seven States out of twenty-four, might deprive Congress of powers which have been expressly delegated. The answer to this, is, that it would be a very extreme case for a single State to claim the resumption of a power, which it had clearly delegated in positive terms. But it seems almost beyond the range of possibility, that six other States should be found to sustain a nullifying State in such a pretension. Should such a case ever occur, as one fourth and upwards of the States resolving to break their pledges, without the slightest pretence, it would shew, that it was time to dissolve the league. If a spirit of friendship and fair dealing, cannot bind together the members of this Union, the sooner it is dissolved, the better. So that this objection is rather nominal, than substantial. But the evil of this objection is, that whilst its admission would relieve us from an imaginary peril, we should be plunged into that certain danger of an unrestricted liberty of Congress to give us, instead of a confederated government, a government without any other limitation upon its power, than the will of a majority.

Other objections have been urged against nullification. It is said that the President or Congress might employ the military and naval force of the United States to reduce the nullifying State into obedience,and thus produce a civil dissention amongst the members of the confederacy. We do not deem it necessary in a community, so conversant with this part of the subject as that of South Carolina, to recapitulate the arguments which have been urged against such an improbable course, both for the want of power, and on the ground of expediency. But we cannot pass over one view, which we think sufficient to quiet all apprehension on that score. We live in an age of reason and intellect. The idea of using force on an occasion of this kind, is utterly at variance with the genius and spirit of the American people. In truth, it is becoming repugnant even to the genius and spirit of the governments of the old world. We have lately seen in England, one of the greatest reforms achieved, which her history records—a reform which her wisest statesmen,twenty years ago, would have predicted could not be accomplished without civil war, brought about by a bloodless revolution.— The cause is manifest. Not only are the people every where better informed, but such is the influence which public opinion exerts over constituted authorities, that the rulers of this earth are more swayed by reason and justice than formerly. Under such evident indications of the march of mind and intellect, it would be to pay but a poor compliment to the people of these States, to imagine, that a measure taken by a Sovereign State, with the most perfect good feeling to her confederates, and to the perpetuity of the Union, and with no other view than to force upon its members, the consideration of a most important constitutional question, should terminate otherwise than peaceably.

Fellow Citizens, it is our honest and firm belief, that nullification will preserve, and not destroy this Union. But we should regret to conceal from you that if Congress should not be animated with a patriotic and liberal feeling in this conjuncture, they can give to this controversy what issue they please. Admit then, that there is risk of a serious conflict with the federal government. We know no better way to avoid the chance of hostile measures in our opponents, than to evince a readiness to meet danger, come from what quarter it will. We should think that the American Revolution was indeed to little purpose, if a consideration of this kind, were to deter our people from asserting their sovereign rights. That revolution, it is well known, was not entered into by our Southern ancestors from any actual oppression, which the people suffered. It was a contest waged for principle, emphatically for principle. The calamities of revolution, strife, and civil war, were fairly presented to the illustrious patriots of those times, which tried the souls of men.— The alternative was either to remain dependant colonies in hopeless servitude, or to become free, sovereign and independent States. To attain such a distinguished rank amongst the nations of the earth, there was but one path, and that the path of glory—the crowning glory of being accounted worthy of all suffering, and of embracing all the calamities of a protracted war abroad, and of domestic evils at home, rather than to surrender their liberties. The result of their labors is known to the world, through the flood of light which that revolution has shed upon the science of government, and the rights of man—in the "lesson it has taught the oppressor, and in the example it has afforded the oppressed"—in the invigoration of the spirit of freedom every where, and in the amelioration it is producing in the social order of mankind.

Inestimable are the blessings of that well regulated freedom, which permits man to direct his labors and his enterprize to the pursuit or branch of industry to which he conceives nature has qualified him, unmolested by avarice enthorned in power. Such was the freedom for which South Carolina struggled when a dependant colony. Such is the freedom of which she once tasted as the first fruit of that revolutionary triumph which she assisted to achieve. Such is the freedom she reserved to herself on entering into the league. Such is the freedom of which she has been deprived, and to which she must be restored, if her commerce be worth preserving, or the spirit of her Laurens and her Gadsden has not fled for ever from our bosoms. It is in vain to tell South Carolina that she can look to any administration of the Federal Government for the protection of her sovereign rights, or the redress of her Southern wrongs. Where the fountain is so polluted, it is not to be expected that the stream will again be pure. The protection to which in all representative governments the people have been accustomed to look, to wit, the responsibility of the governors to be governed, has proved nerveless and illusory; under such a system, nothing but a radical reform in our political institutions can preserve this union. It is full time that we should know what rights we have under the Federal Constitution, and more especially ought we to know whether we are to live under a consolidated government, or a confederacy of States—whether the States be sovereign, or their local Legislatures be mere corporations. A fresh understanding of the bargain, we deem absolutely necessary. No mode can be devised by which a dispute can be referred to the source of all power, but by some one State taking the lead in the great enterprize of reform. Till some one Southern State tenders to the Federal Government an issue, it will continue to have its "appetite increased by what it feeds on." History admonishes us that rulers never have the forecast to substitute in good time reform for revolution. They forget that it is always more desirable that the just claims of the governed should break in on them " through well contrived and well disposed windows, not through flaws and breaches, through the yawning chasms of their own ruin." One State must under the awful prospects before us, throw herself into the breach in this great struggle for constitutional freedom. There is no other mode of awakening the attention of the co-States to grievances which, if suffered to accumulate, must dismember the Union. It has fallen to our lot, fellow citizens, first to quit our trenches. Let us go on to the assault with cheerful hearts and undaunted minds.

Fellow citizens, the die is now cast. We have solemnly resolved on the course which it becomes our beloved State to pursue; we have resolved, that until these abuses shall be reformed, no more Taxes shall be paid here. "Millions for defence, but not a cent for tribute." And now we call upon our citizens, native and adopted, to prepare for the crisis, and to meet it as becomes men and freemen. We call upon all classes and all parties to forget their former differences, and to unite in a solemn determination, never to abandon this contest until such a change be effected in the councils of the nation, that all the citizens of this confederacy shall participate equally in the benefits and the burthens of the Government. To this solemn duty we now invoke you in the name of all that is sacred and valuable to man. We invoke you in the name of that Liberty which has been acquired by you from an illustrious ancestry, and which it is your duty to transmit unimpaired to the most distant generations. We invoke you in the name of that Constitution which you profess to venerate, and of that Union which you are all desirous to perpetuate. By the reverence you bear to these your institutions—by all the love you bear to liberty—by the detestation you have for servitude—by all the abiding memorials of your past glories—by the proud association of your exalted and your common triumphs in the first and greatest of revolutions—by the force of all those sublime truths which that event has inculcated amongst the nations—by the noble flame of republican enthusiasm which warms your bosoms, we conjure you in this mighty struggle to give your hearts and souls and minds to your injured and oppressed State, and to support her cause publicly and privately, with your opinions, your prayers, and your actions. If appeals such as these prove unavailing, we then command your obedience to the laws and the authorities of the State, by a title which none can gainsay. We demand it by that allegiance which is reciprocal with the protection you have received from the State. We admit of no obedience to any authority which shall conflict with that primary allegiance which every citizen owes to the State of his birth or his adoption. There is not, nor has there ever been "any direct or immediate allegiance between the citizens of South Carolina and the Federal Government; the relation between them is through the State." South Carolina having entered into the constitutional compact, as a separate independent political community, as has already been stated, has the right to declare an unconstitutional act of Congress null and void—after her sovereign declaration that the act shall not be enforced within her limits, "such a declaration is obligatory on her citizens. As far as its citizens are concerned, the clear right of the State is to declare the extent of the obligation." This declaration once made, the citizen has no course but to obey. If he refuses obedience, so as to bring himself under the displeasure of his only and lawful sovereign, and within the severe pains and penalties, which by her high sovereign power, the Legislature, will not fail to provide in her self-defence, the fault and the folly must be his own.

And now, fellow citizens, having discharged the solemn duty to which we have been summoned in a crisis big with the most important results to the liberties, peace, safety, and happiness of this once harmonious, but now distracted confederacy, we commend our cause to that great disposer of events, who (if he has not already for some inscrutable purposes of his own, decreed otherwise) will smile on the efforts of truth and justice. We know that "unless the Lord keepeth the city, the watchman waketh but in vain;" but relying as we do, in this controversy, on the purity of our motives, and the honor of our ends, we make this appeal with all the confidence, which in times of trial and difficulty, ought to inspire the breast of the patriot and the Christian. Fellow citizens, do your duty to your country, and leave the consequences to God.

ADDRESS

TO THE

PEOPLE OF THE UNITED STATES,

BY THE

CONVENTION OF THE PEOPLE

OF

SOUTH CAROLINA.

ADDRESS.

To the People of Massachusetts, Virginia, New York, Pennsylvania, North Carolina, Maryland, Connecticut, Vermont, New Hampshire, Maine, New Jersey, Georgia, Delaware, Rhode Island, Kentucky, Tennessee, Ohio, Louisiana, Indiana, Mississippi, Illinois, Alabama, and Missouri.

WE, the people of South Carolina, assembled in Convention, have solemnly and deliberately declared, in our paramount sovereign capacity, that the act of Congress approved the 19th day of May, 1828, and the act approved the 14th July, 1832, altering and amending the several acts imposing duties on imports, are unconstitutional, and therefore absolutely void, and of no binding force within the limits of this State ; and for the purpose of carrying this declaration into full and complete effect, we have invested the Legislature with ample powers, and made it the duty of all the functionaries, and all the citizens of the State, on their allegiance, to co-operate in enforcing the aforesaid declaration.

In resorting to this important measure, to which we have been impelled by the most sacred of all the duties which a free people can owe either to the memory of their ancestors, or to the claims of their posterity, we feel that it is due to the intimate political relation which exists between South Carolina and the other States of this confederacy, that we should present a clear and distinct exposition of the principles on which we have acted, and of the causes by which we have been reluctantly constrained to assume this attitude of sovereign resistance in relation to the usurpations of the Federal Government.

For this purpose, it will be necessary to state briefly, what we conceive to be the relation created by the Federal Constitution, between the States and the General Government; and also what we conceive to be the true character and practical operation of the system of protecting duties, as it affects our rights, our interests, and our liberties.

We hold then, that on their separation from the Crown of Great Britain, the several Colonies became free and independent States, each enjoying the separate and independent right of self-government; and that no authority can be exercised over them, or within their limits, but by their consent respectively given as States. It is equally true, that the Constitution of the United States, is a compact formed between the several States, acting as sovereign communities; that the Government created by it, is a joint agency of the States, appointed to execute the powers enumerated and granted by that instrument; that all its acts not intentionally authorized, are of themselves essentially null and void; and that the States have the right, in the same sovereign capacity in which they adopted the Federal Constitution, to pronounce, in the last resort, authoritative judgment on the usurpations of the Federal Government, and to adopt such measures as they may deem necessary and expedient to arrest the operation of the unconstitutional acts of that Government within their respective limits. Such we deem to be the inherent rights of the States—rights, in the very nature of things, absolutely inseparable from sovereignty. Nor is the duty of a State, to arrest an unconstitutional and oppressive act of the Federal Government, less imperative, than the right is incontestible. Each State, by ratifying the Federal Constitution, and becoming a member of the confederacy, contracted an obligation to "protect and defend" that instrument, as well by resisting the usurpations of the Federal Government, as by sustaining that Government in the exercise of the powers actually conferred upon it. And the obligation of the oath which is imposed, under the Constitution, on every functionary of the States, to "preserve, protect, and defend" the Federal Constitution, as clearly comprehends the duty of protecting and defending it against the usurpations of the Federal Government, as that of protecting and defending it against violation in any other form, or from any other quarter.

It is true, that in ratifying the Federal Constitution, the States placed a large and important portion of the rights of their citizens under the joint protection of all the States, with a view to their more effectual security ; but it is not less true that they reserved a portion still larger, and not less important under their own immediate guardianship, and in relation to which their original obligation to protect their citizens, from whatever quarter assailed, remains unchanged and undiminished.

But clear and undoubted as we regard the right, and sacred as we regard the duty of the States to interpose their sovereign power for the purpose of protecting their citizens from the unconstitutional and oppressive acts of the Federal Government, yet we are as clearly of the opinion, that nothing short of that high moral and political necessity, which results from acts of usurpation, subversive of the rights and liberties of the people, should induce a member of this confederacy to resort to this interposition. Such, however, is the melancholy and painful necessity under which we have declared the acts of Congress, imposing protecting duties, null and void within the limits of South Carolina. The spirit and the principles which animated your ancestors and ours in the councils and in the fields of their common glory, forbid us to submit any longer to a system of legislation, now become the established policy of the Federal Government, by which we are reduced to a condition of colonial vassalage, in all its aspects more oppressive and intolerable than that from which our common ancestors relieved themselves by the war of the revolution. There is no right which enters more essentially into a just conception of liberty, than that of the free and unrestricted use of the productions of our industry. This clearly involves the right of carrying the productions of that industry wherever they can be most advantageously exchanged, whether in foreign or domestic markets. South Carolina produces, almost exclusively, agricultural staples, which derive their principal value from the demand for them in foreign countries. Under these circumstances, her natural markets are abroad ; and restrictive duties imposed upon her intercourse with those markets, diminish the exchangeable value of her productions very nearly to the full extent of those duties.

Under a system of free trade, the aggregate crop of South

Carolina could be exchanged for a larger quantity of manufactures, by at least one third, than it can be now exchanged for under the protecting system. It is no less evident, that the value of that crop is diminished by the protecting system very nearly, if not precisely, to the extent that the aggregate quantity of manufactures which can be obtained for it, is diminished. It is, indeed, strictly and philosophically true, that the quantity of consumable commodities which can be obtained for the cotton and rice annually produced by the industry of the State, is the precise measure of their aggregate value. But for the prevalent and habitual error of confounding the money price with the exchangeable value of our agricultural staples, these propositions would be regarded as self-evident. If the protecting duties were repealed, one hundred bales of cotton, or one hundred barrels of rice, would purchase as large a quantity of manufactures, as one hundred and fifty will now purchase. The annual income of the State, its means of purchasing and consuming the necessaries and comforts and luxuries of life, would be increased in a corresponding degree.

Almost the entire cotton crop of South Carolina, amounting annually to more than six millions of dollars, is ultimately exchanged either for foreign manufactures, subject to protecting duties, or for similar domestic manufactures. The natural value of that crop would be all the manufactures which we could obtain for it, under a system of unrestricted commerce. The artificial value, produced by the unjust and unconstitutional legislation of Congress, is only such part of those manufactures as will remain after paying a duty of fifty per cent. to the Government, or, to speak with more precision, to the Northern manufacturers. To make this obvious to the humblest comprehension, let it be supposed that the whole of the present crop should be exchanged by the planters themselves, for those foreign manufactures, for which it is destined, by the inevitable course of trade, to be ultimately exchanged, either by themselves or their agents. Let it be also assumed, in conformity with the facts of the case, that New Jersey, for example, produces of the very same description of manufactures, a quantity equal to that which is purchased by the cotton crop of South Carolina. We have, then, two States of the same confederacy, bound to bear an equal share of the burthens, and entitled to enjoy an equal share of the benefits of the common government, with precisely the same quantity of productions, of the same quality and kind, produced by their lawful industry. We appeal to your candor, and to your sense of justice, to say whether South Carolina has not a title as sacred and indefeasible to the full and undiminished enjoyment of these productions of her industry, acquired by the combined operations of agriculture and commerce, as New Jersey can have to the like enjoyment of similar productions of her industry, acquired by the process of manufacture? Upon no principle of constitutional right—upon no principle of human reason or justice, can any discrimination be drawn between the titles of South Carolina and New Jersey to these productions of their capital and labor. Yet what is the discrimination actually made by the unjust, unconstitutional, and partial legislation of Congress? A duty, on an average, of fifty per cent., is imposed upon the productions of South Carolina, while no duty at all is imposed upon the similar productions of New Jersey! The inevitable result is, that the manufactures thus lawfully acquired by the honest industry of South Carolina, are worth, annually, three millions of dollars less to her citizens, than the very same quantity of the very same description of manufactures are worth to the citizens of New Jersey—a difference of value produced exclusively by the operation of the protecting system.

No ingenuity can either evade or refute this proposition.— The very axioms of geometry are not more self-evident. For even if the planters of South Carolina, in the case supposed, were to sell and not consume these productions of their industry, it is plain that they could obtain no higher price for them, after paying duties to the amount of $3,000,000, than the manufacturers of New Jersey would obtain for the same quantity of the same kind of manufactures, without paying any duty at all.

This single view of the subject, exhibits the enormous inequality and injustice of the protecting system in such a light, that we feel the most consoling confidence that we shall be fully justified by the impartial judgment of posterity, whatever may be the issue of this unhappy controversy. We confidently appeal to our confederate States, and to the whole world, to decide whether the annals of human legislation furnish a parallel instance of injustice and oppression perpetrated under the forms of a free government. However it may be disguised by the complexity of the process by which it is effected, it is nothing less than the monstrous outrage of taking three millions of dollars annually, from the value of the productions of South Carolina and transferring it to the people of other and distant communities. No human Government, can rightfully exercise such a power. It violates the eternal principles of natural justice, and converts the Government into a mere instrument of legislative plunder. Of all the governments on the face of the earth, the Federal Government has the least shadow of a constitutional right to exercise such a power. It was created principally, and almost exclusively, for the purpose of protecting, improving, and extending that very commerce which, for the last ten years, all its powers have been most unnaturally and unrighteously perverted to cripple and destroy. The power to "regulate commerce with foreign nations," was granted, obviously, for the preservation of that commerce. The most important of all the duties which the Federal Government owes to South Carolina, under the compact of Union, is the protection and defence of her foreign commerce, against all the enemies by whom it may be assailed. And in what manner has this duty been discharged? All the powers of the earth, by their commercial restrictions, and all the pirates of the ocean, by their lawless violence, could not have done so much to destroy our commerce, as has been done by that very Government, to which its guardianship has been committed by the Federal Constitution. The commerce of South Carolina consists in exchanging the staple productions of her soil for the manufactures of Europe. It is a lawful commerce. It violates the rights of no class of people in any portion of the confederacy. It is this very commerce, therefore, which the Constitution has enjoined it upon Congress to encourage, protect, and defend, by such regulations as may be necessary to accomplish that object. But instead of that protection, which is the only tie of our allegiance, as individual citizens to the Federal Government, we have seen a gigantic system of restrictions, gradually reared up, and at length brought to a fatal maturity, of which it is the avowed object and must be the inevitable result, to sweep our commerce from the great highway of nations, and cover our land with poverty and ruin.

Even the States most deeply interested in the maintenance of the protecting system will admit, that it is the interest of South Carolina to carry on a commerce of exchanges with foreign countries, free from restrictions, prohibitory burthens, or incumbrances of any kind. We feel, and we know, that the vital interests of the State, are involved in such a commerce. It would be a downright insult to our understandings, to tell us that our interests are not injured, deeply injured, by those prohibitory duties, intended and calculated to prevent us from obtaining the cheap manufactures of foreign countries for our staples, and to compel us to receive for them the dear manufactures of our domestic establishments, or pay the penalty of the protecting duties, for daring to exercise one of the most sacred of our natural rights. What right, then, human or divine, have the manufacturing States—for we regard the Federal Government as a mere instrument in their hands—to prohibit South Carolina, directly, or indirectly, from going to her natural markets ; and exchanging the rich productions of her soil, without restriction or incumbrance, for such foreign articles as will most conduce to the wealth and prosperity of her citizens? It will not surely be pretended—for truth and decency equally forbid the allegation—that in exchanging our productions for the cheaper manufactures of Europe, we violate any right of the domestic manufacturers, however gratifying it might be to them, if we would purchase their inferior productions at higher prices.

Upon what principle, then, can the State of South Carolina be called upon to submit to a system, which excludes her from her natural markets, and the manifold benefits of that enriching commerce, which a kind and beneficent Providence has provided, to connect her with the family of nations, by the bonds of mutual interest? But one answer can be given to this question. It is in vain that we attempt to disguise the fact, mortifying as it must be, that the principle by which South Carolina is thus excluded, is in strict propriety of language, and to all rational intents and purposes, a principle of colonial dependence and vassalage, identical with that which restrained our forefathers from trading with any manufacturing nation of Europe, other than Great

Britain. South Carolina now bears the same relation to the manufacturing States of this confederacy, that the Anglo American Colonies bore to the mother country, with the single exception that our burthens are incomparably more oppressive than those of our ancestors. Our time, our pride, and the occasion, equally forbid us to trace out the degrading analogy. We leave that to the historian who shall record the judgment which an impartial posterity shall pronounce upon the eventful transactions of this day.

It is in vain that we attempt to console ourselves by the empty and unreal mockery of our representation in Congress. As to all those great and vital interests of the States, which are affected by the protecting system, it would be better that she had no representation in that body. It serves no other purpose but to conceal the chains which fetter our liberties under the vain and empty forms of a representative Government. In the enactment of the protecting system, the majority of Congress is, in strict propriety of speech, an irresponsible despotism. A very brief analysis will render this clear to every understanding. What, then, we ask, is involved in the idea of political responsibility, in the imposition of public burthens? It clearly implies that those who impose the burthens, should be responsible to those who bear them. Every representative in Congress should be responsible, not only to his own immediate constituents, but through them and their common participation in the burthens imposed, to the constituents of every other representative. If in the enactment of a protecting tariff, the majority of Congress imposed upon their own constituents the same burthens which they impose upon the people of South Carolina, that majority would act under all the restraints of political responsibility, and we should have the best security which human wisdom has yet devised, against oppressive legislation.

But the fact is precisely the reverse of this. The majority in Congress, in imposing protecting duties, which are utterly destructive of the interests of South Carolina, not only impose no burthens, but actually confer enriching bounties upon their constituents, proportioned to the burthens they impose upon us. Under these circumstances, the principle of representative responsibility, is perverted into a principle of absolute despotism.

It is this very tie, binding the majority of Congress to execute the will of their constituents, which makes them our inexorable oppressors. They dare not open their hearts to the sentiments of human justice, or to the feelings of human sympathy. They are tyrants by the very necessity of their position, however elevated may be their principles in their individual capacities.

The grave question, then, which we have had to determine, as the sovereign power of the State, upon the awful responsibility under which we have acted, is, whether we will voluntarily surrender the glorious inheritance, purchased and consecrated by the toils, the sufferings, and the blood of an illustrious ancestry, or transmit that inheritance to our posterity, untarnished and undiminished ? We could not hesitate in deciding this question. We have, therefore, deliberately and unalterably resolved, that we will no longer submit to a system of oppression, which reduces us to the degrading condition of tributary vassals ; and which would reduce our posterity, in a few generations, to a state of poverty and wretchedness, that would stand in melancholy contrast with the beautiful and delightful region, in which the providence of God has cast our destinies. Having formed this resolution, with a full view of all its bearings, and of all its probable and possible issues, it is due to the gravity of the subject, and the solemnity of the occasion, that we should speak to our confederate brethren, in the plain language of frankness and truth. Though we plant ourselves upon the Constitution, and the immutable principles of justice, and intend to operate exclusively through the civil tribunals and civil functionaries of the State ; yet, we will throw off this oppression, at every hazard. We believe our remedy to be essentially peaceful. We believe the Federal Government has no shadow of right or authority, to act against a sovereign State of the confederacy, in any form, much less to coerce it, by military power. But we are aware of the diversities of human opinion ; and have seen too many proofs of the infatuation of human power, not to have looked, with the most anxious concern, to the possibility of a resort to military or naval force on the part of the Federal Government ; and in order to obviate the possibility of having the history of this contest stained by a single drop of fraternal blood we have solemnly and irrevocably resolved, that we will regard such a resort as a dissolution of the political ties which connect us with our confederate States; and will, forthwith, provide for the organization of a new and separate Government.

We implore you, and particularly the manufacturing States, not to believe that we have been actuated, in adopting this resolution, by any feeling of resentment, or hostility towards them; or, by a desire, to dissolve the political bonds which have so long united our common destinies. We still cherish that rational devotion to the Union, by which this State has been pre-eminently distinguished, in all times past. But that blind and idolatrous devotion, which would bow down and worship Oppression and Tyranny, veiled under that consecrated title— if it ever existed among us, has now vanished forever. Constitutional Liberty is the only idol of our political devotion; and, to preserve that, we will not hesitate a single moment, to surrender the Union itself, if the sacrifice be necessary. If it had pleased God to cover our eyes with ignorance—if he had not bestowed upon us the understanding to comprehend the enormity of the oppression under which we labor, we might submit to it without absolute degradation and infamy. But the gifts of Providence cannot be neglected, or abused, with impunity. A people, who deliberately submit to oppression, with a full knowledge that they are oppressed, are fit only to be slaves; and all history proves, that such a people will soon find a master. It is the pre-existing spirit of slavery in the people, that has made tyrants in all ages of the world. No tyrant ever made a slave—no community, however small, having the spirit of freemen, ever yet had a master. The most illustrious of those States, which have given to the world examples of human freedom, have occupied territories not larger than some of the districts of South Carolina; while the largest masses of population, that were ever united under a common government, have been the abject, spiritless, and degraded slaves of despotic rulers. We sincerely hope, therefore, that no portion of the States of this Confederacy, will permit themselves to be deluded into any measures of rashness, by the vain imagination, that South Carolina will vindicate her rights and liberties, with a less inflexible and unfaltering resolution, with a population of some half a million, than she would do with a population of twenty millions.

It does not belong to Freemen to count the costs, and calculate the hazards of vindicating their rights and defending their liberties ; and even if we should stand alone in the worst possible emergency of this great controversy, without the co-operation or encouragement of a single State of the confederacy, we will march forward with an unfaltering step, until we have accomplished the object of this great enterprise.

Having now presented, for the consideration of the Federal Government and our confederate States, the fixed and final determination of this State, in relation to the protecting system, it remains for us to submit a plan of taxation in which we would be willing to acquiesce, in a spirit of liberal concession, provided we are met in due time and in a becoming spirit, by the States interested in the protection of manufactures.

We believe that upon every just and equitable principle of taxation, the whole list of protected articles should be imported free of all duty, and that the revenue derived from import duties, should be raised exclusively from the unprotected articles, or that, whenever a duty is imposed upon protected articles imported, an excise duty of the same rate should be imposed upon all similar articles manufactured in the United States. This would be as near an approach to perfect equality as could possibly be made, in a system of indirect taxation. No substantial reason can be given for subjecting manufactures obtained from abroad in exchange for the productions of South Carolina, to the smallest duty, even for revenue, which would not show that similar manufactures made in the United States, should be subject to the very same rate of duty. The former, not less than the latter, are, to every rational intent, the productions of domestic industry, and the mode of acquiring the one, is as lawful and more conducive to the public prosperity, than that of acquiring the other.

But we are willing to make a large offering to preserve the Union ; and with a distinct declaration that it is a concession on our part, we will consent that the same rate of duty may be imposed upon the protected articles that shall be imposed upon the unprotected, provided that no more revenue be raised than is necessary to meet the demands of the Government for Constitutional purposes, and provided also, that a duty, substantially uniform, be imposed upon all foreign imports.

It is obvious, that, even under this arrangement, the manufacturing States would have a decided advantage over the planting States. For it is demonstrably evident that, as communities, the manufacturing States would bear no part of the burthens of Federal Taxation, so far as the revenue should be derived from protected articles. The earnestness with which their representatives seek to increase the duties on these articles, is conclusive proof that those duties are bounties, and not burthens, to their constituents. As at least two-thirds of the federal revenue would be raised from protected articles, under the proposed modification of the Tariff, the manufacturing States would be entirely exempted from all participation in that proportion of the public burthens.

Under these circumstances, we cannot permit ourselves to believe for a moment, that in a crisis marked by such portentous and fearful omens, those States can hesitate in acceding to this arrangement, when they perceive that it will be the means, and possibly the only means, of restoring the broken harmony of this great confederacy. They most assuredly have the strongest of human inducements, aside from all considerations of justice, to adjust this controversy, without pushing it to extremities. This can be accomplished only by the proposed modification of the Tariff, or by the call of a General Convention of all the States. If South Carolina should be driven out of the Union, all the other Planting States, and some of the Western States, would follow by an almost absolute necessity. Can it be believed that Georgia, Mississippi, Tennessee, and even Kentucky, would continue to pay a tribute of fifty per cent. upon their consumption, to the Northern States, for the privilege of being united to them, when they could receive all their supplies through the ports of South Carolina, without paying a single cent of tribute ?

The separation of South Carolina would inevitably produce a general dissolution of the Union ; and as a necessary consequence, the protecting system, with all its pecuniary bounties, to the Northern States, and its pecuniary burthens upon the Southern States, would be utterly overthrown and demolished, involving the ruin of thousands and hundreds of thousands in the manufacturing States.

By these powerful considerations, connected with their own pecuniary interests, we beseech them to pause and contemplate the disastrous consequences which will certainly result from an obstinate perseverance on their part, in maintaining the protecting system. With them, it is a question merely of pecuniary interest, connected with no shadow of right, and involving no principle of liberty. With us, it is a question involving our most sacred rights—those very rights which our common ancestors left to us as a common inheritance, purchased by their common toils and consecrated by their blood. It is a question of liberty on the one hand, and slavery on the other. If we submit to this system of unconstitutional oppression, we shall voluntarily sink into slavery, and transmit that ignominious inheritance to our children. We will not, we cannot, we dare not submit to this degradation, and our resolve is fixed and unalterable that a protecting tariff shall be no longer enforced within the limits of South Carolina. We stand upon the principles of everlasting justice, and no human power shall drive us from our position.

We have not the slightest apprehension that the general government will attempt to force this system upon us by military power. We have warned our brethren of the consequences of such an attempt. But if, notwithstanding, such a course of madness should be pursued, we here solemnly declare that this system of oppression shall never prevail in South Carolina, until none but slaves are left to submit to it. We would infinitely prefer that the territory of the State should be the cemetery of freemen than the habitation of slaves. Actuated by these principles, and animated by these sentiments, we will cling to the pillars of the temple of our liberties, and if it must fall, we will perish amidst the ruins.

J. HAMILTON, Jun., *President of the Convention.*

[Attest.]

ISAAC W. HAYNE, *Clerk.*

PROCLAMATION

BY THE

PRESIDENT

OF THE

UNITED STATES OF AMERICA.

PROCLAMATION.

Whereas, a Convention assembled in the State of South Carolina, have passed an Ordinance, by which they declare "That the several acts and parts of acts of the Congress of the United States, purporting to be laws for the imposing of duties and imposts on the importation of foreign commodities, and now having actual operation and effect within the United States, and more especially" two acts for the same purposes passed on the 28th of May, 1828, and on the 14th of July, 1832, "are unauthorized by the Constitution of the United States, and violate the true meaning and intent thereof, and are null and void, and no law," nor binding on the citizens of that State or its officers: and by the said Ordinance it is further declared to be unlawful for any of the constituted authorities of the State, or of the United States, to enforce the payment of the duties imposed by the said acts within the same State, and that it is the duty of the Legislature to pass such laws as may be necessary to give full effect to the said Ordinance :

And, whereas, by the Ordinance it is further ordained, that in no case of law or equity, decided in the courts of said State, wherein shall be drawn in question the validity of the said Ordinance, or the acts of the Legislature that may be passed to give it effect, or of the said laws of the United States, shall an appeal be allowed to the Supreme Court of the United States, nor shall any copy of the record be permitted or allowed for that purpose ; and that any person attempting to take such appeal, shall be punished as for a contempt of Court :

And, finally, the said Ordinance declares that the people of

South Carolina will maintain the said Ordinance at every hazard; and that they will consider the passage of an act by Congress abolishing or closing the ports of the said State, or otherwise obstructing the free ingress and egress of vessels to and from the said port, or any other act of the Federal Government to coerce the State, shut up her ports, destroy or harrass her commerce, or to enforce said acts otherwise than through the civil tribunals of the country, as inconsistent with the longer continuance of South Carolina in the Union; and that the people of the said State will thenceforth hold themselves absolved from all further obligation to maintain or preserve their political connexion with the people of the other States, and will forthwith proceed to organize a separate Government, and do all other acts and things which sovereign and independent States may of right do.

And, whereas, the said Ordinance prescribes to the people of South Carolina a course of conduct in direct violation of their duty as citizens of the United States, contrary to the laws of their country, subversive of its Constitution, and having for its object the destruction of the Union—that Union, which, coeval with our political existence, led our fathers, without any other ties to unite them than those of patriotism and a common cause, through a sanguinary struggle, to a glorious independence— that sacred Union, hitherto inviolate, which perfected by our happy Constitution, has brought us, by the favor of Heaven, to a state of prosperity at home, and high consideration abroad, rarely, if ever, equalled in the history of nations. To preserve this bond of our political existence from destruction, to maintain inviolate this state of national honor and prosperity, and to justify the confidence my fellow citizens have reposed in me, I Andrew Jackson, President of the United States, have thought proper to issue this my Proclamation, stating my views of the Constitution and laws applicable to the measures adopted by the Convention of South Carolina, and the reasons they have put forth to sustain them, declaring the course which duty will require me to pursue, and appealing to the understanding and patriotism of the people, to warn them of the consequences must inevitably result from an observance of the dictates of the Convention.

Strict duty would require of me nothing more than the exercise of those powers with which I am now, or may hereafter be invested, for preserving the peace of the Union, and for the execution of the laws. But the imposing aspect which opposition has assumed in this case, by clothing itself with State authority, and the deep interest which the people of the United States must all feel in preventing a resort to stronger measures, while there is a hope that any thing will be yielded to reasoning and remonstrance, perhaps demand, and will certainly justify a full exposition to South Carolina and the nation, of the views I entertain of this important question, as well as a distinct enunciation of the course which my sense of duty will require me to pursue.

This Ordinance is founded, not on the indefeasible right of resisting acts which are plainly unconstitutional, and too oppressive to be endured, but on the strange position that any one State may not only declare an act of Congress void, but prohibit its execution—that they may do this consistently with the Constitution—that the true construction of that instrument permits a State to retain its place in the Union, and yet be bound by no other of its laws than those it may choose to consider as constitutional. It is true, they add, that to justify this abrogation of a law, it must be palpably contrary to the Constitution; but it is evident that, to give the right of resisting laws of that description, coupled with the uncontrolled right to decide what laws deserve that character, is to give the power of resisting all laws. For, as by the theory there is no appeal, the reasons alleged by the State, good or bad, must prevail. If it should be said that public opinion is a sufficient check against the abuse of this power, it may be asked why it is not deemed a sufficient guard against the passage of an unconstitutional act by Congress? There is, however, a restraint in this last case, which makes the assumed power of a State more indefeasible, and which does not exist in the other. There are two appeals from an unconstitutional act passed by Congress—one to the Judiciary, the other to the people and the States. There is no appeal from the State decision in theory, and the practical illustration shows that the Courts are closed against an application to review it, both judges and jurors being sworn to decide in its favor. But reasoning on this subject is superfluous, when our social compact in express terms declares, that the laws of the United States, its Constitution, and treaties made under it, are the supreme law of the land ; and for greater caution, adds, " that the Judges in every State shall be bound thereby, any thing in the Constitution or laws of any State to the contrary notwithstanding." And it may be asserted, without fear of refutation, that no Federative Government could exist without a similar provision. Look for a moment to the consequence.

If South Carolina considers the revenue laws as unconstitutional, and has a right to prevent their execution in the port of Charleston, there would be a clear constitutional objection to their collection in every other port, and no revenue could be collected any where ; for all imposts must be equal. It is no answer to repeat that an unconstitutional law is no law, so long as the question of its legality is to be decided by the State itself ; for every law operating injuriously upon any local interest, will be perhaps thought, and certainly represented, as unconstitutional, and it has been shown, there is no appeal.

If this doctrine had been established at an earlier day, the Union would have been dissolved in its infancy. The excise law in Pennsylvania, the embargo and non-intercourse laws in the Eastern States, the carriage tax in Virginia, were all deemed unconstitutional, and were more unequal in their operation than any of the laws now complained of; but, fortunately, none of those States discovered that they had the right now claimed by South Carolina. The war into which we were forced, to support the dignity of the nation and the rights of our citizens, might have ended in defeat and disgrace, instead of victory and honor, if the States, who supposed it a ruinous and unconstitutional measure, had thought they possessed the right of nullifying the act by which it was declared, and denying supplies for its prosecution. Hardly and unequally as those measures bore upon several members of the Union, to the legislature of none did this efficient and peaceable remedy, as it is called, suggest itself. The discovery of this important feature in our constitution was reserved to the present day. To the statesmen of South Carolina belongs the invention, and upon the citizens of that State will unfortunately fall the evils of reducing it to practice.

If the doctrine of a State veto, upon the laws of the Union, carries with it internal evidence of its impracticable absurdity, our constitutional history will also afford abundant proof that it would have been repudiated with indignation, had it been proposed to form a feature in our Government.

In our colonial state, although dependent on another power, we very early considered ourselves as connected by common interest with each other. Leagues were formed for common defence, and before the Declaration of Independence we were known in our aggregate character as the United Colonies of America. That decisive and important step was taken jointly. We declared ourselves a nation by a joint, not by several acts ; and when the terms of our confederation were reduced to form, it was in that of a solemn league of several States, by which they agreed that they would collectively, form one nation, for the purpose of conducting some certain domestic concerns, and all foreign relations. In the instrument forming that Union, is found an article which declares that " every State shall abide by the determinations of Congress on all questions which by that confederation should be submitted to them."

Under the confederation, then, no State could legally annul a decision of the Congress, or refuse to submit to its execution ; but no provision was made to enforce these decisions. Congress made requisitions but they were not complied with. The Government could not operate on individuals. They had no Judiciary, no means of collecting revenue.

But the defects of the confederation need not be detailed. Under its operation, we would scarcely be called a nation. We had neither prosperity at home nor consideration abroad. This state of things could not be endured, and our present happy Constitution was formed ; but formed in vain if this fatal doctrine prevails. It was formed for important objects that are announced in the preamble made in the name and by the authority of the people of the United States, whose delegates framed, and whose conventions approved it. The most important among these objects, that which is placed first in rank, on which all the others rest " is to form a more perfect Union." Now, is it possible that, even if there were no express provisions giving supremacy to the Constitution and laws of the United States over those of the States, it can be conceived, that an instrument made for the purpose of "forming a more perfect Union" than that of the confederation, could be so constructed by the assembled wisdom of our country as to substitute for that confederation a form of government dependent for its existence on the local interest, the party spirit of a State, or of a prevailing faction in a State? Every man of plain unsophisticated understanding, who hears the question, will give such an answer as will preserve the Union. Metaphysical subtlety, in pursuit of an impracticable theory, could alone have devised one that is calculated to destroy it.

I consider, then, the power to annul a law of the United States, assumed by one State, incompatible with the existence of the Union, contradicted expressly by the letter of the Constitution, unauthorized by its spirit, inconsistent with every principle on which it was founded, and destructive of the great object for which it was formed.

After this general view of the leading principle, we must examine the particular application of it which is made in the ordinance.

The preamble rests its justification on these grounds: It assumes as a fact, that the obnoxious laws, although they purport to be laws for raising revenue, were in reality intended for the protection of manufactures, which purpose it asserts to be unconstitutional; that the operation of these laws is unequal; that the amount raised by them is greater than is required by the wants of the Government; and, finally that the proceeds are to be applied to objects unauthorized by the Constitution. These are the only causes alledged to justify an open opposition to the laws of the country, and a threat of seceding from the Union, if any attempt should be made to enforce them. She first virtually acknowledges that the law in question was passed under a power expressly given by the Constitution to lay and collect imposts, but its constitutionality is drawn in question from the motives of those who passed it. However apparent this purpose may be in the present case, nothing can be more dangerous than to admit the position that an unconstitutional purpose, entertained by the members who assent to a law enacted under a constitutional power, shall make that law void; for how is that purpose to be ascertained? Who is to make the scrutiny? How often may bad purposes be falsely imputed? In how many cases are they

concealed by false profession ? In how many is no declaration
of motive made ? Admit this doctrine, and you give to the States
an uncontrolled right to decide ; and every law may be annulled
under this pretext. If, therefore, the absurd and dangerous
doctrine should be admitted, that a State may annul an unconstitutional law, or one that it deems such, it will not apply to the
present case.

The next objection is, that the laws in question operate unequally. This objection may be made with truth to every law
that has been or can be passed. The wisdom of man never
yet contrived a system of taxation that would operate with perfect equality. If the unequal operation of a law makes it unconstitutional, and if all laws of that description may be abrogated by any State for that cause, then indeed is the Federal
Constitution unworthy of the slightest effort for its preservation.
We have hitherto relied on it as the perpetual bond of our
Union. We have received it as the work of the assembled wisdom of the nation. We have trusted to it as to the sheet anchor
of our safety, in the stormy times of conflict with a foreign or
domestic foe. We have looked to it with sacred awe as the palladium of our liberties, and with all the solemnities of religion,
have pledged to each other our lives and fortunes here, and our
hopes of happiness hereafter, in its defence and support. Were
we mistaken, my countrymen, in attaching this importance to
the Constitution of our country? Was our devotion paid to the
wretched, inefficient, clumsy contrivance, which this new doctrine would make it? Did we pledge ourselves to the support
of an airy nothing—a bubble that must be blown away by the
first breath of disaffection? Was this self-destroying, visionary
theory, the work of the profound statesmen, the exalted patriots, to whom the task of constitutional reform was entrusted ?
Did the name of Washington sanction, did the States deliberately ratify such an anomaly in the history of fundamental legislation? No. We were not mistaken ! The letter of this great
instrument is free from this radical fault ; its language directly
contradicts the imputation : its spirit—its evident intent—contradicts it. No; we did not err ! Our Constitution does not
contain the absurdity of giving power to make laws, and another
power to resist them.

The sages, whose memory will always be reverenced, have given us a practical, and, as they hoped, a permanent constitutional compact. The Father of his country did not affix his revered name to so palpable an absurdity. Nor did the States when they severally ratified it, do so under the impression that a veto on the laws of the United States was reserved to them, or that they could exercise it by implication. Search the debates in all their Conventions—examine the speeches of the most zealous opposers of Federal authority—look at the amendments that were proposed. They are all silent—not a syllable uttered, not a vote given, not a motion made to correct the explicit supremacy given to the laws of the Union over those of the States—or to show that implication, as is now contended, could defeat it. No, we have not erred! The Constitution is still the object of our reverence, the bond of our Union, our defence in danger, the source of our prosperity in peace. It shall descend, as we have received it, uncorrupted by sophistical construction, to our posterity; and the sacrifices of local interest, of State prejudices, of personal animosities, that were made to bring it into existence, will again be patriotically offered for its support.

The two remaining objections made by the Ordinance to these laws are, that the sums intended to be raised by them are greater than are required, and that the proceeds will be unconstitutionally employed. The Constitution has given expressly to Congress the right of raising revenue, and of determining the sum the public exigencies will require. The States have no control over the exercise of this right, other than that which results from the power of changing the representatives who abuse it, and thus procure redress. Congress may undoubtedly abuse this discretionary power, but the same may be said of others with which they are vested. Yet the discretion must exist somewhere. The Constitution has given it to the Representatives of all the People, checked by the Representatives of the States, and by the Executive power. The South Carolina construction gives it to the Legislature or Convention of a single State, where neither the people of the different States nor the State in their separate capacity, nor the Chief Magistrate elected by the people, have any representation. Which is the most discreet disposition of the power ? I do not ask you, fellow citizens, which is the Constitutional disposition—that instrument speaks a language not to be misunderstood. But if you were assembled in general convention, which would you think the safest depository for this discretionary power in the last resort. Would you add a clause giving it to each of the States, or would you sanction the wise provisions already made by your Constitution ? If this should be the result of your deliberations, when providing for the future, are you, can you—be ready to risk all that we hold dear, to establish for a temporary and a local purpose, that which you must acknowledge to be destructive, and even absurd, as a general provision ? Carry out the consequences of this right vested in the different States, and you must perceive that the crisis your conduct presents at this day would recur whenever any law of the United States displeased any of the States, and that we should soon cease to be a nation.

The Ordinance, with the same knowledge of the future that characterizes a former objection, tells you that the proceeds of the tax will be unconstitutionally applied. If this could be ascertained with certainty, the objection would, with more propriety, be reserved for the law so applying the proceeds, but surely cannot be urged against the laws levying the duty.

These are the allegations contained in the Ordinance. Examine them seriously, my fellow citizens—judge for yourselves. I appeal to you to determine whether they are so clear, so convincing, as to leave no doubt of their correctness : and even if you should come to this conclusion, how far they justify the reckless, destructive course, which you are directed to pursue. Review these objections, and the couclusions drawn from them once more. What are they ? Every law, then, for raising revenue, according to the South Carolina Ordinance, may be rightfully annulled, unless it be so framed as no law ever will or can be framed. Congress have a right to pass laws for raising revenue, and each State has a right to oppose their execution—two rights directly opposite to each other ; and yet is this absurdity supposed to be contained in an instrument drawn for the express purpose of avoiding collisions between the States and the General Government, by an assembly of the most enlightened statesmen and purest patriots ever embodied for a similar purpose.

In vain have these sages declared that Congress shall have power to lay and collect taxes, duties, imposts, and excise—in vain have they provided that they shall have power to pass all laws which shall be necessary and proper to carry those powers into execution; that those laws and that Constitution shall be the "supreme law of the land; and that the judges in every State shall be bound thereby, any thing in the Constitution or laws of any State to the contrary notwithstanding." In vain have the people of the several States solemnly sanctioned these provisions, made them their paramount law, and individually sworn to support them whenever they were called on to execute any office. Vain provisions! ineffectual restrictions! vile profanation of oaths! miserable mockery of legislation! If a bare majority of the voters in any one State may, on a real or supposed knowledge of the intent with which a law has been passed, declare themselves free from its operation—say here it gives too little, there too much, and operates unequally—here it suffers articles to be free that ought to be taxed, there it taxes those that ought to be free—in this case the proceeds are intended to be applied to purposes which we do not approve; in that the amount raised is more than is wanted. Congress, it is true, are invested by the Constitution, with the right of deciding these questions according to their sound discretion. Congress is composed of the Representatives of all the States and all the people of the States; but we, part of the people of one State, to whom the Constitution has given no power on the subject, from whom it has expressly taken it away; we, who have solemnly agreed that this Constitution shall be our law—we, most of whom have sworn to support it—we, now abrogate this law, and swear, and force others to swear, that it shall not be obeyed—and we do this not because Congress have no right to pass such laws—this we do not allege; but because they have passed them with improper views.

They are unconstitutional from the motives of those who passed them, which we can never with certainty know, from their unequal operation, although it is impossible from the nature of things that they should be equal—and from the disposition which we presume may be made of their proceeds, although that disposition has not been declared. This is the plain meaning of the Ordinance in relation to laws which it abrogates for alleged unconstitutionality. But it does not stop there. It repeals, in express terms, an important part of the Constitution itself, and of laws passed to give it effect, which have never been alleged to be unconstitutional. The Constitution declares that the judicial powers of the United States extend to cases arising under the laws of the United States, and that such laws, the Constitution and treaties, shall be paramount to the State Constitution and laws.

The judiciary act prescribes the mode by which the case may be brought before a Court of the United States by appeal, when a State tribunal shall decide against this provision of the Constitution. The Ordinance declares there shall be no appeal; makes the State law paramount to the Constitution of the United States; forces judges and jurors to swear they will disregard its provisions; and even makes it penal in a suitor to attempt relief by appeal. It further declares that it shall not be lawful for the authorities of the United States, or of that State, to enforce the payment of duties imposed by the revenue laws within its limits.

Here is a law of the United States, not even pretended to be unconstitutional, repealed by the authority of a small majority of the voters of a single State. Here is a provision of the Constitution which is solemnly abrogated by the same authority.

On such expositions and reasonings, the Ordinance grounds not only an assertion of the right to annul the laws of which it complains, but to enforce it by a threat of seceding from the Union, if any attempt is made to execute them.

The right to secede is deduced from the nature of the Constitution, which, they say, is a compact between the sovereign States, who have preserved their whole sovereignty, and, therefore, are subject to no superior; that because they made the compact, they can break it when, in their opinion, it has been departed from by the other States. Fallacious as this course of reasoning is, it enlists State pride, and finds advocates in the honest prejudice of those who have not studied the nature of our Government sufficiently to see the radical error on which it rests.

The people of the United States formed the Constitution, acting through the State Legislatures in making the compact, to meet and discuss its provisions, and acting in separate Conventions when they ratified these provisions; but the terms used in its construction, show it to be a Government in which the people of all the States collectively are represented. We are one people in the choice of the President and Vice President. Here the States have no other agency than to direct the mode in which the votes shall be given. The candidates having the majority of all the votes are chosen. The electors of a majority of States may have given their votes for one candidate, and yet another may be chosen. The people then, and not the States, are represented in the Executive branch.

In the House of Representatives there is this difference, that the people of one State do not, as in the case of President and Vice President, all vote for the same officers. The people of all the States do not vote for all the members, each State electing only its own Representatives. But this creates no material distinction. When chosen, they are all representatives of the United States, not representatives of the particular State from which they come. They are paid by the United States, not by the State, nor are they accountable to it for any act done in the performance of their legislative functions; and, however they may in practice, as it is their duty to do, consult and prefer the interests of their particular constituents when they come in conflict with any other partial or local interest, yet it is their first and highest duty as representatives of the United States, to promote the general good.

The Constitution of the United States, then, forms a Government, not a league; and whether it be formed by compact between the States, or in any other manner, its character is the same. It is a Government in which all the people are represented, which operates directly on the people individually, not upon the States; they retained all the power they did not grant. But each State having expressly parted with so many powers as to constitute jointly with the other States a single nation, cannot from that period possess any right to secede, because such secession does not break a league, but destroys the unity of a nation; and any injury to that unity is not only a breach which would result from the contravention of a compact, but it is an offence against the whole Union. To say that any State may at pleasure secede from the Union, is to say that the United States are not a nation; because it would be a solecism to contend that any part of a nation might dissolve its connexion with the other parts, to their injury or ruin, without committing any offence.

Secession, like any other revolutionary act, may be morally justified by the extremity of oppression, but to call it a constitutional right, is confounding the meaning of terms; and can only be done through gross error, or to deceive those who are willing to assert a right, but would pause before they made a revolution, or incurred the penalties consequent on a failure.

Because the Union was formed by compact, it is said the parties to that compact may, when they feel themselves aggrieved, depart from it; but it is precisely because it is a compact that they cannot. A compact is an agreement or binding obligation. It may, by its terms, have a sanction or penalty for its breach, or it may not. If it contains no sanction, it may be broken with no other consequence than moral guilt; if it have a sanction, then the breach incurs the designated or implied penalty. A league between independent nations, generally, has no sanction other than a moral one; or, if it should contain a penalty, as there is no common superior, it cannot be enforced. A Government, on the contrary, always has a sanction, express or implied; and, in our case, it is both necessarily implied and expressly given. An attempt by force of arms to destroy a Government, is an offence, by whatever means the constitutional compact may have been formed; and such Government has the right, by the law of self-defence, to pass acts for punishing the offender, unless that right is modified, restrained, or resumed by the constitutional act. In our system, although it is modified in the case of treason, yet authority is expressly given to pass all laws necessary to carry its power into effect, and under this grant provision has been made for punishing acts which obstruct the due administration of the laws.

It would seem superfluous to add any thing to show the nature of that Union which connects us; but as erroneous opinions on this subject are the foundation of doctrines the most destructive to our peace, I must give some further developement of my views upon this subject. No one, fellow citizens, has a higher reverence for the reserved rights of the States, than the Magistrate who now addresses you. No one would make greater personal sacrifices, or official exertions, to defend them from violation; but equal care must be taken to prevent on their part an improper interference with, or resumption of, the rights they have vested in the nation. The line has not been so distinctly drawn, as to avoid doubts in some cases of the exercise of power. Men of the best intentions and soundest views may differ in their construction of some parts of the Constitution; but there are others on which dispassionate reflection can leave no doubt. Of this nature appears to be the assumed right of a secession. It rests, as we have seen, on the alleged undivided sovereignty of the States, and on their having formed in this sovereign capacity a compact which is called the Constitution, from which, because they made it, they have the right to secede. Both of these positions are erroneous, and some of the arguments to prove them so have been anticipated.

The States severally have not retained their entire sovereignty. It has been shown that in becoming parts of a nation, not members of a league, they surrendered many of their essential parts of sovereignty. The rights to make treaties—declare war—levy taxes—exercise exclusive judicial and legislative powers—were all of them functions of sovereign power. The States, then, for all these important purposes, were no longer sovereign. The allegiance of their citizens was transferred, in the first instance, to the Government of the United States; they became American citizens, and owed obedience to the Constitution of the United States, and to the laws made in conformity with the powers it vested in Congress. This last position has not been, and cannot be denied. How then can that State be said to be sovereign and independent, whose citizens owe obedience to laws not made by it, and whose magistrates are sworn to disregard those laws, when they come in conflict with those passed by another? What shows conclusively that the States cannot be said to have reserved an undivided sovereignty, is, that they expressly ceded the right to punish treason—not treason against their separate power—but treason against the United States. Treason is an offence against sovereignty, and sovereignty must reside with the power to punish it. But the reserved rights of the States are not less sacred, because they have for their common interest made the General Government the depository of these powers. The unity of our political character (as has been shown for another purpose) commenced with its very existence. Under the Royal Government we had no separate character—our opposition to its oppression began as United Colonies.

We were the United States under the confederation, and the name was perpetuated, and the Union rendered more perfect, by the Federal Constitution. In none of these stages did we consider ourselves in any other light than as forming one nation. Treaties and alliances were made in the name of all. Troops were raised for the joint defence. How, then, with all these proofs, that under all changes of our position, we had, for designated purposes and with defined powers, created National Governments—how is it, that the most perfect of those several modes of union, should now be considered as a mere league, that may be dissolved at pleasure? It is from an abuse of terms. Compact is used as synonymous with league, although the true term is not employed, because it would at once show the fallacy of the reasoning.

It would not do to say that our Constitution is only a league : but, it is labored to prove it a compact, (which in one sense it is) and then to argue that as a league is a compact, every compact between nations must of course be a league, and that from such an engagement every sovereign power has a right to secede. But it has been shown, that in this sense the States are not sovereign, and that even if they were, and the National Constitution had been founded by compact, there would be no right in any one State to exonerate itself from its operations.

So obvious are the reasons which forbid this secession, that it is necessary only to allude to them. The Union was formed for the benefit of all. It was produced by mutual sacrifices of interests and opinions. Can those sacrifices be recalled? Can the States, who magnanimously surrendered their title to the Territories of the West, recall the grant? Will the inhabitants of the inland States agree to pay the duties that may be imposed without their assent by those on the Atlantic, or the Gulf, for their own benefit? Shall there be a free port in one State, and onerous duties in another? No one believes that any right exists in a single State to involve all the others in these and countless other evils, contrary to the engagements solemnly made. Every one must see that the other States, in self defence, must oppose at all hazards.

These are the alternatives that are presented by the Convention. A repeal of all the acts for raising revenue, leaving the Government without the means of support; or, an acquiescence in the dissolution of our Union, by the secession of one of its members. When the first was proposed, it was known that it could not be listened to for a moment. It was known that if force was applied to oppose the execution of the laws, it must be repelled by force—that Congress could not, without involving itself in disgrace, and the country in ruin, accede to the proposition; and yet, if this is not done in a given day, or if any attempt is made to execute the laws, the State is, by the Ordinance, declared to be out of the Union.

The majority of a Convention assembled for the purpose, have dictated these terms, or rather this rejection of all terms, in the name of the people of South Carolina. It is true that the Governor of the State speaks of the submission of their grievances to a Convention of all the States; which, he says, they " sincerely and anxiously seek and desire." Yet this obvious and constitutional mode of obtaining the sense of the other States on the construction of the Federal compact, and amending it, if necessary, has never been attempted by those who have urged the State on to this destructive measure. The State might have proposed the call for a General Convention to the other States; and Congress, if a sufficient number of them concurred, might have called it. But the first Magistrate of South Carolina, when he expressed a hope that, " on a review by Congress, and the functionaries of the General Government, of the merits of the controversy," such a Convention will be accorded to them, must have known that neither Congress, nor any functionary of the General Government, has authority to call such a Convention, unless it be demanded by two-thirds of the States. This suggestion, then, is another instance of the reckless inattention to the provisions of the Constitution with which this crisis has been hurried on, or the attempt to persuade the people that a constitutional remedy had been sought, and refused. If the Legislature of South Carolina " anxiously desire" a General Convention to consider their complaints, why have they not made application for it in the way the Constitution points out ? The assertion that they " earnestly seek" it, is completely negatived by the omission.

This, then, is the position in which we stand. A small majority of the citizens of one State in the Union, have elected delegates to the State Convention : that Convention has ordained, that all the revenue laws of the United States, must be repealed, or that they are no longer a member of the Union. The Governor of that State has recommended to the Legislature the raising of an army to carry the secession into effect, and that he may be empowered to give clearances to vessels in the name of the State. No act of violent opposition to the laws has yet been committed; but such a state of things is hourly apprehended, and it is the intent of this instrument to proclaim not only that the duty imposed on me by the Constitution, " to take care that the laws be faithfully executed," shall be performed to the extent of the power vested in me by law, or of such others as the wisdom of Congress shall devise and entrust to me for that purpose ; but, to warn the citizens of South Carolina, who have been deluded into an opposition to the laws, of the danger they will incur by obedience to the illegal and disorganizing Ordinance of the Convention—to exhort those who have refused to support it, to persevere in their determination to uphold the Constitution and the laws of their country, and to point out to all the perilous situation into which the good people of that State have been led—and that the course they are urged to pursue is one of ruin and disgrace to the very State whose rights they affect to support.

Fellow citizens of my native State, let me not only admonish you as the first Magistrate of our common country, not to incur the penalty of its laws, but use the influence that a father would over his children whom he saw rushing to certain ruin. In that paternal language, with that paternal feeling, let me tell you, my countrymen, that you are deluded by men who are either deceived themselves, or wish to deceive you.

Mark, under what pretences you have been led on to the brink of insurrection and treason, on which you stand ! First, a diminution of the value of your staple commodity, lowered by over-production in other quarters, and the consequent diminution in the value of your lands, were the sole effects of the tariff laws. The effect of those laws is confessedly injurious, but the evil was greatly exaggerated by the unfounded theory you were taught to believe, that its burthens were in proportion to your exports, not to your consumption of imported articles. Your pride was roused by the assertion, that a submission to those laws was a state of vassalage, and that resistance to them was equal, in patriotic merit, to the opposition our fathers offered to the oppressive laws of Great Britain. You were told that this opposition might be peaceable—might be constitutionally made ; that you might enjoy all the advantages of the Union, and bear none of its burthens.

Eloquent appeals to your passions, to your State pride, to your native courage, to your sense of real injury were used to prepare you for the period when the mask which concealed the hideous features of disunion should be taken off. It fell, and you were made to look with complacency on objects which, not long since, you would have regarded with horror. Look back at the arts which have brought you to this state—look forward to the consequences to which it must inevitably lead! Look back to what was first told you as an inducement to enter into this dangerous course ! The great political truth was repeated to you, that you had the revolutionary right of resisting all laws that were palpably unconstitutional and intolerably oppressive —it was added that the right to nullify a law rested on the same principle, but that it was a peaceable remedy. This character which was given to it, made you receive, with too much confidence the assertions that were made of the unconstitutionality of the law, and its oppressive effects. Mark, my fellow-citizens, that by the admission of your leaders, the unconstitutionality must be palpable ; or it will not justify either resistance or nullification! What is the meaning of the word palpable, in the sense in which it is here used ?—that which is apparent to every one : that which no man of ordinary intellect will fail to perceive. Is the unconstitutionality of these laws of that description? Let those among your leaders who once approved and advocated the principle of protective duties, answer the question; and let them choose whether they will be considered as incapable, then of perceiving that which must have been apparent to every man of common understanding, or as imposing upon your confidence, and endeavoring to mislead you now. In either case, they are unsafe guides in the perilous path they urge you to tread. Ponder well on this circumstance, and you will know how to appreciate the exaggerated language they address to you. They are not champions of liberty, emulating the fame of our Revolutionary Fathers; nor are you an oppressed people, contending, as they repeat to you, against worse than colonial vassalage. You are free members of a flourishing and happy Union. There is no settled design to oppress you.

I have urged you to look back to the means that were used to hurry you on to the position you have now assumed, and forward to the consequences it will produce. Something more is necessary. Contemplate the condition of that country of which you still form an important part! Consider its government, uniting in one bond of common interest and general protection, so many different States, giving to all their inhabitants the proud title of American citizens, protecting their commerce, securing their literature and their arts, facilitating their intercommunication, defending their frontiers, and making their name respected in the remotest part of the earth! Consider the extent of its territory, its increasing and happy population, its advances in arts which render life agreeable, and in the sciences which elevate the mind! See education spreading the lights of religion, humanity, and general information into every cottage in this wide extent of our territories and states. Behold it as the asylum where the wretched and the oppressed find a refuge and support! Carolina is one of these proud States: her arms have defended, her best blood has cemented this happy Union. Look on this picture of happiness and honor, and say—we, too, are citizens of America; and then add, if you can, without horror and remorse, this happy Union we will dissolve—this picture of peace and prosperity we will deface; this free intercourse we will interrupt—these fertile fields we will deluge with blood— the protection of that glorious flag we renounce; the very name of Americans we discard. And for what, mistaken men ! —for what do you throw away these inestimable blessings—for what would you exchange your share in the advantages and honor of the Union ? For the dream of a separate independence —a dream interrupted by bloody conflict with your neighbors and a vile dependence on a foreign power. If your leaders could succeed in establishing a separation, what would be your situation ? Are you united at home—are you free from the apprehension of civil discord, with all its fearful consequences ? Do our neighboring republics, every day suffering some new revolution, or contending with some new insurrection ; do they excite your envy ? But the dictates of a high duty oblige me solemnly to announce that you cannot succeed.

You have indeed felt the unequal operation of laws which may have been unwisely, not unconstitutionally passed ; but that inequality must necessarily be removed. At the very moment when you were madly urged on to the unfortunate course you have begun, a change in public opinion had commenced. The nearly approaching payment of the public debt, and the consequent necessity of a diminution of duties, had already produced a considerable reduction, and that too on some articles of general consumption in your State. The importance of this change was understood, and you were authoritatively told, that no further alleviation of your burthen was to be expected, at the very time when the condition of the country imperiously demanded such a modification of the duties as should reduce them to a just and equitable scale. But, as if apprehensive of the effect of this change in allaying your discontents, you were precipitated into the fearful state in which you find yourselves.

The laws of the United States must be executed—I have no discretionary power on the subject—my duty is emphatically pronounced in the Constitution. Those who told you that you might peaceably prevent their execution, deceived you—they could not have been deceived themselves. They know that a forcible opposition could alone prevent the execution of the laws, and they know that such opposition must be repelled. Their object is disunion ; but be not deceived by names ; disunion by armed force is treason. Are you really ready to incur its guilt? If you are, on the heads of the instigators of the act be the dreadful consequences—on their heads be the dishonor, but on yours may fall the punishment—on your unhappy State will inevitably fall all the evils of the conflict you force upon the Government of your country. It cannot accede to the mad project of disunion, of which you would be the first victims—its first Magistrate cannot, if he would, avoid the performance of his duty—the consequences must be fearful for you, distressing to your fellow-citizens here, and to the friends of government throughout the world. Its enemies have beheld our prosperity with a vexation they could not conceal—it was a standing refutation of their slavish doctrines, and they will point to our discord with the triumph of malignant joy. It is yet in your power to disappoint them.

There is yet time to show that the descendants of the Pinckneys, the Sumpters, the Rutledges, and of the thousand other names which adorn the pages of your revolutionary history, will not abandon that Union, to support which, so many of them fought, and bled, and died. I adjure you, as you honor their memory; as you love the cause of freedom, to which they dedicated their lives, as you prize the peace of your country, the lives of its best citizens, and your own fair fame, to retrace your steps. Snatch from the archives of your State the disorganizing edict of its Convention; bid its members to re-assemble and promulgate the decided expression of your will to remain in the path which alone can conduct you to safety, prosperity and honor—tell them that compared to disunion all other evils are light, because that brings with it an accumulation of all—declare that you will never take the field unless the star-spangled banner of your country shall float over you—that you will not be stigmatized when dead, and dishonored and scorned while you live, as the authors of the first attack on the Constitution of your country! Its destroyers you cannot be. You may disturb its peace—you may interrupt the course of its prosperity—you may cloud its reputation for stability—but its tranquillity will be restored, its prosperity will return, and the stain upon its national character will be transferred, and remain an eternal blot on the memory of those who caused the disorder.

Fellow citizens of the United States! The threat of unhallowed disunion—the names of those, once respected, by whom it is uttered—the array of military force to support it—denotes the approach of a crisis in our affairs on which the continuance of our unexampled prosperity, our political existence, and perhaps that of all free government, may depend. The conjuncture demanded a free, a full and explicit enunciation, not only of my intentions, but of my principles of action ; and as the claim was asserted of a right by a State to annul the laws of the Union, and even to secede from it at pleasure, a frank exposition of my opinions in relation to the origin and form of our government, and the construction I give to the instrument by which it was created, seemed to be proper. Having the fullest confidence in the justness of the legal and constitutional opinion of my duties, which has been expressed, I rely with equal confidence on your undivided support in my determination to execute the laws ; to preserve the Union by all Constitutional means ; to arrest, if possible, by moderate but firm measures, the necessity of a recourse to force ; and if it be the will of Heaven that the recurrence of its primeval curse on man for the shedding of a brother's blood, should fall upon our land, that it be not called down by any offensive act on the part of the United States.

Fellow citizens! The momentous case is before you. On your undivided support of your Government, depends the decision of the great question · it involves, whether your sacred Union will be preserved, and the blessings it secures to us as one people, shall be perpetuated. No one can doubt that the unanimity with which that decision will be expressed, will be such as to inspire new confidence in republican institutions ; and that the prudence, the wisdom, and the courage which it will bring to their defence, will transmit them unimpaired and invigorated to our children.

May the Great Ruler of nations grant that the signal blessings with which he has favored ours, may not, by the madness of party or personal ambition, be disregarded and lost; and may His wise Providence bring those who have produced this crisis, to see their folly, before they feel the misery of civil strife ; and inspire a returning veneration for that Union, which, if we dare to penetrate His designs, He has chosen as the only means of attaining the high destinies to which we may reasonably aspire.

In testimony whereof, I have caused the Seal of the United States to be hereunto affixed, having signed the same with my hand.

Done at the City of Washington, this 10th day of December, in the year of our Lord, one thousand eight hundred and thirty-two, and of the independence of the United States, the fifty-seventh.

By the President.

ANDREW JACKSON.

EDW. LIVINGSTON,
     Secretary of State.

RESOLVES

OF THE

LEGISLATURE

OF

NEW HAMPSHIRE.

State of New Hampshire.

Resolved by the Senate and House of Representatives in General Court convened, That the sentiments contained in the Proclamation of the President of the United States, dated December 10, 1832, meet with the entire approbation of this Legislature, and that we hail in those sentiments, and in the general measures of his administration, and particularly in the salutary exercise of his Veto, a Chief Executive Magistrate, whose devoted patriotism and moral courage are equal to any crisis, and under the guidance of whose wisdom the ancient landmarks of the Constitution will be preserved, and the confidence reposed in him, as manifested in his recent election by a vast majority of the American people, will be fully justified.

And resolved further, That the Secretary of State be directed to transmit a copy of this resolution to the President of the United States, and to each of our Delegates in Congress, and the Governor of each State in the Union.

FRANKLIN PIERCE,
Speaker of the House of Representatives.

BENNING M. BEAN,
President of the Senate.

[A true copy.]

RALPH METCALF, *Secretary of State.*

RESOLVES

OF THE

LEGISLATURE

OF

MAINE.

State of Maine.

In Senate, February 1, 1833.

The Joint Select Committee, to which was referred so much of
the Governor's Message as relates to the difficulties existing
between South Carolina and the General Government, and
the Documents from South Carolina, and several other States,
upon the same subject, have had the same under consideration, and

REPORT:

That they have given their anxious and serious attention to
the several documents referred to their consideration; all of
which have grown out of the unhappy controversy now subsisting between South Carolina and the General Government.
Most, if not all of them, contain speculative views of the nature
and objects of our political system. In the several communications, there is observable a wide diversity of sentiment; and in
some, especially those from South Carolina, the conclusions
adopted are made the subjects of a very extended and elaborate
argument. To review and compare with each other the several
opinions and doctrines set forth in these several communications, to examine fully the various arguments and objections
which they oppose to each other, and to investigate what, if any,
errors of fact, of principle, or of reasoning, may be contained in
any, or all of them, would seem to be a task of great labor, and
one not likely, perhaps, to result in any corresponding benefit.
   This State, on two occasions, has heretofore expressed her
opinion upon the subject of Federal Relations. It is believed,

that the Report and Resolutions of 1827, relative to Internal Improvements, and the Report and Resolutions of 1831, upon the same subject, contain a general outline of the sentiments of Maine, as regards the origin and purposes of our political system, the powers conferred upon the General Government by the Constitution, and the rights reserved to the People and the States. As a declaration of our principles and opinions, as to the relative powers and duties of the General Government and the several State Governments, we deem it unnecessary, therefore, at the present time, to do more than simply refer to the several Reports and Resolutions above alluded to.

Without entering into the discussion of political theories, we have chosen rather to take a practical view of the unhappy difficulties which agitate the public tranquillity, and alarm the public mind. Viewing with the deepest feelings of regret, the excitement which pervades our sister State, and the rash and presumptuous measures to which it has led, and deprecating those measures as utterly inconsistent with the spirit of forbearance and compromise in which our Union had its origin and by a perseverance in which it can alone be maintained, we cannot, at the same time, forget that this excitement, this disturbance of the public tranquillity, and all the dangers which this unnatural controversy threatens to bring upon the country, have for their origin and moving cause the policy of the protective system. Under this aspect of public affairs, it has seemed to your Committee the more useful course to respectfully interpose the voice of this State for conciliation and forbearance. There are none among us who would justify the untimely and ruinous resistance which South Carolina threatens against the existing laws of the United States, of whose injustice she complains. On the other hand, a large majority of the citizens of Maine ever have entertained—they still entertain the most undoubting convictions of the impolicy and oppression of high protecting duties.

Under these circumstances, and with these views, the Committee submit the following Resolves.

J. WILLIAMSON, Chairman.

RESOLVES.

Resolved, That we are not insensible to the wrongs and sufferings of our brethren of South Carolina, under the unjust and oppressive burdens imposed upon them by the Tariffs of high protective duties. But while we deplore their grievances, and are ready to unite with them in any and every peaceful and lawful mode of redress, we cannot, nor will we give our countenance or support to their projected scheme for relief. We regard nullification as neither a safe, peaceable, or constitutional remedy, but as unsound and dangerous in theory and in practice tending directly to civil commotion, disunion, and anarchy. We implore them to pause in their precipitate career, to suspend their rash and revolutionary measures, and trust to that redeeming spirit of justice which is a ruling characteristic of the American people.

Resolved, That the acts of Congress, usually denominated Tariff laws, so far as they were passed palpably and solely for the purpose of protecting and fostering particular branches of industry, are unequal in their operation, and contrary to the spirit, true intent, and meaning of the Federal Compact.

Resolved, That it is due to a spirit of mutual conciliation, to the demands of justice, to a decent respect for the opinions and interests of large portions of the community, and absolutely necessary to the preservation of the Union, that the Tariff laws should be gradually (but speedily) abated to the imposition of such duties only as are required for the purpose of a revenue sufficient to defray the ordinary expenses of the General Government, confined to its appropriate objects, and economically administered.

Resolved, That we heartily approve the policy and measures of President Jackson's administration, and in the present difficult and threatening aspect of public affairs, we look with confidence to the patriotism, vigilance, and firmness of our Chief

Magistrate, as sure pledges that all his efforts will be directed to preserve unimpaired the union, happiness, and glory of our Republic.

Resolved, That the patriotic spirit and tone of the President's recent Proclamation, relating to the extraordinary proceedings of South Carolina, meet our warmest approbation and we approve of the principles and policy avowed therein, as expounded, not in accordance with the federal doctrine of consolidation, but with the democratic doctrine of State rights, and a limitation of action of the Federal Government to the powers expressly delegated to it by the Constitution, and in accordance with the several messages of President Jackson, to Congress, and the uniform tenor of the acts of his administration ; and in support of all constitutional measures adopted by him to preserve the Union, we tender him our undivided support.

Resolved, That the Secretary of State be, and hereby is directed to transmit a copy of these Resolves, with the Preamble, to each of the Representatives in Congress from this State.

Resolved, That the Governor be, and hereby is requested to transmit a copy of these Resolves, with the Preamble to the Executive of each of the other States of this Union, and the President of the Senate of the United States.

In the House of Representatives, February 18, 1833.
    Read and passed.

NATHAN CLIFFORD, *Speaker.*

In Senate, February 19, 1833.
    Read and passed.

FRANCIS O. J. SMITH, *President.*

February 20, 1833.
    Approved.

SAMUEL E. SMITH, *Governor.*

[A true copy.]

Attest :—R. G. GREENE, *Secretary of State.*

RESOLVES

OF THE

LEGISLATURE

OF

MASSACHUSETTS.

Commonwealth of Massachusetts.

HOUSE OF REPRESENTATIVES, January 9, 1833.

Ordered, That Messrs. CROWNINSHIELD, of *Boston,*
     "   SHAW, of *Lanesborough,*
     "   LINCOLN, of *Worcester,*
     "   HOLMES, of *Rochester,* and
     "   ROBINSON, of *Marblehead,*
with such as the Senate may join, be a Committee to consider
so much of the Governor's Address as relates to the proceedings
of the late Convention of the people of South Carolina, and the
purposes and policy thereof, and also the Resolutions of the
State of Pennsylvania thereon : Sent up for concurrence.

L. S. CUSHING, *Clerk.*

IN SENATE, January 10th, 1833.

Concurred, and Messrs. Everett, Hoar, Barton and Burnell
are joined.

ATTEST,   CHAS. CALHOUN, *Clerk.*

Commonwealth of Massachusetts.

In Senate, February 15, 1833.

The Joint Select Committee, appointed to consider so much of the Governor's Address as relates to the proceedings of the late Convention of the people of South Carolina, and the purposes and policy thereof: and to whom have been referred Resolutions of the States of Pennsylvania, New Hampshire, Illinois, North Carolina and Delaware upon that subject, have attended to the duty assigned them, and beg leave to submit the following

REPORT :

In the partial Report which they have already submitted, the Committee have stated in general terms the character of the proceedings of the late Convention of the people of South Carolina; and the subject is now so familiar to the public, that it does not seem necessary to enter very fully into a recapitulation of facts. It is generally known that this Convention, which appears to have been assembled agreeably to the forms prescribed by the Constitution of the State, met at Columbia on the 22d of last November :—that almost immediately after, and with very little deliberation, it proceeded to pass an Act, denominated an Ordinance, declaring null and void all the laws of the United States which impose duties upon the importation of foreign goods, particularly those of the 19th of May, 1828, and the 14th of June, 1832; prohibiting the execution of them within the State of South Carolina, and making it the duty of the Legislature to pass such laws as should be necessary to give full effect to the Ordinance, and to prevent the enforcement and arrest the execution of the laws aforesaid :—that the Legislature, at a session subsequent to the meeting of this Convention, has in fact passed certain laws for these purposes, which were to go into operation on the first day of this month, and which, if executed, must bring the constituted authorities of the United States and of South Carolina, into open collision.

The papers in the hands of the Committee include a printed copy of this Ordinance of the Convention, transmitted by its order to His Excellency the Governor, and also printed copies of a long report of the committee which drafted the Ordinance, and of addresses in the name of the Convention to the people of the United States and of South Carolina. These documents undertake to justify the proceedings of the Convention, on the ground that the duties on the importation of foreign goods were laid, in part at least, for the purpose of protecting domestic industry : that the General Government is not invested by the Constitution with the power of laying duties for this purpose, and that, whenever the General Government assumes powers which, in the opinion of any one of the States, are not given to it by the Constitution, the State which entertains this opinion may, without violating the Constitution, declare the act by which the power so assumed has been exercised, null and void, and prevent the execution of it within its limits. It also appears to have been supposed by the Convention, that, on the adoption of such measures by any one State, it would become the duty of the General Government to suspend the execution of the law complained of, at least within the limits of the complaining State, and to apply to the people in the form prescribed for amending the Constitution, for a grant of the power supposed to have been unconstitutionally assumed :—that, if the power should on this application be refused by the people, it would be the duty of the General Government definitively to repeal the law by which it had been exercised, and that if, on the contrary, it should be granted, it would then become the duty of the complaining State to acquiesce. There seems, however, to be some uncertainty in the views of this part of the subject entertained by that portion of the citizens of South Carolina upon whom the responsibility for the semeasures rests : as the Legislature of the State, instead of leaving it to the General Government to propose to the people in the form prescribed for amending the Constitution a grant of the power of laying duties upon the importation of foreign goods, have themselves, at their late session, passed resolutions, proposing to the other States to hold a Convention for the purpose of settling this and other questions which they consider as doubtful.

It is affirmed, in these addresses and reports, that the laws of the United States, imposing duties upon the importation of foreign goods, thus declared to be null and void, are exceedingly burthensome and oppressive to the people of South Carolina.— This proposition is not made out by the statement of any facts which tend to prove the existence of actual distress; and it is remarkable that the Governor of South Carolina, in his address to the Legislature, at the opening of their late session, congratulates them upon the extraordinary prosperity of the State. The Convention attempt to maintain their assertion of the ruinous tendency of the impost laws, by laying down certain abstract principles in political economy, which are very paradoxical, and as the Committee believe, entirely erroneous. It is unnecessary, however, for the purpose of the present report, to enter upon a particular examination of these doctrines, because the justification of the proceedings of South Carolina does not, after all, depend in any degree upon the question of their truth or falsehood. Whatever may be the real operation of the impost laws upon the peculiar interests of that State,—were it as unfavorable as the Committee believe it to be beneficial and salutary, it is admitted that the State would have no right to seek redress in the form in which it is now sought, unless the enactment of these laws involve an assumption by the General Government of powers not granted by the Constitution. No abuse of constitutional power, however glaring and intolerable, would on the theory of the Convention, justify a resort to nullification.

The question of the real operation of the impost laws upon the prosperity of South Carolina, may therefore be laid entirely out of the case. Nor, although the justification of the proceedings of the Convention is to be sought, on the ground taken by that body, in the supposed unconstitutional character of these laws, do the Committee deem it important for the present purpose to inquire particularly how far this supposition is well founded. Entertaining, themselves, no doubt whatever, that the power of laying duties on imported foreign goods, with a view to any appropriation of them which, in the discretion of the Government, may be required by the common defence and general welfare, is given by the Constitution, the Committee are also persuaded, that were this a doubtful point, or were it even conceded that the General Government has no such power, the proceedings of South Carolina would not, on that account, be any the more defensible. The objection to them is, that they propose an unconstitutional and illegal method of obtaining relief from a supposed political grievance. It is therefore unnecessary to inquire, whether this grievance be real or imaginary, since the objection, if substantiated, is equally valid in either contingency.

Omitting, therefore, any consideration of the expediency or constitutionality of the laws imposing duties on imported foreign goods, the Committee will confine themselves to the single inquiry, how far the proceedings of the Convention of South Carolina are consistent with the Constitution and Laws of the Country? Even in this restricted shape, the subject is far too extensive to be examined, in a full and satisfactory manner, within the limits assigned by usage to a document of this kind. The Committee can only undertake to present a few of the considerations that bear most strongly and obviously upon the leading points of the argument.

The suggestion that would probably first occur to an impartial mind, on examining the account of these proceedings, is the apparent want of consistency and precision in the reasoning and conduct of the Convention, admitting even the correctness of the general principles on which they profess to act. It would be natural to expect, that in a case of so novel a character, and of such extraordinary interest and importance, every step would be carefully guarded, and no conclusions drawn, which did not follow, in the strictest manner, from their supposed premises. This, however, is far from being the case. The Committee have already remarked the difference between the theories of the Convention and the Legislature, as to the second step in the process of nullification. While the Convention appear to suppose that after a State has annulled an act of Congress, it becomes the duty of the General Government to apply to the States for a grant of the disputed power, the Legislature have addressed themselves directly to the States, and proposed a Convention. The want of consistency in the texture of the Ordinance, is not less apparent. The whole reasoning of that act, and the accompanying papers, supposes that the right of a State to annul an act of Congress, can only exist in the case of an assumption by that body, of powers not delegated by the Constitution; and for the purpose of bringing the impost laws within this rule, the Convention attempt, at great length, to prove that they do, in fact, involve such an assumption. Thus far their conduct, if not justifiable, is consistent; but after first annulling the Tariff laws, the Convention proceed, in open defiance of their own rules and reasoning, to annul an important provision of another law, which has never been regarded by any one as unconstitutional, and which the Convention themselves do not even pretend to represent as being so. While the Judiciary law gives the right of appeal from the State Courts to the United States, in all cases involving any question of the validity of an act of Congress, the Ordinance prohibits any such appeal in all cases involving any question of the validity of the acts of Congress which it professes to annul. This is done without even the ceremony of affirming, or attempting to prove, that this provision of the Judiciary act involves an assumption of power not delegated by the Constitution.

This feature in the Ordinance renders it, perhaps, in some degree, superfluous to examine the reasoning by which the Convention undertake to justify its leading provisions. If they can venture to annul one act of Congress, without even pretending to assert that it is unconstitutional, it is not easy to see why they should be at so much pains to make this out, in regard to another, before they subject it to the same process: nor does it seem to be very necessary to inquire, how far they succeed in establishing this proposition, when their proceedings so clearly shew, that if be necessary to their argument, it is in no way necessary to their action. But without enlarging upon this consideration, the Committee will proceed to examine, very concisely, the nature of the reasoning by which the Convention undertake to prove, that any one State has a right to annul an act of Congress, which, in the opinion of such State, involves an assumption of power not delegated by the Constitution. The substance of the argument is understood to be as follows :

The Constitution is a compact between the States, which were, at the time of forming it, and are now distinct communities, politically independent of each other. It confers, on the General Government, certain specific powers, and the assumption by that Government of any power not so delegated, is a breach of the compact. But in this, as in all other cases of compacts or treaties between independent States, a breach of the compact by one party, exempts the rest from the obligation they were under to observe it ; and each is, of course, the only judge for itself, whether the compact is or is not observed.

Or, in still more concise language :

The States were independent of each other at the time when they formed the Constitution ; therefore they are independent of each other now.

This argument appears to the Committee to be defective in both its parts. It is far from being a settled and acknowledged point, that the States can fairly be considered as having been absolutely independent of each other at the time when the present Constitution was formed ; and if this were even admitted, it would by no means follow, that they possess, and may exercise under the Constitution, and consistently with it, the rights belonging to mutually and absolutely independent States.

1. It is far from being a settled point, that the States can fairly be considered as having been absolutely independent of each other at the time when the Constitution was formed and adopted. It is well known, that this is a question upon which the ablest statesmen, and purest patriots in the country have differed, and at this moment continue to differ, in opinion. The President of the United States, in his late Proclamation upon the subject of the proceedings of South Carolina, expressed his belief, that the Acts of the Union which preceded the Declaration of Independence, had combined the States into ONE PEOPLE, and that it was in their joint capacity as such, that they formed the Constitution. His predecessor has publicly professed the same sentiment. On the other hand, Presidents Jefferson and Madison, with various other citizens of the highest

respectability, many of whom had concurred in the forming of the Constitution, consider the States as having been, from the time of the Declaration of Independence, until the adoption of the Constitution, distinct communities, entirely independent of each other.

This diversity of views, among individuals of equal talent and unsuspected integrity, will not appear very extraordinary, when it is recollected that during the period in question, the country was in a revolutionary state. Its condition was analogous to that of England during the interval between the overthrow of the arbitrary government of the Stuarts, and the settlement of the Constitution in 1688 ; or that of France, between the destruction of the old monarchy in 1789, and the final sanction of the present charter, after the three great days of July 1830. In both the cases alluded to, it is well known, that political institutions, of various and opposite characters, rapidly succeeded each other, and that neither country could be said, with propriety, to possess a regular and settled government. They were in a state of transition from one form of political existence to another, and this was substantially the condition of the United States from the Declaration of Independence until the adoption of the Constitution. It was not only a natural, but, as the Committee conceive, a necessary result of this condition, that political events of different and even contradictory characters, should successively occur, and that individuals, as they have been led, by circumstances, to attach greater or less importance to one or another of these events, should draw different conclusions as the existing forms of government. On the one hand, the States acted, for many purposes, as distinct communities, claiming to be politically independent of each other; while, on the other hand, they organized a Union among themselves, with a Congress of Delegates at the head of it, who exercised most of the powers of a General Government. It would, perhaps, be difficult to reconcile all the acts and powers of Congress and the State Governments at that time, with any consistent and precise political theory ; and the failure of the experiment tends to confirm the opinion, that the elements which entered into the structure of the old confederacy, were incoherent and self-contradictory. The Committee are inclined to believe, as they have already remarked, that the future historian will consider the whole period in question as a revolutionary one, and the form of the government as unsettled and fluctuating, until it was finally fixed, for the first time, by the adoption of the present Constitution.

2. But the Committee deem it unnecessary to dwell upon this point, since, were it even admitted that the States, at the time when they formed the Constitution, were distinct communities, politically independent of each other, it would by no means follow, as the Convention of South Carolina appear to suppose, that they are still in that condition, and that the Union is a League or Confederacy of mutually and absolutely independent States. The rights and obligations of the parties to a contract, are determined by its nature and terms, and not by their condition previously to its conclusion. As respects the latter point, the only question is, were the parties legally, or in cases when they are not subject to a Common Government, morally capable of making such a contract? If this question be answered in the affirmative, the previous condition of the parties, in other respects, is immaterial; and in order to ascertain to what the contract binds them, we have only to inquire what the contract is.

Now there can be no doubt, that independent States are morally as capable of forming themselves into a body politic, as independent individuals. A great proportion of the political societies which now exist, or of which we know the history, were constituted in this way. Hence, were it even admitted, that the States were distinct and independent communities at the time when they framed the Constitution, the fact would no more prove, that they are distinct and independent communities now, than the fact that the two parties to a contract of marriage were single before its conclusion goes to prove that they are single afterwards. If the States were, at the time when they framed the Constitution, as there cannot be a doubt, morally capable of forming a contract, involving the entire surrender of their political independence, it is quite apparent that, in order to ascertain their rights and obligations under the Constitution, we have to look exclusively to the nature and terms of that instrument, without regard to the mutual relations of the parties before they made it.

Reposing mainly, as has been said, for the justification of their proceedings, upon the argument that the States were independent at the time when the Constitution was adopted, and must therefore of course be independent now, the Convention has in a great measure lost sight of the course of reasoning which is proper to the subject, and have made but little effort to establish their doctrines, by reference either to the general nature of the Constitution, or to its specific provisions. Some considerations appertaining to this branch of the inquiry, are however to be found in their publications, and to them the Committee will now very briefly direct their attention.

Of these considerations the most important is, that the General Government, created by the Constitution of the United States, is a Government invested with specific and limited powers, having no general and indefinite powers, excepting such as are necessary to carry the specified ones into effect, and that the powers not conferred upon the General Government are reserved to the States. This is, no doubt, true in fact : but that it was not intended in making this arrangement, to maintain the States in possession of an absolute political independence, with a right of judging for themselves when the General Government exceeds its powers, and annulling any acts involving such excess, is apparent, as well from other particular provisions of the Constitution, as from the general scope and purpose of that instrument.

1. In all cases the general purpose of a contract is one of the most important elements to be taken into view in ascertaining the rights and obligations resulting from it, because the general purpose controls, to a certain extent, the construction of all the particular provisions. It would be absurd to interpret any particular part of an instrument in such a way as would suppose in the parties an intention manifestly contrary to the general object of the whole ; as for example, to interpret one of the clauses in a contract of marriage in such a way as would suppose that it was the intention of the parties to remain single. Now it is quite apparent from the general scope and purpose of the Constitution of the United States, that it was not the intention of the parties who framed it, whether considered in their joint or individual capacity, to retain the character of absolute political independence. It is one of that class of agreements commonly

denominated social compacts, the principal object of which is to combine the parties forming them into one body politic, or political society, under a common Government. This is apparent on the face of the instrument. 'We, the people of the United States, in order to form a more perfect Union, establish justice, ensure domestic tranquillity, provide for the common defence, promote the general welfare, and secure the blessings of liberty to ourselves and our posterity, do ordain and establish this Constitution for the United States of America.' That such is the general scope of the instrument is not contested by the warmest advocates of the doctrines maintained by the Convention of South Carolina. But the precise object which the parties to a social compact have in view in forming themselves into one political society, is to terminate the relation of mutual independence which previously existed between them. If the contract contained a clause providing that the parties should retain their political independence, it would be self-contradictory; and to interpret a doubtful passage or particular provision in such a a way as to attribute to the parties such an intention, would, as the Committee have remarked, involve the same absurdity as to interpret a clause in a marriage contract on the supposition that the parties intended to remain single. It is of the essence of a social compact or Constitution of Government, that the parties to it surrender their absolute political independence, and become members of a society whose will is admitted to be the common law. To declare this will, agreeably to the forms prescribed in the Constitution,—in other words, to make and alter the laws as occasion may require, is the office of the Government. No individual or other member of the body politic can possibly as such, exercise the power of making or annulling the laws, for the obvious reason that laws derive their character as such, from being the acts of the Government, and that if an individual, or other member of the body politic, should succeed in giving to his own will the force of law, that is, in compelling the society to obey it, he would at the same time cease to be a citizen, and would concentrate in his own hands the Government of the country. In some extreme cases of intolerable oppression, the individual and other members of the body politic are justifiable in forcibly opposing the execution of the law; but even in these cases there is no claim of any constitutional or legal right to repeal or annul it. The claim is to resist, in the exercise of the natural and inalienable right of self defence, the execution of what is admitted at the time to be, in form, at least, a law.

2. The general scope and objects of the Constitution preclude therefore the idea that it was the intention of the parties to it to retain their absolute political independence, or that they possess any right under it to annul the acts of the General Government. The same conclusions result with equal certainty from a view of its particular provisions. Had it been intended that the States should possess the important power of annulling or repealing at discretion the acts of the General Government, this power would undoubtedly have been given to them in express terms. It is not even pretended that the Constitution contains any such express concession. Not only is there no express concession to this effect, but the idea that any thing of the kind was intended, is precluded by several provisions of an opposite character. The Constitution gives to the Supreme Court cognizance of all cases arising under the Constitution, and the laws and treaties made under the authority of the United States.— This involves the right of deciding, in the last resort, whether a law is constitutional, which the Carolina doctrine claims for the States. The Convention have accordingly found themselves under the necessity of annulling the section of the judiciary act by which provision was made for carrying this clause of the Constitution into effect without even pretending that it was unconstitutional. Again : ' This Constitution, and the laws and treaties made in pursuance of it, are the Supreme Law of the land, any thing in the Constitution and laws of any State to the contrary notwithstanding.' By this provision, any act of a State, whether performed in its sovereign or legislative capacity, pretending to annul an act of the General Government, is declared in advance to be null and void. As respects the pretention that the States retain under the Constitution their absolute political independence, it may be remarked that, were there no other objection to the dectrine, it would be satisfactorily refuted by the clause which regulates the form of making amendments. It is there provided that any amendment of the Con-

stitution which may be proposed by two thirds of both Houses of Congress, and ratified by three fourths of the States, shall be binding on the rest. It is hardly necessary to add, that a community which is not only bound to obey laws which twenty three other communities have a common agency in making, but which is bound to acquiesce in any changes in the form of the common Government that may be proposed by a certain number of these other communities, can have no claim to the character of absolute independence.

It is apparent therefore, as well from the general objects of the Constitution as from the tenor of its particular provisions, that it was not the intention of the parties who formed it to retain their entire independence, or to exercise the power of annulling the acts of the General Government created by it. The fact that the Government is invested with specific and not indefinite powers, has no tendency to prove the existence of such an intention, and has in fact no bearing at all upon the subject. The question at issue is, how much power the body politic of the United States of America possesses over the individual States of which it is composed. To the decision of this question, it is obviously quite immaterial whether the powers attributed by the Constitution to the General Government, are definite or indefinite. These are exercised upon the individual citizen, and not upon the States, and neither their extent, nor the mode in which they are determined, can have any effect in settling the mutual relations between the States and the United States of America. The powers of all Governments are prescribed and limited, if not by written instruments, at least by usage and by the moral law. When they transgress the limits prescribed for them, the people cure the evil either by a change in the administration effected in consistency with the forms of the Constitution, or if the case be extreme, by recurring to the natural right of violent resistance to the law. When the powers of the Government are defined by a written instrument, an attempt at usurpation is more likely to be distinctly seen and promptly attended to. But no new remedy is created, and in this, as in all other cases, the people must tolerate the existence of the evil until it can be removed by the silent efficacy of the ballot-box, or must recur at once to forcible resistance. There is, and can be in the nature of things, no middle path between these two courses. Every attempt to prevent by force, the execution of the laws,—by whatever name it may be called,—is, in its nature, revolutionary, and can only be defended by such considerations as would justify an act of rebellion.

On the whole, the Committee have been led to conclude from the best consideration which they have been able to give to the subject, that the right claimed by South Carolina, for the several States, of annulling at discretion any act of the General Government which they may deem unconstitutional, has no foundation in the letter or spirit of the Constitution, Nor is it countenanced in any degree by the practice under that instrument. For nearly half a century, during which the Government has been in operation, no case has occurred of an attempt by a State to annul one of its acts, although serious discontents have from time to time existed in different quarters, which would probably have led to the adoption of such a course had it been recognized by public opinion as constitutional. The only authority of a practical kind which has ever been adduced in support of it, is that of certain Resolutions adopted by the State Legislatures of Virginia and Kentucky, in 1798—9. Were it admitted that these Resolutions go the full length of the Carolina doctrine, they would still afford no actual precedent, and could only be regarded as an expression of the opinion temporarily prevailing in the Legislatures of these two States, but never even by them reduced to practice. These celebrated Resolutions have however been recently explained in reference to this very question, by the distinguished Statesman who drafted one set of them, and was at the time the confidential friend and political associate of the author of the other, to intend nothing more than an assertion, in strong terms, of the universally acknowledged right of constitutional opposition to measures regarded as oppressive, and in extreme cases, of forcible resistance. This explanation of his own intentions, and those of his immediate political friends, of course settles the construction to be put upon these Resolutions, and removes the only shadow of practical authority and precedent, that has ever been claimed by the advocates of the doctrine of Nullification.

As this doctrine receives no countenance from the theory of the Constitution, or the practice under it, it is the less necessary to dwell upon its practical tendency, a topic which would afford very strong corroborating arguments against it, if, as a strict question of right, it could be considered as doubtful. It hardly requires any argument to shew that the exercise, by each of the twenty-four States, of a right to annul, at discretion, any act of the General Government which they might deem unconstitutional, is wholly incompatible with a consistent and settled administration of the public affairs. Any law which might be supposed, correctly or not, to operate with peculiar hardship upon a particular State, would naturally appear, under the excitement of the moment, to be unconstitutional; and as, in a community so vast as ours, there can hardly ever be a time when there is not some law which, for some reason, is particularly offensive to some one State, the process of nullification, if once recognized, would be constantly going on in one quarter or another. Every new attempt of the kind would shake the Government to its foundations, and it would not probably require the occurrence of many to reduce our happy Union to a state of dissolution, more complete and hopeless than even that of the Old Confederacy. The Committee refrain from enlarging upon these results, the necessity of which is, however, apparent, to the most superficial observation. The question is argued by Carolina, chiefly as one of mere right; and the answer on that ground only, is, in the opinion of the Committee, so clearly against her, that it would be needless to attempt to sustain it by any considerations of mere expediency.

With this view of the subject referred to them, and under a conviction that it is proper and expedient that the opinion of the General Court of this Commonwealth should be distinctly expressed upon it, the Committee respectfully submit the accompanying Resolves, which embody the most important principles that have now been suggested.

The Committee have felt a very deep regret at finding themselves called upon to express opinions unfavorable to the proceedings of a State so distinguished in the annals of the country, and so remarkable for the lofty and generous character of its sons as that of South Carolina. In so doing, they would not be understood to impeach the motives by which the State has been governed, or to intimate that it has been actuated by any other purpose, than that of procuring relief from a supposed grievance. The Committee are well aware, that the purest patriots and wisest statesmen may be led, under the influence of mistaken views and excited feelings, into very dangerous measures. The present proceedings in South Carolina are, in their opinion, of that description. But the Committee indulge a confident hope, that by the exercise of the necessary firmness and discretion, on the part of the General Government, the danger may be averted, and that South Carolina herself, recovering from the delusion under which, for some time past she has appeared to labor, may continue to maintain her accustomed place among the most enlightened and patriotic States in the Union.

Before concluding their Report, the Committee deem it a duty to themselves and to the Legislature, to advert very briefly to some remarks which have been made upon the tendency of the Resolves accompanying their former Report, and adopted by the almost unanimous vote of both branches of the General Court. In certain quarters of high respectability, where the Resolves have been brought under discussion, it has been intimated that they favor the doctrine of Nullification, because they express the sentiment that the Legislature is not bound, silently, to acquiesce in measures considered by them as subversive of the spirit of the Constitution ; and this in the way of instruction to the delegation of the Commonwealth in Congress, for the purpose of preventing the adoption of these measures. The difference between a proceeding of this kind, and an attempt to annul and prevent the execution of existing laws, is too obvious to be overlooked. That the General Government may adopt an unconstitutional measure, is of course possible ; and no one can doubt that any portion of the people have a right, in an orderly and peaceable manner, to express their opinion upon the character of any of the measures of the General Government. But when this is done in advance, for the purpose not of denouncing an existing law, but of preventing a threatened mischief, it is not easy to see how the most fastidious judge can find any thing at which to take offence.

But were it even true, that the Legislature of this Commonwealth had expressed the intention of forcibly resisting the execution of an unconstitutional law, it would not therefore follow, that they had countenanced the doctrine of Nullification. The right of forcible resistance to the laws, in cases of extreme oppression, is undisputed. If such a case should ever occur, Massachusetts will openly take her stand upon that undisputed and indefeasible natural right. Nullification undertakes to reconcile resistance with submission; to obey and break the law at one and the same time. It must be justified, if at all, on principles entirely different from those which justify the natural right of resistance, and on principles which have never been professed, countenanced or practised upon by the Government or people of this Commonwealth.

All which is respectfully submitted.

For the Committee,

A. H. EVERETT.

RESOLVES

In relation to the Proceedings of the Convention of South Carolina.

Whereas, The People of South Carolina, assembled by their Delegates in Convention, have recently passsed an act, denomited an Ordinance, purporting to annul certain acts of the Government of the United States, and to arrest their execution within the limits of that State, and have transmitted a copy of the same to His Excellency the Governor, with an accompanying address to the people of this Commonwealth, setting forth the reasons by which they justify this extraordinary measure; and

Whereas, It is important that the opinion of the General Court of this Commonwealth should be publicly and distinctly expressed upon those proceedings, in order that their silence may not be construed into acquiescence in the propriety of the same, or approbation of the reasons alleged in justification of them: therefore

Resolved, by the Senate and House of Representatives of the Commonwealth of Massachusetts, in General Court assembled, That the Constitution of the United States of America, is a solemn Social Compact, by which the people of the said States, in order to form a more perfect union, establish justice, insure domestic tranquillity, provide for the common defence, promote the general welfare, and secure the blessings of liberty for themselves and their posterity, formed themselves into one body politic, under a common Government: that this Constitution, and the laws of the United States made in pursuance thereof, and all treaties made under the authority of the same, are the supreme law of the land, any thing in the Constitution or laws of any State to the contrary notwithstanding: and that no citizen, State, or other member of the body politic, has a right in any shape, or under any pretext, to annul or prevent the execution of the said Constitution, laws, or treaties, or any of them, excepting in such extreme cases as justify a violent resistance to the laws on the principle of the natural and indefeasible prerogative of self-defence against intolerable oppression.

Resolved, That the right claimed by the Convention of South Carolina for that State, of annulling any law of the United States which it may deem unconstitutional, is unauthorized by the letter or spirit of the Constitution—not supported by any contemporaneous exposition of that instrument, or by the practice under it :—inconsistent with the nature of political society, and tending, in practice, to the subversion of public tranquillity, and the complete overthrow of the Government.

Resolved, That the President of the United States is empowered, and in duty bound by the express provisions of the Constitution, and by his oath of office, to take care that the laws are faithfully executed :—that when attempts are made to disturb by force the execution of the laws, it is the duty of the President to employ the means which are placed at his disposal by the Constitution and laws for the purpose of defeating them ; that the Proclamation of the 10th December last, is a judicious, well timed and salutary measure, well calculated to prevent the necessity of recurring to others of a different character :—that we approve the determination therein expressed by the President, to enforce the laws; and that we are prepared to support him and the other constituted authorities of the Union, in all the necessary, suitable, constitutional and legal measures, which they may be called upon to adopt for that purpose.

Resolved, That while we find ourselves compelled to express an unfavorable opinion of the recent proceedings of South Carolina, we entertain no sentiments of unkindness towards our fellow citizens of that State :—that we look back with pride and satisfaction to the brilliant services rendered by South Carolina in the struggle for Independence, and have ever regarded her as among the most distinguished members of the Union :—that we deeply regret that measures adopted in good faith, and in a strictly constitutional form, by the constituted authorities of the country, should have been considered by the people of that State as intended to build up another section of the Union at their expense :—that we are, and always have been ready and desirous to listen in a sincere spirit of conciliation to any propositions for changing, in a constitutional and legal manner, any part of the existing legislation, and to give them all the attention to which they are fairly entitled :—and that we earnestly entreat our brethren and fellow citizens of South Carolina, to desist from the irregular, violent and unconstitutional attempts to obtain redress for their supposed grievances, in which they are now engaged, the result of which, if further pursued, can only be to create collision between the General and State Governments, endanger the public tranquillity, and seriously compromise the safety of the persons immediately concerned in them.

Resolved, That His Excellency the Governor be requested to transmit a copy of these Resolves, and the Report preceding them, to the President of the United States, the Governors of all the States, and to each of the Senators and Representatives of this Commonwealth in Congress.

In Senate, March 1, 1833.

Read twice, and passed.

Sent down for concurrence.

B. T. PICKMAN, *President*.

House of Representatives, March 9, 1833.

Read twice, and passed in concurrence.

W. B. CALHOUN, *Speaker*.

March 11, 1833.

Approved.

LEVI LINCOLN.

RESOLVES

OF THE

LEGISLATURE

OF

NEW YORK.

REPORT.

THE right claimed by the State of South Carolina, to make void the laws of the United States within her territory, is so fully set forth in the Ordinance and Documents before the Legislature, and so well understood, that a precise statement, in this report, of its nature and extent, would be superfluous.

The Committee have considered the claim, thus set up, with the attention due to the high respectability of the source from which it emanated, and to the very grave consequences that would unavoidably result from its establishment: and they concur with the Governor in regarding it as a pretension, "not merely unauthorized by the Constitution of the United States, but fatally repugnant to all the objects for which it was framed."

The unfounded nature of the authority asserted by South Carolina, has been so clearly demonstrated in the Proclamation of the President of the United States, which has been published by order of the Legislature, and is now on its files; and is so fully confirmed by the concurring opinions of the people of every other State in the Union; that it cannot be necessary that the Committee should attempt to shed any additional light upon a subject, in respect to which, the argument may, with so much truth, be said to be exhausted.

The duty of the President to exercise the authority vested in him by the Constitution and laws of the United States; to enforce the latter in the State of South Carolina, notwithstanding the unjustifiable attempt on the part of that State to arrest the due execution thereof, is obvious and imperative. And the Committee are well satisfied that they represent truly the opinions of the Government and People of the State of New York, when they reciprocate the assurance given by the Governor, that in the performance of that great and responsible duty, by the exercise of necessary and proper means, the President may count on their support and co-operation.

With this brief statement of the principal matter referred to them, the Committee would prefer to leave the subject. Considered only with reference to the present aspect of the affair, it might not be strictly necessary to say more ; and they deprecate too sincerely the asperities which usually grow out of diversities of opinion upon doctrinal points, not to be anxious to avoid them as far as it can properly be done. The more especially are they impressed with the propriety of such a course, in reference to the present posture of our public affairs, when the hearts and minds of our citizens should be exclusively directed to the measures best calculated to preserve the happy union of these States in the spirit of affection and brotherly love in which it was established. The Committee however, are too well advised of the desire of the Legislature that their opinion should be distinctly expressed upon some points of deep interest, growing out of the assumptions of right contained in the Ordinance of South Carolina, and the commentary of the President thereon in his recent Proclamation and Message, to feel themselves at liberty to exercise a discretion upon the subject.

In the performance of the duty assigned them, they will submit the dictates of their best judgment, in that spirit of liberality and forbearance which, under any circumstances, it would give them pleasure to cherish, but which, under those that now exist, they consider it a sacred duty to observe.

They believe that this duty cannot be better discharged than by a frank and explicit avowal of the principles which, in their opinion, ought to be applied to the construction of the Constitution of the United States, and to control in that respect the administration of the government established by it. They regard it the more important to do so, from the attempts which have been made to bring into discredit political principles which the people of this State have so long and so ardently cherished ; and upon the maintenance of which, in all their purity, the Committee firmly believe the safety of our institutions, and the future welfare of the country, mainly depend. The reassertion of those principles at a period like the present, when there is reason to fear that they may suffer from misapprehension or misrepresentation, is, in the opinion of the Committee, a matter of paramount obligation.

There is no reasonable ground to doubt, that the great body of the American people are fervently attached to the Union of the States, and sincerely desirous that the partition and limitations of power intended to be established by the Federal Constitution, and the republican principle on which it rests, should be preserved inviolate. They have, however, greatly differed as to the most effectual and least exceptionable means, of effecting those objects; and as to the true source of the dangers to which our political system was exposed.

These differences arose in the Convention which framed the Constitution; attended every step of its formation and establishment, and have never ceased to exist. Consolidation on the one hand, tending to monarchy in the head, and on the other, anarchy, consequent upon the insubordination and resistance of the members, were the evils anticipated at its formation, and have ever since been dreaded by the respective parties.

A portion of the people believed, that unless great vigor was imparted to the Federal arm, it would not be able to sustain itself against the power and influence of the States, and effect the great objects which all desired to accomplish, through the agency of the Federal Government. Others supposed, that the natural tendency of the new system would be towards consolidation; and that unless the powers delegated to the government, thus created, were granted with a sparing hand, scrupulously and vigilantly guarded, and the remaining powers and sovereignty of the States amply protected, there would be reason to apprehend that the revolution of 1776 would be shorn of its honors and its benefits; and the consequence ultimately would be, a return to that form of government which had been thrown off at so much cost. No candid and intelligent observer can have failed to witness the enduring effects of these early differences, nor be ignorant of the unceasing influence they have exercised on public affairs. On every recurrence to the conflicting principles by which they were generated, we have seen on the one side, a strong inclination to yield, readily, to that construction, and to that course of measures, which might best serve to strengthen the Federal Government, and extend the sphere of its action ; a disposition which at all times, but with various success, has been resisted by those, who entertain different views, as to the best means of securing the efficacy and harmony, and of preserving the equilibrium and constant stability of the entire system. It is not the intention of the Committee to enter into a particular consideration of the reasons, by which these conflicting opinions are respectively sustained; nor to advert to them, farther than is necessary to the distinct and intelligible explanation of their own views, upon the subject referred to them.

The Committee are advocates for the reserved rights of the States, and a strict construction of the Constitution of the United States. Experience has, they think, fully demonstrated the wisdom of the determination of the Convention to commit to the Federal Government, the management of such concerns only, as appertain to the relations of the States with each other, and with foreign nations, and certain other matters particularly enumerated in the Constitution : leaving the great mass of the business of the people, relating as it does mainly to their domestic concerns, to the legislation of the States. They were wisely regarded as the safest depositories of the latter powers. This course was moreover due to the reserved sovereignty of the States, and required by an enlightened estimate of the dangers to the harmony of National Legislation, inseparable from the great diversity in the interests and conditions of the different States. A sincere adherence to this partition of legislation amongst the respective governments, and an honest and inflexible observance of the specifications and restrictions by which it was defined, in the sense designed by the Convention, and as understood by the people in the adoption of the Constitution, are in the best judgment of the Committee, indispensably necessary to its preservation.

Time, and the course of events, have solved the great problem that divided the Convention. It is now apparent that the tendency of the system is to encroachments by the Federal Government upon the reserved rights of the States, rather than to an unwillingness on the part of the States to submit to a full exercise of the powers which were intended to be delegated to the General Government. So manifest has this tendency been

rendered to the people of the United States, that at several interesting eras in our history, they have been induced by the ex-
cesses to which it led, to rise in their strength, and drive from
power, the agents employed in giving it effect. Such was their
course in the memorable civil revolution of 1800 : and the same
sovereign remedy, upon the same impulse, and, it is hoped, with
similar effect, was applied by the people in 1828. Whilst these
scenes have passed before our eyes, and stand forth upon the
page of our history, for our edification and security, not an instance has occurred in which the resistance of a single State, to
the measures of the Federal Government, has excited sufficient
sympathy or countenance from her sister States, to afford cause
for a well grounded apprehension of detriment to the Union, by
an improper combination amongst its members. Even at this
critical emergency in our public affairs, when so much discredit
is apprehended to the sacred cause of State rights from the ex-
cesses of South Carolina, the confidence of the Committee in the
correctness of that cause is strengthened by the exemplary conduct of her sister States. When we witness the fervent zeal that
pervades them all, and see so many who have the same cause of
complaint as South Carolina, and who are equally solicitous for
a redress of their grievances, rising superior to local interests,
exhibiting to the world the most sublime spectacle of devoted
patriotism, and throwing their great moral and physical weight
into the scale of the Union, who can doubt that now, as in the
late war, the federal arm, in the hour of its greatest peril, will
be upheld by the State authorities ? The Committee are cheer-
ed by this animating indication of fidelity, not merely because
they see in it the unequivocal evidence of the safety of that
Union which they so highly cherish, but on account of the favorable influence which the complete establishment of the principles to which they have avowed their attachment, is calculated to exercise on the future administration of this government.
In " the support of the State governments in all their rights as
the most competent administrators of our domestic concerns and
the surest bulwarks against anti-republican tendencies : and the
preservation of the general government in its whole constitutional vigor, as the sheet-anchor of our peace at home and safety
abroad," the Committee recognize the highest duties of every

public functionary ; and in the encouragement derived from the approving voice of a virtuous and grateful people, the best security for their faithful performance.

Of the deeply interesting questions arising upon the Ordinance and other documents referred to the Committee, there is none of more immediate importance, than the claim which is advanced, that a single State has a right to withdraw herself, against the wishes of her co-States, from the Union, whenever, in her sole judgment, the acts of the Federal Government shall be such as to justify the step.

The Committee cannot approve this doctrine. Anxious as they are to sustain the sovereignty of the States in its full force, they do not feel it to be less their duty to " preserve," in the language of Mr. Jefferson, "the General Government, in its whole constitutional vigor." There is no conflict of duty between these sentiments ; so far from it, that, in the opinion of the Committee, no man can be a good citizen, who is disloyal to either. No apprehension too alarming, can be entertained as to the injurious consequences which may result from the principles attempted to be established. The Committee have witnessed, with deep regret, that an impression has gone abroad, that the assertion of this right was embraced in the proceedings of the Legislatures of Virginia and Kentucky, in 1798 and 1799. Whatever authority there may be for the right of secession, it certainly cannot, in the opinion of the Committee, claim any from those proceedings. They took place at a very dark and portentous period in our history ; when the encroachments of the Federal Government, and the general temper of the times had filled the hearts of many of our firmest patriots with alarm.

The respect of the people of this State, for those emanations of lofty and devoted patriotism, is at this day as great, and their devotion to the principles they inculcated, as sincere as it was in 1800. And the Committee cannot, as they conceive, render a more acceptable service to the Republic, than by separating them from a doctrine which, however sincerely it may be entertained by others, is rejected by our citizens, with a degree of unanimity heretofore unknown to political controversy. A very brief exposition of the nature and history of those proceedings, is all that is essential for that purpose. The portions of the

Virginia Resolutions, upon the alien and sedition laws, (and there is not, in this respect, sufficient difference between them and those of Kentucky, to make the separate examination of each necessary) from which such a deduction is attempted to be made, are in the following words :

" That this Assembly doth explicitly and peremptorily declare, that it views the powers of the Federal Government, as resulting from the Compact, to which the States are parties, as limited by the plain sense and intention of the Instrument constituting that Compact ; as no farther valid than they are authorized by the grants enumerated in that Compact ; and that, in case of a deliberate, palpable and dangerous exercise of other powers, not granted by the said Compact, the States who are parties thereto, have a right, and are in duty bound, to interpose, for arresting the progress of the evil, and for maintaining within their respective limits, the authorities, rights and liberties appertaining to them."

" That the good people of this Commonwealth, having ever felt, and continuing to feel the most sincere affection for their brethren of other States : the truest anxiety for establishing and perpetuating the union of all ; and the most scrupulous fidelity to that Constitution which is the pledge of mutual friendship, and the instrument of mutual happiness ; the General Assembly doth solemnly appeal to the like dispositions in the other States, in confidence that they will concur with this Commonwealth in declaring, as it does hereby declare, that the acts aforesaid are unconstitutional ; and, that the necessary and proper measures will be taken by each, for co-operating with this State in maintaining unimpaired, the authorities, rights and liberties reserved in the States respectively, or to the people."

These resolutions were met by several of the State Legislatures to whom they had been communicated, by counter resolutions, protesting against them with much warmth, chiefly on the ground that the act of a State Legislature, declaring a law of the United States unconstitutional, was, in itself, an unconstitutional assumption of authority, and an unwarrantable interference with the exclusive jurisdiction of the Supreme Court of the United States : accompanied, in some instances, with severe denunciations against their disorganizing tendency.

The resolutions of the protesting States were, at a succeeding session of the Virginia Legislature, referred to and reported upon, at large, by a Committee of that body. Their report was written by Mr Madison, and led to a re-affirmance by Virginia, of the unconstitutionality of the alien and sedition laws, and a re-assertion of the doctrines of the original resolutions. This masterly exposition of the true principles of the Constitution, and of the abuses which had been practised under it, contributed more than any event, to that radical change in the public sentiment of the country, which was consummated by the election of Mr. Jefferson, and has, from that day to the present, been justly regarded as the genuine text book of political orthodoxy. The Committee do, unhesitatingly, and with great satisfaction, embrace this occasion to avow their decided approbation of its doctrines; and they feel, that they would be wanting in gratitude and duty, if they were not to express their conviction of the benefits which have been derived from their influence : of the extent to which, in their opinion, the future operations of our political institutions are dependent upon the continued respect and confidence of the people in them : as well as their unfeigned admiration of the unsurpassed disinterestedness and inflexible fidelity, with which those doctrines have, through evil and through good report, been sustained by that truly patriotic member of the confederacy.

That the judicial department of the Federal Government, was the exclusive expositor of the Constitution, in cases submitted to its judgment, in the last resort, was freely admitted. But, it was contended by that Committee—" First, that there may be instances of usurped power, which the forms of the Constitution would never draw within the control of the judicial department : Secondly, that if the decision of the judiciary be raised above the authorities of the sovereign parties to the Constitution, the decisions of the other departments not carried by the forms of the Constitution before the Judiciary, must be equally authoritative and final with the decisions of that department. That the resolutions of the General Assembly, related to those great and extraordinary cases in which all the forms of the Constitution may prove ineffectual against infractions dangerous to the essential rights of the parties to it. That the resort to the judiciary must necessarily be deemed the last, in relation to the authorities of the other departments of the Government : not in relation to the rights of the parties to the constitutional compact, from which the judicial as well as the other departments hold their delegated trusts. On any other hypothesis, the delegation of judicial power would annul the authority of the power delegating it ; and the concurrence of this department with others in usurped powers, might subvert forever, and beyond the possible reach of any rightful remedy, the very Constitution which all were instituted to preserve." That " a declaration that proceedings of the Federal Government are not warranted by the Constitution, was a novelty neither among the citizens nor the Legislatures of the States ;"—" nor could the declarations of either, whether affirming or denying the constitutionality of the measures of the Federal Government ; or whether made before or after judicial decisions thereon, be deemed in any point of view an assumption of the office of a judge. The declarations in such cases are expressions of opinion, unaccompanied with other effect than what they may produce on opinion by exciting reflection. The expositions of the judiciary, on the other hand, are carried into immediate effect by force. The former may lead to a change in the legislative expression of the general will— possibly to a change in the opinion of the judiciary." Hence it was urged that there was no impropriety in the declaration by the Legislature that the alien and sedition laws were unconstitutional : nor was there any valid objection to the communication of that resolution to her sister States ; nor in the invitation which was given to them to concur therein ; nor in asking for the adoption of " necessary and proper measures by each, for co-operating with her in maintaining unimpaired the authorties, rights, and liberties reserved in the States respectively, or to the people."

But what were those measures which the Legislature of Virginia deemed " necessary and proper" to meet the exigency in the affairs of the country so truly alarming as that which then existed, and to which their proceedings had reference ? Was it to oppose, by State authority, the regular administration of justice in any case in law or equity committed by the Constitution to the Federal Judiciary ? Did they relate to resistance by a member of the confederacy, to the execution of the laws of the United States, passed in conformity to the provisions of the Constitution ; or embrace the revocation by a State of the powers which had, with so much solemnity, and under such high penalties, been granted by the people of the respective States to the Federal Government ? Far, very far from it. Anticipations of this character were entertained when those resolutions were under discussion in the Virginia Legislature, and they were consequently denounced as the harbinger of civil commotion. These denunciations were met and refuted by the advocates of the resolutions, not only after they had been submitted to the other States, but when they were first submitted to the Legislature of that State. They were introduced by John Taylor, of Caroline.

In reply to these predictions, he said, " Suppose a clashing of opinion should exist between Congress and the States, respecting the true limits of the constitutional territories, it was easy to see that if the right of decision had been vested in either party, that party deciding in the spirit and interest of party, would inevitably have swallowed up the other. The Constitution must not only have foreseen the possibility of such a clashing, but also the consequence of a preference on either side as to its construction ; and out of this foresight must have arisen the fifth article, by which two-thirds of Congress may call upon the States for an explanation of any such controversy as the present, by way of amendment to the Constitution, and thus correct an erroneous construction of its own acts, by a minority of the States ; whilst two-thirds of the States are also allowed to compel Congress to call a convention, in case so many should think an amendment necessary, for the purpose of checking the unconstitutional acts of that body. Thus, so far as Congress may have power, it might exert it to check the usurpations of a State, and so far as the States may possess it, an union of two-thirds in one opinion might effectually check the usurpations of Congress. And under this article of the Constitution, the incontrovertible principle before stated might become practically useful, otherwise no remedy did exist for the only case which could possibly destroy the Constitution, namely, an encroach-

ment by Congress or the States upon the rights of the other.
* * * * Mr. Taylor then proceeded to apply these observ-
ations to the threats of war, and the apprehension of civil
commotion, towards which the resolutions were said to have a
tendency. Are the republicans, said he, possessed of fleets and
armies? If not, to what could they appeal for defence and support? To nothing except public opinion. If that should be
against them, they must yield. * * * * How could the
fifth article of the Constitution be brought into practical use,
even upon the most flagrant usurpations? War or insurrection,
therefore, could not happen," &c. * * * * " Such, however, he hoped would be the respect to public opinion, that he
doubted not but that the two reprobated laws would be sacri-
ficed, to quiet the apprehensions even of a single State, without
the necessity of a convention or a mandate from three-fourths of
the States, whenever it shall be admitted that the quiet and happiness of the people is the end and design of Government."

Similar sentiments were advanced by the other supporters of
the resolutions. Mr. Mercer said "that force was never thought
of by any one. The preservation of the Federal Constitution,
the cement of the Union, with its original powers, was the object of the resolutions."

But all pretence for misapprehension or misconstruction upon
this head is put at rest by the direct explanations of the Virginia
Legislature, in the report which was made and received their
sanction in the session of 1799; in which, in relation to the
means referred to in the resolutions, and in answer to the objection that they might have been such as conflicted with the order
and stability of the Union, they say, 'In the example given by
the State, of declaring the alien and sedition acts to be unconstitutional, and of communicating the declaration to the other
States, no trace of improper means has appeared. And if the
other States had concurred in making a like declaration, supported too by the numerous applications flowing immediately
from the people, it can scarcely be doubted, that these simple
means would have been as sufficient as they are unexceptionable.

" It is no less certain that other means might have been employed which are strictly within the limits of the Constitution.
The Legislatures of the States might have made a direct repre-

sentation to Congress, with a view to obtain a rescinding of the two offensive acts ; or they might have represented to their respective Senators in Congress their wish that two-thirds thereof would propose an explanatory amendment to the Constitution; or two-thirds of themselves, if such had been their option, might, by an application to Congress, have obtained a convention for the same object.

" These several means, though not equally eligible in themselves, nor probably to the States, were all constitutionally open for consideration. And if the General Assembly, after declaring the two acts to be unconstitutional, the first and most obvious proceeding on the subject, did not undertake to point out to the other States a choice among the farther measures that might become necessary and proper, the reserve will not be misconstrued by liberal minds into any culpable imputation."

Such was the understanding of the import and the intent of the resolutions by him who introduced them ; by those who supported them ; by the Committee to which they were at a subsequent session referred ; and by the Legislature which adopted their exposition.

It is a matter of undoubted historical fact, that the Virginia resolutions were drawn up by Mr. Madison, and those of Kentucky by Mr. Jefferson.

In the dispensation of an all-wise Providence, Mr. Madison's useful and brilliant life has been prolonged to this late period of existence. He has borne his testimony against the justice of any of the inferences which the Committee have felt it their duty to repel ; and they are unadvised of any act or declaration of Mr. Jefferson, who, in the confidence and affections of his fellow citizens, was only second to the Father of his Country, which conflicts with the known views of his great coadjutor. The Committee are well aware that the advocates of nullification have attempted to sustain that doctrine by expressions contained in an unpromulgated draft of the Kentucky resolutions found among his papers, in which is set forth the right of a State to nullify an act of Congress, passed in respect to a subject upon which its action is expressly inhibited, or upon which it had no authority to legislate at all. A suggestion which, if it were possible to make a paper so circumstanced whenever it may be found, the basis of so solemn an act, is clearly inapplicable to the case under consideration, inasmuch as it expressly declares, that for "an abuse of delegated power," (the most that could by possibility be made of the revenue laws) "the members of the General Government being chosen by the people, a change by the people would be the Constitutional remedy." But the published writings of that great man are replete with the evidences of his avowed opinions, inconsistent with the supposition that he believed in the right of a single State either to make constitutional resistance to the laws of the United States or to dissolve the Union by withdrawing herself from it, when in her sole judgment, the circumstances were sufficient to justify the act.

In a letter to Mr. Destutt Tracy, in January, 1811, he says, "Dangers of another kind might more reasonably be apprehended from this perfect and distinct organization, civil and military, of the States, to wit : that certain States from local and occasional discontents, might attempt to secede from the Union. This is certainly possible ; and would be befriended by this regular organization. But it is not probable that local discontents can spread to such an extent as to be able to face the sound parts of so extensive a Union—and if ever they should reach the majority, they would then become the regular government, acquire ascendency in Congress, and be able to redress their own grievances by laws peaceably and constitutionally passed."

In a letter to Elbridge Gerry, of January, 1812, he uses these significant and emphatic expressions :—"What, then, does this English faction with you mean ? Their newspapers say rebellion, and that they will not remain united with us, unless we will permit them to govern the majority. If this be their purpose, their anti-republican spirit, it ought to be met at once. But a government like ours should be slow in believing this, should put forth its whole might when necessary to suppress it, and promptly return to the paths of reconciliation. The extent of our country secures it, I hope, from the vindictive passions of the petty incorporations of Greece. I rather suspect that the principal office of the other seventeen States, will be to moderate and restrain the local excitement of our friends with you, when they (with the aid of their brethren of the other States, if they need it,) shall have brought the rebellious to their feet."

In a letter to Major John Cartwright, as late as June, 1824, he says, "But, you may ask, if the two departments, (meaning the General and State Governments,) should claim each the same subject of power, where is the common umpire to decide ultimately between them ? In cases of little importance or urgency, the prudence of both parties will keep them aloof from the questionable ground ; but if it can neither be avoided nor compromised, a convention of the States must be called, to ascribe the doubtful power to that department which they may think best. You will perceive by these details, that we have not yet so far perfected our Constitutions as to venture to make them unchangeable. But still, in their present state, we consider them not otherwise changeable than by the authority of the people, on a special election of representatives for that purpose expressly : They are until then the *lex legum.*"

The Committee have felt it their duty to say thus much, in order to separate the doctrines of 1798, from the principle now in question. So far, at least, as they are contained in and depend on documents which deserve to be held in respectful remembrance whilst the Constitution endures.

Neither do the Committee concur in the opinion that the right of secession necessarily results from the sovereignty of the States. It appears to the Committee, and they express their views with unfeigned deference to the highly respectable opinions of those who differ with them, that this impression arises from erroneously regarding the sovereignty of the respective States as unqualified, and the association a mere confederacy of free and sovereign States. If such were the case, if the union were a mere league, the result contended for might follow ; but the Committee do not so understand the system. The States, on the contrary, as it was competent for the people of each, acting in their highest sovereign character, have voluntarily established, by express grant, a sovereignty in some respects concurrent with, and in other respects superior to, their own. This authority thus established, though founded on a compact, is nevertheless a government which is made by that compact sovereign and independent as to the powers granted to it, in the same manner as the States are sovereign and independent as to powers not granted. The people of the respective States have stipulated that their legislatures, and all their executive and judicial officers, shall be bound by oath or affirmation to support the Constitution of that government. For a breach of their allegiance to it, they have voluntarily subjected themselves to the highest penalties known to human laws; and to maintain its sovereignty, they have invested this government of their own creation with the purse and sword of the nation. The faithful performance of this contract is certainly matter of high obligation on all the parties to it; and no condemnation by the people can be too severe upon such as are so lost to the obligation under which they rest, to each other, to the people, and to the cause of free government throughout the world, as to be guilty of its intentional violation. But, of the fact and consequences of such a breach, in cases where no other umpire has been designated, it is the right of each party to judge for itself; not for the Federal Government exclusively, as was contended by the States which protested against the Virginia and Kentucky resolutions in 1799; nor for each State solely, as is now contended. No right is reserved to the people of any State to absolve themselves from the performance of duties which they have so solemnly assumed, without the consent of the other party or parties to the compact. Each State, on surrendering a portion of its sovereignty, acquired, in consequence thereof, a right to the perpetual adherence of each of its co-States to that Union which is so necessary to, and was established for, the security of all.

The articles of Confederation abound with declarations that the Union then formed should be perpetual; and the present Constitution was established for the avowed purpose of making it more perfect. New York entered into the formation of it expressly " to render the Federal Constitution adequate to the exigencies of the Government, and the preservation of the Union." Deficient, indeed, would have been the work which came from the hands of those great men who framed the Constitution, the final adoption of which was hailed with so much joy by the people, if it thus contained the elements of its own destruction.

When a State shall attempt to withdraw herself from the Confederacy, it is for her co-States to decide whether they will re-

linquish the rights which they acquired when they surrendered
a portion of their sovereignty—consent to a dissolution, and endeavor to establish a new Government; or whether they will
insist on the preservation of the Union as it is. Without the
recognition of this right, the Union could not have existed to the
present day. Strip the States of this right, and a system which
but yesterday excited the respect and admiration of the world,
must soon, very soon, serve only as an additional argument in
the mouths of monarchists and absolutists against the capacity
of man for self-government.

Let it not, however, be supposed that the Committee are the
advocates of unconditional submission. Such are not their
views. They concur fully in the sentiment, " that the authority
of constitutions over governments, and of the sovereignty of the
people over constitutions, are truths which are at all times necessary to be kept in mind." Or, in the language of our own
State, " that the powers of Government may be re-assumed by
the people, whenever it shall become necessary to their happiness." In respect to State governments, this control can be
constitutionally exercised by a bare majority of the people; and
in the Federal Government, by a specified number of the States.
But this is not the only mode by which the people can redress
intolerable grievances. There is another, which cannot be better described than has been done by Mr. Madison. " And in
the event (says he) of the failure of every constitutional resort,
and an accumulation of usurpations and abuses, rendering pass-
ive obedience and non-resistance a greater evil than resistance
and revolution, there can remain but one resort, the last of all—
an appeal from the cancelled obligations of the compact, to
original rights and the law of self-preservation. This is the *ultima
ratio* under all governments, whether consolidated, confederated,
or a compound of both. And it cannot be doubted that a single
member of the Union, in the extremity supposed, but in that
only, would have a right, as an extra and ultra-constitutional
right, to make the appeal."

It was to this species of separation, which God in his infinite
mercy avert! that the Committee understand Mr. Jefferson as
referring, when he alluded to the farther measure of redress
which might be resorted to in extreme cases, and spoke of Vir-

ginia's " standing by her arms." It was this great calamity that
he sought to avoid, when he so eloquently and feelingly invoked
his native State never to think of it, until the sole alternatives
left, were a dissolution of the Union, or submission to a Government, without limitation or power.

The history given by the President, of the formation of our
Government, has drawn forth conflicting opinions in respect to
its accuracy ; and lest the Committee might be regarded as having omitted any portion of their duties, they will, upon this subject, also, with deference to the views of others, but frankly
state their own.

The character of our Government, so far as that is effected by
the manner in which the Federal Constitution was framed and
adopted, has been always a matter of more or less contention.
Differences of opinion upon the subject, have been in some degree fostered by a seeming discrepancy between the preamble
of the Constitution, and historical facts ; and perhaps in a still
greater degree, by the different senses in which the term
" States," is used by different persons. If we use that term, not
merely as denoting particular sections of territory, nor as referring to the particular governments, established and organized
by the political societies within each, but as referring to the
people composing those political societies, in their highest sovereign capacity (as the Committee think that in this respect the
term should be used) it is incontrovertible, that the States must
be regared as parties to the compact. For it is well established, that, in that sense, the Constitution was submitted to the
States ; that in that sense, the States ratified it. This is the explanation which is given of the matter in the report to the Virginia Legislature, which has already received the sanction of
the Committee. It is in this sense of the term " States," that
they form the constituency from which the Federal Constitution
emanated, and it is by the States, acting either by their Legislatures, or in Convention, that any valid alterations of the instrument can alone be made. It is by so understanding the
subject, that the preamble is reconciled with facts, and that it is
a Constitution established by "the people of the United States,"
not as one consolidated body, but as members of separate and
independent communities, each acting for itself, without regard

to their comparative numbers. It was in this form that the Constitution of the United States was established by the people of the different States, with the same solemnity that the Constitutions of the respective States were established; and, as the Committee have heretofore insisted, with the same binding force in respect to the powers which were intended to be delegated to the Federal Government. The effects which are likely to be produced by the adoption of either of the different versions of the Constitution, which have at different times been contended for, it is not the intention of the Committee to discuss. The positive provisions and restrictions of that instrument, could not be directly abrogated by the recognition of either. The comparative weight and influence which would be attached to the allegations and remonstrances of the States, in respect to the supposed infractions of the Compact, might, however, be very different, whether they are regarded as sovereign parties of the Compact, acting upon their reserved rights, or as forming only indiscriminate portions of the great body of the people of the United States, thus giving a preponderence to mere numbers, incompatible with the frame and design of the Federal Constitution.

The diversities of opinion which have arisen upon this subject, have been more or less injurious according to their influence in inclining or disinclining the minds of those who entertain them, to a faithful observance of the landmarks of authority between the respective Governments. Professions are easily made; and the best evidence of a correct appreciation of the nature and design of the system by a public agent, is to be found in the general bearing of his official acts. If his conduct be characterized by a desire to administer the Government upon the principles which his constituents have elected, and by a determination to repudiate the dangerous heresy, that the Constitution is to be interpreted, not by the well understood intentions of those who framed and those who adopted it, but by what can be made out of its words by ingenious interpretation; if he honestly believes that the people are the safest depository of power, and acts up to that belief, by evincing an unwillingness to exercise authority which was not intended to be granted, and which the States and the people might not, on open application, be willing to grant; if he has steadily opposed the adoption of all schemes, however magnificent and captivating, which are not warranted by the Constitution—which, from the inequality of their benefits and burthens, are calculated to sow discord where there should be union, and which are too frequently the offspring of that love of personal authority and aggrandizement which men in power find it so difficult to resist. If he has done all in his power to arrest the increase of monopolies, under all circumstances so adverse to public liberty, and the equal interests of the community. If his official career has been distinguished by unceasing assiduity to promote economy in the public expenditures, to relieve the people from all unnecessary burthens, and generally to preserve our republican system in that simplicity and purity which were intended for it—under which it has hitherto been so successful, by which it can alone be maintained ; and on account of which it has, until this moment, stood in such enviable and glorious contrast with the corrupt systems of the old world. If such be the traces of his official course, and if in maintaining it he shall have impressed all mankind with the conviction that he regards as nothing, consequences which are merely personal to himself, when they come in contact with duty to his country, the people of the United States will not doubt his attachment to the true principles of that Constitution which he has so faithfully administered and so nobly supported. Such, the Committee take pride in saying, has been the official course of our present Chief Magistrate—a course by which, in the judgment of the people of this State, he has established for himself imperishable claims to their gratitude, respect, and confidence.

The Committee have thus explained their views upon the several delicate and deeply interesting questions before them, with that frankness which becomes the solemn occasion on which they act, and which should always characterize the movements of a sovereign State upon matters involving her relations with her sister States. In doing so, they have felt it to be their duty to vindicate and explain the political principles which are entertained by themselves, and, as they believe, by a majority of the good people of this State. In the performance of this act of justice and duty, they have endeavored to avoid all impu-

tations upon the motives of those who may differ from them·
The same independence and toleration which they claim for
themselves, they are disposed to extend to others. Amidst the
conflict of interest and feelings with which those, who are
charged with the conduct of public affairs at this interesting
crisis, are obliged to struggle, there is happily one opinion
which has not yet met with a dissenting voice in all the land;
and which it is fervently hoped, is too deeply implanted in the
minds and hearts of the people to be ever eradicated. It is a
thorough conviction, that anarchy, degradation, and interminable distress, will be, must be, the unavoidable results of a dissolution of the union of these States. Associated with this undeniable and undenied truth, and growing out of it, there are, we
trust, two other sentiments of eqnal universality—a determination to maintain the Union at all hazards, and a willingness to
make liberal concessions, nay sacrifices, for the preservation of
peace and reciprocal good will amongst its members. Upon
this great conservative platform, all sincere friends of the Union,
all who honor and truly respect the parting admonitions of the
Father of his country, all who prefer that country to their own
ambitious views and personal aggrandizement, and who are disposed to give the Executive of the United States a cordial and
efficient support, can meet, and act in concert to promote the
greatest of all earthly objects. Here all may earn the enduring
respect and confidence of the people, by an honorable sacrifice
of personal and party feelings on the altar of their country's
safety. We may differ as to the time, the manner, or the extent
of the measures to be employed, whether of conciliation or coercion. It cannot be expected, at the present crisis, that honest
and unprejudiced minds should all happen to arrive at the same
conclusion. But such differences should not occasion heart
burnings, much less resentments. Our fathers differed in like
manner in the establishment of our Government; and it is in
vain for us to hope for exemption from similar embarrassments;
the causes which produced them have not yet ceased to operate;
they have been planted by the hand of nature, and cannot be
entirely removed by that of man. Those, to whose valor and
disinterested patriotism we are indebted for this glorious system
under which we have so long and so happily lived, overcame

them by mutual concession and compromise. If every man looks only to his own interests, or every State to its own favorite policy, and insists upon them, this Union cannot be preserved. We must not deceive ourselves upon this point, or suffer others to deceive us. Our errors, in this respect, may lead to consequences which can never be recalled; and over which we and our posterity may have occasion to shed bitter tears of repentance; we must take higher counsel than that which is derived from our pockets or our passions; we must be just, and, if need be, generous; and the deep and overpowering attachment of the great mass of the people to the Union, the fidelity, energy, and fortitude of their character, directed by the illustrious man so providentially at the head of the Government, will carry us safely through the dangers which threaten our beloved country.

It remains only to reciprocate, as the Committee doubt not the two Houses will readily do, the magnanimous and enlightened sentiments expressed by the Governor, upon the subject which has caused the present embarrassments in our public affairs. Most cheerfully, therefore, do they respond to his declarations, which "disclaim for New York all desire to aggrandize herself at the expense of her sister States, or to pervert to local purposes, a system of government intended for the common benefit of all;" which assert her estimate of the value of the Union and her devotion to it; and which avow her willingness, if the operation of existing laws be adverse to those views, to consent to such a modification of them as will remove all just ground of complaint, and afford substantial relief to every real grievance. In these sentiments the committee recognize the best policy as well as the true glory of these States; a policy, "which cultivates peace and harmony by observing justice."

The opinion of this State in favor of the constitutional power of Congress, to afford encouragement and protection to domestic products, by the establishment for that object of suitable commercial regulations, has been too often declared to need repetition. Neither time nor circumstances have contributed to change its convictions, either of the existence or importance of this right. Without it, it would not be possible for the Federal Government to carry into effect one of the principal objects of its institution: and the United States would, in relation to our own exports, be left altogether at the mercy of foreign nations. The possession of the right, however, and the manner and extent of its exercise are very different matters. Whatever causes of serious apprehension for the stability of the Union may heretofore have arisen from this source, it appears to the Committee that they have been greatly lessened by the payment of the national debt, and the disposition of the Executive of the United States, and, as the Committee firmly believe, of the great body of the people, to make such a modification of the tariff as becomes by that event just and practicable. The repeated recommendations of the President to reduce the revenue to what is requisite to defray the expenses of the government, necessarily incurred within the pale of the Constitution, and under a strictly economical administration of our affairs, have been so distinctly and emphatically sanctioned by the people of this State, as to leave no room for doubt or cavil as to their cheerful acquiescence in the measure. Indeed, the Committee are yet to learn, that there is any man in this great community who advocates or would justify the collection of taxes from the people for any other purpose, and certainly not for the sole one of taking money from the pockets of one class of our people to put into those of another. All that is asked, is, that the amount of duties thus raised, and so expended, shall be levied in such a manner as to afford reasonable encouragement and protection to our own manufactures and other productions, to enable them to compete with similar articles, the manufacture or production of other countries. With such qualifications as may be necessary to prevent injustice, and to preserve inviolate that sound rule of legislation, which requires that all public burthens should be borne in a fair proportion to the ability of the contributors, and the extent of the security which they derive from the government. In other words, that too large a share of the public taxes be not imposed upon those articles of prime necessity to the poor, to the exoneration of articles of luxury, which are used only by the rich. And further, that the reduction of duties thus rendered practicable by the payment of the public debt, though ultimately certain, should not be sudden or capricious, but tempered to the condition of existing establishments—establishments which have grown up and been encouraged by our legislation, and whose claims to the favor and indulgence of the government and people are founded upon the public faith. To a claim so reasonable the Committee are unwilling to believe that the real friends of the Union any where can object. Men may resist to the uttermost the imposition of unreasonable burthens for the protection of articles, in the manufacture and production of which they are not immediately concerned. But, there are, surely, no American citizens who, exempt from such impositions, would not prefer to encourage those of their own country, in preference to the fruits of foreign labor.

It is not in behalf of New York, particularly, that these considerations are urged. For it is notorious that this State is not the principal seat of manufacturing establishments. But justice dictates the same course whatever and wherever be its application.

The rules by which this distribution and reduction of the public burthens are to be effected, must from the nature of things, be more or less arbitrary and uncertain. But if the subject be undertaken and prosecuted in good faith—if the tariff system be not made subservient to the purposes of personal ambition, nor to the cravings of individual cupidity, but treated as a matter of business, affecting deeply the private concerns of every man in every quarter of the Union, there is no doubt of the ability of Congress to adopt such rules as will be satisfactory to the nation.

That the bill of the last session will not reduce the revenue to the proposed standard is certain. The anticipated excess is estimated at between six and seven millions of dollars. Whether the late act should be permitted to go into operation with the intention of modifying the system at the next session of Congress; or whether the object in view shall be effected at the present session, by a law which, though passed now, shall have a gradual operation, is an important point in the difficult and deeply interesting question to be decided. The Committee are by no means insensible to the embarrassment arising from the existence of the Ordinance of the State of South Carolina, and regret that any such obstruction should have been thrown in the way of a regular expression of the public will. They could never advise any legislation by Congress under the dictation of any power; and they have very little fear, that any such will be desired by the Executive, or sanctioned by that body. It must, however, be borne in mind, that South Carolina is not the only State which considers herself injuriously affected by the existing law, and seeks relief from its operation; that there are many other States who are, in this respect, similarly circumstanced, whose alienation from the Union would be the greatest calamity that could befal us, but who have shown as much devotion to the Union, and have manifested as much repugnance to the measures of South Carolina as any. It is then for the justice and sound discretion of Congress to decide, whether, whilst all proper measures are adopted to maintain the laws of the United States in the State of South Carolina, in the same manner as if no such Ordinance had been passed, they may not without detriment to the honor and dignity of the Government, now act upon a matter which has been so specially and urgently submitted to them by the Executive. We may be assured that there is sufficient intelligence and virtue in the people to judge those greatly deprecated measures by themselves, uninfluenced by prejudices of any sort on the one hand, or by the cotemporaneous measures of the Government on the other. Nor is it a matter of slight importance to the people of this State to consider whether the acts of South Carolina ought to occasion a collection from them of about one million of dollars annually, a sum three times as large as is required for the entire expenses of our State Government, when the President informs us that it is not needed for the public service.

The duty of deciding upon these grave matters, rests, as has been justly observed by the Governor, so far as this State has a voice in the discussion, with those who represent us in the Congress of the United States. There, the Committee think, with a general expression of the sense of the Legislature, it ought and may with safety be left. It would, doubtless, be competent for the Legislature to give explicit advice and instruction to their representatives upon the subject; but from the obvious superiority in position of our representatives in Congress, to take a better view of the whole ground than that which is possessed by us, and from the great extent to which the question as to the most proper time for action, as well as the particular provisions which ought to be made, are dependent on facts and details, of which it is impossible that we can be as capable of judging as they are, the Committee think the Legislature will best consult their duty and the interests of all, by confining themselves, at this time, to the general expression of opinion which is now most respectfully proposed.

If by a faithful adherence to the principles here advanced in their behalf, the people of this State can contribute to the restoration and preservation of that fraternal affection in which the Union was originally founded, by which it was once cemented, and which is so essential to its preservation, it will be to them a source of much joy and deep gratitude to the Supreme Disposer of events, for the agency they have been permitted to exercise in effecting so great a good. But if, on the contrary, their well-meant efforts prove unavailing; if the offerings of peace and good will which have been freely and so sincerely tendered by them, in conjunction with their co-States who participate in the same sentiments, shall be rejected ; if, in the providence of God, it be decreed that this Government and this happy Union, the affairs of which have been hitherto so successfully directed by it, are to be put to the final test, the Government and people of this State will meet the crisis with the sustaining consciousness, that they have done all that duty enjoined and honor permitted to avert the worst calamity that could befall the country.

The Committee respectfully suggest, for the consideration of the Legislature, the following resolutions.

RESOLVES.

State of New York.

In Senate, February 16th, 1833.

Resolved, (if the Assembly concur,) That we approve of the general views and conclusions of the preceding Report.

Resolved, (if the Assembly concur,) That we regard the Union of these States as indispensable to their prosperity and happiness: that we participate fully in the desire which has been manifested by the President, to restore harmony, and conciliate affection amongst all the people of the United States, by a seasonable and equitable modification of the Tariff, adapting it to the present condition of the country : that we approve the measures he has adopted and recommended to sustain the authority and execute the laws of the United States ; and that the Government and people of this State will cordially co-operate with him in the exercise of all the means which may be necessary and proper to secure those objects.

Resolved, (if the Assembly concur,) That we regard the right of a single State, to make void within its limits the laws of the United States, as set forth in the Ordinance of South Carolina, as wholly unauthorized by the Constitution of the United States, and in its tendency subversive of the Union and the Government thereof.

Resolved, (if the Assembly concur,) That we do dissent from the doctrine, that a single State has a right to withdraw itself from the Union against the wishes of its co-States, whenever in its sole judgment the acts of the Federal Government shall be such as to justify the step.

Resolved, (if the Assembly concur,) That the Governor be requested to transmit a copy of the foregoing Report and Resolutions, to the Executive of the State of South Carolina, and to the Executives of the other States respectively, to the end that they may be communicated to the Legislatures thereof, and also a copy of the same to the President of the United States, and to each of our Senators and Representatives in Congress.

By order,

J. F. BACON,
Clerk of the Senate.

In Assembly, February 23d, 1833.

Resolved, That this House do concur with the Senate, in their said Resolutions.

By order,

FRANCIS SEGER,
Clerk of the Assembly.

RESOLVES

OF THE

LEGISLATURE

OF

NEW-JERSEY.

State of New=Jersey.

WHEREAS the people of the State of South Carolina, in Convention assembled, have, by an ordinance, dated twenty-fourth of November, eighteen hundred and thirty-two, declared and ordained that the several acts and parts of acts of the Congress of these United States, purporting to be laws for the imposing of duties and imposts on the importation of foreign commodities, are unauthorised by the constitution, violate the true intent and meaning thereof, and are null and void and not binding upon the said State, its officers or citizens and have proclaimed their determination to enforce said ordinance at every hazard, denied the authority of the general government to enforce the revenue laws within the said State of South Carolina, and transmitted a copy of such ordinance, together with an appeal to the people of the United States, to the Executive of this State: AND WHEREAS the high obligations we owe to our common country, as a member of this great confederacy, as well as the due preservation of the inestimable privileges we enjoy under this free and happy government, secured by the toils and cemented by the blood of our common ancestors, has rendered it an imperative duty to proclaim our opinions upon this important subject—THEREFORE, in the name and in behalf of the people of the State of New Jersey, and as their legal representatives,

1. *Be it Resolved, by the Council and General Assembly of said State,* That the Constitution adopted and sanctioned by the people of these United States, as well as our early history, our common interest, our habits, our intercourse, our love of freedom, the honor, strength and durability of our country, proclaim that

all the States of this Union make one indivisible nation united in prosperity and adversity, in peace as in war, by the sacred and indissoluble bond of their Union.

2. *Resolved*, That we deprecate the acts and proceedings of our brethren of the State of South Carolina, as opposed to the fundamental principles upon which the government of these United States is based, as violating the spirit and meaning of the Federal Constitution, and tending to rend asunder those ties of common interest and fraternal regard, of mutual dependance and reciprocal obligation, which are alike our pride, our glory, and our strength, and which have proclaimed us to the world a United People.

3. *Resolved*, That when South Carolina, together with all the other States, acceded to this Union, and adopted the Constitution, she and they became thereby irrevocably bound that all controversy upon the constitutionality of an act of Congress, should be finally adjudicated by the Supreme Court of these United States. The sacred charter of our liberties never contemplated that each state had reserved to itself an ultimate appeal to its own citizens in their sovereign capacity.

4. *Resolved*, That the manufactures of America, are one of the elements of our Independence and greatness ; not oppressing but advancing hand in hand with agriculture and commerce. These three sources of National prosperity, demand equally the fostering protection of Government ; to crush either would be to paralyze all ; and to the General Government, alone, standing on an elevation to survey the whole ground, belongs the information, the wisdom, and the power to apportion just patronage wherever circumstances may require.

5. *Resolved*, That the Constitution of the United States, now contains within itself, an ample provision for its amendment, and for the remedy of every evil which may arise from unforeseen events, or ambiguous construction. When this provision shall be legally called into operation, we shall be prompt to concede all to justice, much to fraternal feeling, and somewhat even to local excitement and mistaken enthusiasm. But it cannot comport either with dignity or sound policy to yield aught in the face of threatened disunion and an armed resistance to the laws.

6. *Resolved,* That the principles contained in the Proclamation, and late Message of the President of the United States, meet our entire approbation; and that we will sustain the Chief Magistrate of the Union in the Constitutional enforcement of these principles.

7. *Resolved,* That we implore our Fellow Citizens of South Carolina, allied as they are to us, by all the heart stiring and inspiriting recollections of the eventful struggle, that made us an independent nation, maturely to ponder over the present crisis in their affairs, and magnanimously to return to more temperate councils, and a juster sense of that obedience to the general will which constitutes the lasting security, and should be the glory and the ornament of every member of this confederacy. But should our fellow citizens of South Carolina, contrary to our reasonable expectations, unsheath the sword, it becomes our solemn and imperative duty to declare, that no separate nation ought or can be suffered to intrude into the very centre of our Territory.

8. *Resolved,* That the Governor be requested to transmit a copy of these resolutions to the President of the United States, to each Senator and Representative in Congress, from this State, and to the Governors of the respective States of the Union.

House of Assembly, February 18th, 1833.

These re-engrossed Joint Resolutions having been three times read in the House of Assembly.

Resolved, That the same do pass.

By order of the House.

JOHN P. JACKSON, *Speaker of Assembly.*

In Council, February 18th, 1833.

These re-engrossed Joint Resolutions having been three times read in the Council and compared.

Resolved, That the same do pass.

By order of Council.

ELIAS P. SEELEY, *Vice President.*

I, JAMES D. WESTCOTT, Secretary of the State of New-Jersey, do certify, that the foregoing is a true copy of the Joint Resolutions of the Legislative Council and General Assembly of the State of New-Jersey, passed February 18th, A. D. one thousand eight hundred and thirty three, as compared with the original, now remaining on file in my office.

In testimony whereof, I have hereunto set my hand and affixed the seal of my said office, at the city of Trenton, in said State, this 18th day of February, A. D. one thousand eight hundred and thirty-three.

JAMES D. WESTCOTT.

RESOLVES

OF THE

LEGISLATURE

OF

PENNSYLVANIA.

RESOLVES

Relative to the Union of the States and the Constitution of the United States.

Resolved by the Senate and House of Representatives of the Commonwealth of Pennsylvania, in General Assembly met, That the Constitution of the United States, and the laws of the United States made in pursuance of the Constitution, are the supreme law of the land, to which every citizen of the United States owes obedience ; and that no authority whatever can release him from his obligation to obey, or require him to take any oath, or enter into any engagement inconsistent with such obligation ; and that any pretension on the part of a State, or any portion thereof, so to release any citizen of the United States, or so to require of him, is unconstitutional, and without the least foundation of right, and can afford neither shelter nor excuse for offences he may commit against the laws of the United States.

Resolved, That no portion of the citizens of the United States, have a rightful power to render invalid an act of the Congress of the United States, duly made by the people's representatives, and approved by the Executive, in the mode prescribed by the Constitution ; nor to nullify the same, either generally, or within particular districts ; but that every such act of Congress continues in full force every where within the United States, notwithstanding any such asserted nullification ; and all persons who resist its execution, offend against the Constitution and laws of the United States, and are liable to prosecution and punishment for such offence.

Resolved, That no State has a right to withdraw from the Union, and to declare itself independent of it ; and that every attempt to do so, would be a virtual infraction of the Constitution of the United States, justifying and requiring the use of constitutional measures to suppress it.

Resolved That the faithful execution of all laws of the United States, made in the mode prescribed by the Constitution, is a duty enjoined upon the President of the United States, in the constitutional discharge of which he is entitled to, and ought to receive the aid and support of every citizen of the Union.

Resolved, That it is the clear and indisputable right of Congress, to impose duties upon importations, and of the Government of the United States to collect the duties payable by law upon goods imported into every part of the Union ; and that every resistance to the collection of the same, is an offence against the Constitution and laws of the United States, and that the offenders are liable to prosecution and punishment for such offence.

Resolved, That in enforcing, by all constitutional means, the laws passed by Congress, for imposing and collecting duties upon goods imported into the United States, and all other acts of the Congress of the United States ; and in bringing to punishment all persons, who, under any pretence, may offer resistance to them. the Commonwealth of Pennsylvania will, if necessary, aid and assist the Government of the United States, by all the means in her power.

Resolved, That we pledge ourselves, jointly and individually to sustain the Chief Magistrate of the United States, in all constitutional measures calculated to preserve and perpetuate the union of the States.

Resolved, That the Governor be requested to transmit a copy of these Resolutions to the President of the United States, and to each Senator and Representative in Congress from this Commonwealth, and to the several Governors of the respective States and Territories of these United States.

SAMUEL ANDERSON,

Speaker of the House of Representatives.

JESSE R. BURDEN,

Speaker of the Senate.

Approved, the twentieth day of December, A. D. one thousand eight hundred and thirty-two.

GEO. WOLF.

SECRETARY'S OFFICE, PENNSYLVANIA, }
HARRISBURG, December 21, 1832. }

This is to certify, that the foregoing Resolutions are truly copied from the original roll in this office.

Witness my hand and seal.

SAML. M'KEAN.

RESOLVES

OF THE

LEGISLATURE

OF

DELAWARE.

REPORT.

The Committee to whom was referred so much of the Governor's Message as relates to the communication from the Governor of the State of South Carolina, respectfully submit the following

REPORT:

THE communication from the Governor of South Carolina is composed of documents ordered by a Convention of the people of that State, held in November last, to be transmitted to the Governors of the several States for the information of their respective Legislatures. These documents consist of a report of a Committee of twenty-one, to the Convention, on the subject of the several acts of Congress imposing duties for the protection of domestic manufactures, with the Ordinance to Nullify the same, an address to the people of that State, and an address to the people of the United States. Your Committee have examined the papers with great care, and with that respectful attention which is due to the source from which they emanate, but they cannot disguise their astonishment at the position assumed by the Convention and the arguments by which it is attempted to be sustained. The position taken by the Convention is, that they have a right to suspend the operation of certain acts of Congress within the limits of the State by declaring those acts null and void, on the ground of their supposed unconstitutionality. This extraordinary right is assumed not as a revolutionary measure, but as one that results from the nature of the compact, created by the Constitution, and as in perfect harmony with its principles. It becomes necessary, therefore, to settle distinctly, the nature of that instrument, in order to decide the question of this right.

The ground taken by the Convention on this subject is, " that the Federal Constitution is a treaty, a confederation, an alliance, by which so many sovereign States agree to exercise their sovereign powers conjointly, upon certain objects of external concern, in which they are equally interested." That the Federal Government is the common agency of the sovereign States, and possesses no more inherent sovereignty than an incorporated town, that it is a mere political corporation, " and that it is the moral obligation alone which each state has chosen to impose on herself, and not the want of sovereignty" which restrains her from exercising all those powers which have been granted to the Federal Government. And this is declared by the Convention to be the true nature of the compact. The principle with which they set out, and upon which the whole doctrine is built, is thus laid down in the address to the people of the State—page 4. " The Constitution of the United States, as is admitted by cotemporaneous writers, is a compact between sovereign States." This is the corner stone of the whole system of Nullification. For if it be true that the Constitution is a mere treaty or compact between sovereign States, which now possess all the sovereignty they ever had, and among whom there can be no common arbiter, the rest of the doctrine follows as a matter of course. The question then arises, is this proposition true? Your Committee conceive that it is false in both its branches. It is neither a compact between sovereign States, nor is so admitted to be, by cotemporaneous writers, at least of any credit.

The first and most natural source to look to, for the settlement of this question, is the instrument itself. Since it is apparent that it would be utterly useless to reduce an agreement or compact to writing, that it would be useless to establish a written constitution for any government or any people, if the crude notions and wild conceits of any individual may be substituted for the terms of the instrument. This is more particularly true with regard to such an instrument as the Constitution of the United States, which was the work, in the first instance, of a general convention from the different States, and was afterwards submitted to the conventions of the people in each of the States.

So that not a word or letter, and certainly not a single principle contained in it can be supposed to have escaped the severest srcutiny, and the whole must therefore have the highest sanction.

Upon opening that instrument, the first principle which presents itself is, that it purports to be the act of the American people. It is not stated to be a compact between New Hampshire, Massachusetts, Rhode Island, and the other ten sovereign States, and which would have been the appropriate, and indeed the only preamble, if the idea intended to be conveyed was, that of a compact or treaty between those sovereign States ; but on the contrary, it is declared to be the act of the American people. The language is, "We the people of the United States do ordain and establish this Constitution for the United States of America." The principle here established is, that the government created by that Constitution is the act of the people of the United States, and not the act of the States, as sovereignties. As this principle lies at the foundation of the whole system, it is impossible that it should have escaped the attention of the General Convention, and of the thirteen State conventions which passed upon it. They could not have been ignorant of, or inattentive to, the difference of the two principles involved in the question, whether the instrument to which they assented, was a Constitution of Government to be established by the people, or a treaty or compact between thirteen sovereign States. To suppose them ignorant, is to suppose them incompetent to their task, and to suppose them inattentive, is to suppose them culpably negligent of their duty. But we will show that they were neither the one or the other.

The very first question, as might naturally be supposed, that presented itself to the General Convention was, whether the Constitution they were about to form should be a compact among the States, or the act of the people. The particular business of the Convention was opened by Governor Randolph, who submitted to their consideration, on the 29th May, 1787, various resolutions, with a view to settle the principles on which they were to proceed. The first of those resolutions was in these words—" Resolved, that the articles of confederation ought to be so corrected and enlarged as to accomplish the objects proposed by their institution, namely, common defence, security of liberty and general welfare."—Elliott's Debates, vol. 4, p. 41. Now it must be recollected that the articles of confederation were, in point of fact, and in terms, a compact between the different States as sovereignties. The instrument itself purports to be such, and is described in the preamble as " Articles of confederation and perpetual union between the States of New Hampshire, Massachusetts Bay, Rhode Island and Providence Plantations," &c. As Governor Randolph's proposition was merely to correct and enlarge those articles, if it had been adopted, the nature of the compact would have been the same, and it would have continued to stand on the footing of an agreement among the States as sovereignties. The very point now at issue was therefore brought at once, and directly before the Convention. On the same day the Convention resolved to go into Committee of the whole, on the State of the Union, and the propositions of Governor Randolph were referred to that Committee. On the following day, May 30th, these resolutions were taken up for consideration, and the particular one in question being the first in order, was, on his own motion, postponed ; and another, offered likewise by him, was, after debate, adopted as a substitute, in the following words : " Resolved that a National Government ought to be established, consisting of a Supreme Legislative, Judiciary, and Executive." On this question, six States, namely, Massachusetts, Pennsylvania, Delaware, Virginia, North Carolina and South Carolina voted in the affirmative ; Connecticut voted in the negative, and New York was divided. Elliott's Debates, vol. 4, p. 49. Mr. Yates, a member of the Convention from New York, who was opposed to the present Constitution, and afterwards withdrew from the Convention because he thought they were exceeding their powers, kept minutes of the debates while he was there, which are published in the fourth volume of Elliott's Debates, and has thus thrown much light on the questions that were agitated ; and may be considered for that purpose, as of the highest authority. In his minutes of the debate on that day, he observes, " this last resolve had its difficulties, the term supreme required explanation. It was asked whether it was intended to annihilate the State Governments ? It was answered only so far as the powers intended to be granted to the new government should clash with the States, when the latter should yield."—Yates' Minutes, p. 50.   It was thus decided that the articles of confederation should be laid aside, and the principle of a compact among the States as sovereignties abandoned.   Accordingly, we find that on the 6th June following, when the fourth resolution offered by Governor Randolph, was under consideration, which provided that the members of the first branch of the National Legislature should be elected by the people, a motion having been made to strike out the word " people," and substitute the word " Legislatures," of the several States, the motion was lost by a vote of eight States to three. In the debate on that point, Mr. Madison is reported by Mr. Yates, to have observed " that when we agreed to the first resolve of having a National Government, consisting of a Supreme Executive, Judicial and Legislative power, it was then intended to operate to the exclusion of a Federal Government, and the more extensive we made the basis, the greater probability of duration, happiness and order."—Yates' Minutes, p. 63.

The first resolution was afterwards modified so as to read thus : " Resolved that the Government of the United States ought to consist of a Supreme Legislative, Judiciary and Executive." The reason for which is stated by Mr. Luther Martin, one of the delegates from Maryland, and a most determined opponent of the proposed system at the time, to have been that they were afraid that the word national might tend to alarm.—Yates' Minutes, p. 22.

The principle was thus therefore clearly established and remained unchanged, that the new government was not to be placed on the footing of a compact among the States as sovereigns ; but was to emanate from the people and be established by their authority.   On the twenty-third of July the resolution thus modified, was, together with the others which had been elaborated in the debate that had been carried on in the Committee of the whole, referred to a Committee of five for the purpose of reporting a Constitution.   It is evident that the Committee appointed for the purpose, were bound, in drafting the instrument, to preserve that fundamental principle.   Accordingly, on the 6th of August, the Committee reported the draught of a Constitution, the preamble to which began in these words : " We the people of the States of New Hampshire, Massachusetts, &c.

do ordain and establish the following Constitution for the government of ourselves and our posterity."—Elliot's Debates, vol. 4, p. 116. The principle was here distinctly set forth, but as it might have afforded some room for cavil, and it was determined that there should not be a loop to hang a doubt upon, the phraseology was changed, and that of the present Constitution adopted, "We the people of the United States," &c. If it is possible for human language or for human conduct to express the intentions of the mind, nothing can be clearer than the intention of the General Convention on this point. If regard then be had to the instrument itself, it is, and it purports to be, a Constitution of Government established by the people of the United States. For this purpose it was not at all necessary that they should be assembled in one body, in one place, or by one authority. It was sufficient for them to assemble in their respective states, at their usual places of election, and under the usual authority. When once assembled and they proceeded to ratify the instrument, it became to all intents and purposes their act. Nor does it at all affect the question that it was provided, that the ratification of a certain number of the States should be necessary for its establishment. That was a mere condition which amounted to no more than a declaration, that the experiment was not worth the trial, unless such a portion of the people should concur. So far as this particular subject is concerned, the term States is a mere description of the people by classes, and is of no more moment in the argument than if the provision had been, that it should not take effect unless ratified by two millions of people, or by two hundred and forty counties, or one hundred districts. The provision was a condition precedent which ceased to be of importance the moment it was fulfilled.

The tenth amendment of that Constitution which provides that "the powers not delegated to the United States by the Constitution, nor prohibited by it to the States, are reserved to the States respectively or to the people," illustrates and confirms the view here taken of the character of the instrument and the source of its authority. But if in addition to this, the frame of government be considered which deprives the States of almost all the essential rights of sovereignty, and makes them amenable to the tribunals of the United States' Government, whose decisions are conclusive in relation to all controversies arising under the Constitution or laws of the United States, it becomes a matter of surprise that any doubt should have been expressed on the subject.

It thus appears that the Constitution is not a treaty or compact between sovereign States, and it remains to show that such was the opinion of cotemporaneous writers. Reference has already been made to the work of Mr. Yates who was a member of the Convention from New York, and whose minutes of the debates are of the highest degree of authenticity, and which in the passage already cited, as well as in others, confirms the position taken by your Committee. In the debate on the 29th June, the first clause of the seventh proposition being under consideration, which respected the suffrage of each State in the first branch of the Legislature, Mr. Madison who was so much relied on by the Carolina Convention as an authority, in the celebrated resolutions of 1798, expressed himself as follows, as reported by Mr. Yates : " Some gentlemen are afraid that the plan is not sufficiently national, while others apprehend that it is too much so. If this point of representation was once well fixed, we would come nearer to one another in sentiment. The necessity would then be discovered of circumscribing more effectually the State governments, and enlarging the bounds of the general government. Some contend that States are sovereigns, when in fact, they are only political societies. There is a gradation of power in all societies, from the lowest corporation to the highest sovereign. The States never possessed the essential rights of sovereignty. These were always vested in Congress. Their voting as States in Congress, is no evidence of sovereignty. The State of Maryland voted by counties—did this make the counties sovereign ? The States at present are only great corporations having the power of making by-laws, and these are effectual only if they are not contradictory to the general confederation. The States ought to be placed under the control of the general government. If the power is not immediately derived from the people, in proportion to their numbers, we may make a paper confederacy, but that will be all. We know the effects of the Old Confederation, and without a general government this will be like the former."—Yates' Minutes, p. 114.

In the debate on the 5th June, the last or 15th proposition of Governor Randolph, being under consideration, which provided that the work of the convention should be submitted to assemblies of representatives to be chosen by the people expressly for that purpose. Mr. Yates resports that " Mr. Madison endeavored to enforce the necessity of this resolve, because the new National Constitution ought to have the highest source of authority—at least, paramount to the powers of the respective constitutions of the States ; points out the mischiefs that had arisen in the Old Confederation, which depends upon no higher authority than the confirmation of an ordinary act of the Legislature."—Yates' Minutes, p. 62.

Mr. Luther Martin, who was a delegate from the State of Maryland, in the General Convention, and violently opposed to the new system at the time, in his report to the Legislature of Maryland, on the subject of the proceedings of the Convention, thus details the arguments used by himself and his friends : " It was urged, that the Government we were forming, was not in reality a Federal, but a National Government, not founded on the principles of the preservation, but the abolition or consolidation of all State governments. That we appeared totally to have forgot the business for which we were sent, and the situation of the country for which we were preparing our system. That we had not been sent to form a Government over the inhabitants of America, considered as individuals, that as individuals they were all subject to their respective State governments, which governments would still remain, though the Federal Government should be dissolved. That the system of government we were entrusted to prepare, was a government over these thirteen States ; but that in our proceedings, we adopted principles which would be right and proper only on the supposition that there were no State governments at all, but that all the inhabitants of this extensive continent were in their individual capacity without government, and in a state of nature. That, accordingly, the system proposes the Legislature to consist of two branches, the one to be drawn from the people at large, immediately in their individual capacity, the other to be chosen in a more select manner, as a check upon the first. It is in its very introduction, declared to be a compact between the people of the United States, as individuals ; and it is to be ratified by the people at large in their capacity as individuals ; all which it was said would be quite right and proper, if there were no State governments, if all the people of this continent were in a state of nature, and we were forming one National Government for them as individuals, and is nearly the same as was done in most of the States, when they formed their governments over the people who compose them."—Yates' Minutes, pages 19, 20. Notwithstanding these arguments, the Constitution was prepared and adopted on the principles which were thus opposed ; and we have here the commentary of one of the ablest lawyers that this country ever produced, who was himmself a member of the Convention, and opposed to the system, upon that very instrument ; and putting it beyond all doubt and controversy, that it was the design of the Convention to abandon the principle of a compact among the States as sovereigns, and substitute for it, that of a government established by the people. The same view of the subject is presented in the Federalist, a work which was written at the time for the express purpose of explaining and recommending the new Constitution, and which was the joint production of three of the ablest men of the day, and has been regarded and relied upon, both in and out of Congress, and even in the courts of justice, as presenting a most able, authentic, and correct exposition of its principles. The conclusion of the twenty-second number, in which some of the evils of the Old Confederation, are pointed out, is as follows : " It has not a little contributed to the infirmities of the existing Federal system, that it never had a ratification by the people. Resting on no better foundation than the consent of the several Legislatures, it has been exposed to frequent and intricate questions concerning the validity of its powers ; and has, in some instances, given birth to the enormous doctrine of a right of legislative repeal. Owing its ratification to the law of a State, it has been contended that the same authority might repeal the law by which it was ratified. However gross a heresy it may be, to maintain that a party to a compact has a right to revoke that compact, the doctrine itself has had respectable advocates

The possibility of a question of this nature, proves the necessity of laying the foundations of our National Government deeper than in the mere sanction of delegated authority. The fabric of the American empire, ought to rest on the solid basis of the consent of the people. The streams of national power ought to flow immediately from that pure original fountain of all legitimate authority."

It is unnecessary to multiply quotations. The question is not under what name the Government established by the Constitution would be classed by political writers ; whether it would be called a Federal Government, or a National Government, or a compound of the two—but simply from whom does it derive its powers ? whether from the States as sovereigns ? or from the people ? It thus appears from the Constitution itself, from the journal of the Convention, from the debates on its proceedings, from the reports of its enemies, and from the arguments of its friends, that the principle on which it was founded, was, that it was to be a government emanating from, and established by the people. If any thing more were wanting to make assurance doubly sure, the ratification by the State of Virginia, where more opposition was experienced than in any other State, and more debate was had on the subject, the solemn act of ratification by that State recognizes the fact in so many words. It is as follows :

" We, the delegates of the people of Virginia, &c. do, in the name and behalf of the people of Virginia, declare and make known, that the powers granted under the Constitution, being derived from the people of the United States, may be resumed by them, whensoever the same shall be perverted to their injury or oppression ; and that every power not granted thereby, remains with them, and at their will," &c.—Elliott's Debates, vol. 4, p. 215.

It is thus established beyond a doubt, whether we regard the instrument itself, or its cotemporaneous history, that the Constitution is a form of government established by the people, and not a compact or treaty among the States. If this be true, then the whole system of nullification topples into ruin.

The principle on which that system is built, is, that the Constitution is a treaty between sovereign States and the General

Government—an agency for them. The moment this foundation is destroyed, the whole system of reasoning fails with it. If the General Government be one, established by the people of the United States, then they owe it allegiance, and may be guilty of treason towards it. Its laws are supreme, and no portion of the people can abrogate them. The State Governments are component but subordinate parts of the system. They are as necessary and useful in their sphere as the General Government, but that portion of the people of the United States, who constitute a particular State, can have no more right to nullify or suspend a law of the United States, than a smaller portion of them, as a county of a particular State, or than any individual : in other words, the union of any number, whether great or small, can give no greater or other right than that which belongs to each individual, as a constitutional measure. It is to be recollected, that the ground taken by the Nullification Party, is, that Nullification is a right consistent with the Constitution, and peaceable in its nature. In order to sustain that position, it was essential to show that the Constitution is a treaty between sovereign States, and that in such case there could be no common arbiter, but that each was entitled to construe the instrument for itself, and was bound only by moral obligation to observe its stipulations, and was therefore the judge of their infraction, and of the measure and mode of redress. But so far from this being true, it has been shown that the Constitution is a form of government established by the people of the United States ; and having provided a tribunal for the settlement of all controversies arising under its provisions, or the laws of the United States, it necessarily follows, that no other mode of decision can be resorted to as consonant with its principles.

If the ground had been taken, that it was a revolutionary measure, and justified on the great principle of self-preservation, it would have had the merit of being intelligible ; and, if true, would have enlisted the sympathies of other States, and, indeed, of other nations. In such a case it would be an appeal to arms, and the legal consequences of such a step would have to be met. The case would then be one of an insurrection of a portion of the people against the Government, in consequence of alleged oppression. But it was clearly seen, that the real state of the case would not justify such a measure. It was clearly seen, that neither the rest of the people of the United States, nor any portion of the world, could be made to believe that in the midst of so much general happiness and prosperity, in a time of profound peace, with an overflowing treasury, and under such a Government as that of the United States, such a case of oppression could be made out, as would justify rebellion. It was therefore necessary to resort to this doctrine of nullification, for the purpose of disguising the real nature of the measure, and to give to a contemplated resistance the air of constitutional right. The act of nullification is, itself, nullity, and the consequences are treason.

The State governments, it is true, are sovereign for some purposes; but have, by the Constitution of the United States, been stripped of most of the essential attributes of sovereignty—such as the right to declare war, make peace, enter into treaties and alliances, coin money, &c. It is a matter of no sort of importance, which instrument happened to precede the other in point of time, whether the Constitution of the State, or the Constitution of the United States. The latter instrument having been declared the supreme law, and being the work of the same people, necessarily controls and abridges any sovereign power vested in the State Governments under the State Constitutions. It is needless to pursue the subject further; it is apparent that the State of South Carolina has no such right as she claims under the Constitution. And if she can justify the measure at all, it must be on the ground of intolerable oppression, and the unconstitutionality of the acts complained of; but, on this ground, the rights of her whole body of citizens, or any portion of them, are no other and no greater than those of the humblest individual in the community; but they cannot trammel up the consequences. Their political organization as a State, may furnish readier means of resistance and greater probabilities of success, but the consequences are the same. They cannot sanctify or legalize resistance, and the predicament in which the individual may stand, if mistaken in his judgment, is that of a traitor to his country.

The view here taken of the origin of the Government, and the nature of the Constitution, is confirmed by the solemn decisions of that great tribunal which has been created by that instrument, and which is the sole and proper one for the settlement of all controversies arising under it. The language of the Supreme Court, as delivered by Chief Justice Marshall, in the case of M'Cullough against the State of Maryland, is as follows : " In discussing this question, the counsel for the State of Maryland have deemed it of some importance in the construction of the Constitution, to consider that instrument not as emanating from the people, but as the act of sovereign and independent States. The powers of the General Government, it has been said, are delegated by the States, who alone are truly sovereign ; and must be exercised in subordination to the States, who alone possess supreme dominion. It would be difficult to sustain this proposition. The Convention which framed the Constitution, was indeed elected by the State Legislatures. But the instrument, when it came from their hands, was a mere proposal, without obligations or pretentions to it. It was reported to the then existing Congress of the United States, with a request that it might ' be submitted to a Convention of Delegates chosen in each State, by the people thereof, under the recommendation of its Legislature, for their assent and ratification.' This mode of proceeding was adopted ; and by the Convention, by Congress, and by the State Legislatures, the instrument was submitted to the people. They acted upon it in the only manner in which they can act safely, effectually, and wisely on such a subject, by assembling in Convention. It is true, they assembled in their several States—and where else should they have assembled ? No political dreamer was ever wild enough to think of breaking down the lines which separate the States, and of compounding the American people into one common mass. Of consequence, when they act, they act in their States. But the measures they adopt, do not on that account cease to be the measures of the people themselves, or become the measures of the State Governments. From these conventions the Constitution derives its whole authority. The Government proceeds directly from the people, is ' ordained and established' in the name of the people ; and is declared to be ordained in order to form a more perfect union, establish justice, ensure domestic tranquillity, and secure the blessings of liberty to themselves and to their posterity."—Wheaton's Rep. vol. 4, p. 403.

The same principles are recognized as being true in the late admirable Proclamation of the President of the United States.

As to the doctrine of Nullification, your Committee would scarcely have considered it worth the trouble of discussion, but for the grave sanction that has thus been given to it by the Convention of South Carolina. They would have treated it as one of those conceits which might have formed the subject of debate in a Moot Court of a law school, but would never have conceived it possible that it could enter into the business realities of life.

Under the view which had been taken of the subject, it is scarcely necessary to inquire into the grounds of complaint, since they are not deemed strong enough, even on the part of the Convention, to warrant a revolutionary measure—or, in other words, rebellion ; and the particular subject of attention under the communication, is the attitude assumed by the State on the ground of her sovereign power.

But your Committee cannot forbear from expressing the opinion, that their views of political economy are as erroneous as their constitutional principles. They conceive that it would be no difficult matter to show that the distress of South Carolina may be imputed to very different causes than those assigned, and might be traced with much more semblance of reason, among other causes, to the increased production of their principal staple, both here and in other parts of the world ; but your Committee refrain from touching further on this subject. They cannot perceive that the people of South Carolina have any constitutional cause of complaint. If there is distress among them, it is a matter in which we deeply sympathize. But if in the due administration of the General Government, any measure has borne hardly upon them, we know of but one remedy under the Constitution and Laws, and that is in the exercise of the elective franchise.

Your Committee abstain from the expression of any hopes or wishes on the subject, they lament the delusion under which they believe a portion of the people of that State labor. But they are free to say, that as the people of this State were the first to adopt the present Government, they will be the last to abandon it ; and that whenever and wherever the exigency may arise they will be found on the side of the Constitution and the Country.

Your Committee therefore report the following Resolutions :

RESOLVES.

WHEREAS, a Convention of the people of the State of South Carolina has undertaken, by an ordinance passed in November last, to declare certain acts of Congress, for imposing duties and imposts on the importation of foreign commodities, null and void, and not binding on the State, its officers and citizens ; and has prohibited the enforcement of those laws within the limits of that State, and has also prohibited any appeal from the decisions of the State Courts, wherein the authority of the ordinance shall be drawn in question, to the United States Courts : And whereas, this measure has been communicated by order of the Convention to the Governor of this State, for the purpose of being laid before the Legislature, and it is expedient that the sense of the people of this State should be expressed in relation thereto—Therefore,

Resolved by the Senate and House of Representatives of the State of Delaware, in General Assembly met, That the Constitution of the United States is not a treaty or compact between sovereign States, but a form of Government emanating from, and established by, the authority of the people of the United States of America.

Resolved, That the Government of the United States, although one of limited powers, is supreme within its sphere, and that the people of the United States owe to it an allegiance which cannot be withdrawn, either by individuals or masses of individuals, without its consent.

Resolved, That the Supreme Court of the United States is the only and proper tribunal for the settlement, in the last resort, of controversies in relation to the Constitution and the Laws of Congress.

Resolved, That if in the regular action of the Government, mischief of any kind be produced, the proper remedy is to be found in the elective franchise, and the responsibility of its officers.

Resolved, That in cases of gross and intolerable oppression, which in a Government like that of the United States, can be little else than a hypothesis, the natural right of self defence remains ; but which must, in the nature of things, be an appeal to arms, and subject to all the consequences of resistance to the constituted authorities. In such a case the measure is revolutionary, and the result remains in the hands of the Almighty.

Resolved, That the Convention of South Carolina can have no other or greater right to annul or resist the laws of Congress, than any assemblage of an equal number of individuals in any part of the United States ; nor can any assemblage, however large, have any other or greater right, for such a purpose, than belongs to each individual citizen, considered as a constitutional measure.

Resolved, That it is a subject of regret, that such a delusion should exist among any portion of the citizens of that State, towards whom the people of this State, entertain the kindest feelings, with whom they stood side by side in the war of the revolution, and in whose defence their blood was freely spilt. But if the measure which has been adopted is intended as the precursor of resistance to the government, the people of Delaware will not falter in their allegiance, but will be found now as then, true to their country and its government.

Resolved, That we cordially respond to the sentiments on this subject, contained in the able Proclamation of the President of the United States, and shall be at all times prepared to support the Governmont in the exercise of its constitutional rights, and in the discharge of its constitutional duties.

Resolved, That the Governor be requested to transmit a copy of these Resolutions and the accompanying Report of the Committee to the President of the United States, to each of our Senators and our Representatives in Congress, and to the Governors of the respective States and Territories of the United States of America.

JOSHUA BURTON,
Speaker of the Senate.

THOMAS DAVIS,
Speaker of the House of Representatives.

Passed at Dover, January 16th, 1833.

RESOLVES

OF THE

LEGISLATURE

OF

VIRGINIA.

RESOLVES.

WHEREAS, the General Assembly of Virginia, actuated by an ardent desire to preserve the peace and harmony of our common country—relying upon the sense of justice of the people of each and every State of the Union, as a sufficient pledge that their Representatives in Congress, will so modify the acts laying duties and imposts on the importation of foreign commodities, commonly called the Tariff Acts, that they will no longer furnish cause of complaint to the people of any particular State ; believing, accordingly, that the people of South Carolina are mistaken in supposing that Congress will yield them no relief from the pressure of those acts, especially as the auspicious approach of the extinguishment of the public debt affords a just ground for the indulgence of a contrary expectation; and confident that they are too strongly attached to the union of the States, to resort to any proceedings which might dissolve or endanger it, whilst they have any fair hope of obtaining their object by more regular and peaceful measures ; persuaded, also, that they will listen willingly and respectfully to the voice of Virginia, earnestly and affectionately requesting and entreating them to rescind or suspend their late Ordinance, and await the result of a combined and strenuous effort of the friends of union and peace, to affect an adjustment and reconciliation of all public differences now unhappily existing ; regarding, moreover, an appeal to force on the part of the General Government, or on the part of the Government of South Carolina, as a measure which nothing but extreme necessity could justify or excuse in either ; but, apprehensive at the same time, that if the present state of things is allowed to continue, acts of violence will occur, which may lead to consequences that all would deplore, cannot but deem it a solemn duty to interpose and mediate between the high contending parties, by the declaration of their opinions and wishes, which they trust that both will consider and respect. Therefore,

1. *Resolved, by the General Assembly, in the name and on behalf of the people of Virginia,* That the competent authorities of South Carolina be, and they are hereby earnestly and respectfully requested and entreated to rescind the Ordinance of the late Convention of that State, entitled " An Ordinance to Nullify certain Acts of the Congress of the United States, purporting to be laws laying duties and imposts on the importation of foreign commodities ;" or, at least to suspend its operation until the close of the first session of the next Congress.

2. *Resolved,* That the Congress of the United States be, and they are hereby earnestly and respectfully requested and entreated, so to modify the Acts laying duties and imposts on the importation of foreign commodities, commonly called the Tariff Acts, as to effect a gradual but speedy reduction of the resulting revenue of the General Government, to the standard of the necessary and proper expenditure for the support thereof.

3. *Resolved,* That the people of Virginia expect, and in the opinion of the General Assembly, the people of the other States have a right to expect, that the General Government, and the Government of South Carolina, and all persons acting under the authority of either, will carefully abstain from any and all acts whatever, which may be calculated to disturb the tranquillity of the country, or endanger the existence of the Union.

AND, WHEREAS, considering the opinions which have been advanced and maintained by the Convention of South Carolina, in its late Ordinance and Addresses, on the one hand, and by the President of the United States, in his Proclamation, bearing date the 10th day of December, 1832, on the other, the General Assembly deem it due to themselves, and the people whom they represent, to declare and make known their own views in relation to some of the important and interesting questions which these papers present. Therefore,

4. *Resolved by the General Assembly,* That they continue to regard the doctrines of State Sovereignty and State Rights, as

set forth in the Resolutions of 1798, and sustained by the Report thereon of 1799, as a true interpretation of the Constitution of the United States, and of the powers therein given to the General Government; but that they do not consider them as sanctioning the proceedings of South Carolina, indicated in her said Ordinance; nor as countenancing all the principles assumed by the President in his said Proclamation—many of which are in direct conflict with them.

5. *Resolved*, That this House will, by joint vote with the Senate, proceed on this day to elect a Commissioner, whose duty it shall be to proceed immediately to South Carolina, and communicate the foregoing Preamble and Resolutions to the Governor of that State, with a request that they be communicated to the Legislature of that State, or any Convention of its citizens, or give them such other direction, as in his judgment may be best calculated to promote the objects which this Commonwealth has in view; and that the said Commissioner be authorized to express to the public authorities and people of our sister State, in such manner as he may deem most expedient, our sincere good will to our Sister State, and our anxious solicitude that the kind and respectful recommendations we have addressed to her, may lead to an accommodation of all the difficulties between that State and the General Government.

6. *Resolved*, That the Governor of the Commonwealth be, and he hereby is requested to communicate the foregoing Preamble and Resolutions to the President of the United States, to the Governors of the other States, and to our Senators and Representatives in Congress.

VIRGINIA—*City of Richmond, to wit* :

I, GEORGE W. MUNFORD, Clerk of the House of Delegates, and Keeper of the Rolls of the Commonwealth of Virginia, do hereby certify and make known, that the foregoing is a true copy of a Preamble and Resolutions adopted by the General Assembly of Virginia, on the 26th day of January, 1833.

Given under my hand, this 8th of February, 1833.

GEORGE W. MUNFORD, *C. H. D*
And Keeper of the Rolls of Virginia.

RESOLVES

OF THE

LEGISLATURE

OF

NORTH CAROLINA.

RESOLVES.

Resolved, That the General Assembly of the State of North Carolina doth entertain, and doth unequivocally express a warm attachment to the Constitution of the United States.

Resolved, That the General Assembly doth solemnly declare a devoted attachment to the Federal Union, believing that on its continuance depend the liberty, the peace and prosperity of these United States.

Resolved, That whatever diversity of opinion may prevail in this State, as to the constitutionality of the acts of Congress imposing duties on imports for protection, yet, it is believed, a large majority of the people think those acts unconstitutional; and they are united in the sentiment, that the existing Tariff is impolitic, unjust and oppressive ; and they have urged, and will continue to urge its repeal.

Resolved, That the doctrine of Nullification as avowed by the State of South Carolina, and lately promulgated in an Ordinance, is revolutionary in its character, subversive of the Constitution of the United States and leads to a dissolution of the Union.

Resolved, That our Senators in Congress be instructed, and our Representatives be requested to use all constitutional means in their power, to procure a peaceable adjustment of the existing controversy between the State of South Carolina and the General Government, and to produce a reconciliation between the contending parties.

Resolved further, That a copy of these resolutions, be respectfully communicated by his Excellency the Governor of this State, to the President of the United States, the Governors of the several States, and to our Senators and Representatives in Congress.

Read three times and ratified in General Assembly, this 5th day of January, 1833.

LOUIS D. HENRY, S. H. C.
W. D. MOSELY, S. S.

RESOLVES

OF THE

LEGISLATURE

OF

OHIO.

RESOLVES

On the subject of the South Carolina Ordinance.

WHEREAS, His Excellency the Governor, has transmitted to this General Assembly, the Ordinance of the late Convention of the people of South Carolina, together with the proceedings of that body, whose object appears to be, a resistance to the collection of duties, imposts, &c. upon foreign commodities, imported into that State, by nullifying the acts of Congress, providing for the levying and collecting such duties.   And this General Assembly cannot but view, with the deepest regret, the avowed determination of a majority of the citizens of the State of South Carolina, to resist the operation of the laws of the General Government, in the manner pointed out by the ordinance adopted by their late Convention ; and we have no doubt that such a course, if persisted in, must inevitably lead to consequences the most disastrous, and ruinous to the peace, prosperity and happiness of our common country.

Being connected, as we are, with our brethren of South Carolina by the strongest ties of consanguinity, and endeared by the mutual reciprocity of friendly intercourse and national attachment, and being sensible of the importance of our connexion as States, belonging to the same Federal Union, we cannot but deprecate every effort or measure which is calculated, in the remotest degree, to operate to the severance of any of those ties, or render doubtful the permanent existence of our Confederacy. And entertaining, as we do, the most implicit confidence in the wisdom, justice, and integrity of the General Government, we are well persuaded that no partial evil would be permitted to exist in any particular section of the Union, should it not be apparent that such evil was fully overbalanced by a general benefit afforded by the same policy, out of which that evil was found to spring up.   Such evils, if such exist, we should endeavor to remedy in a spirit of moderation and good faith, to the end, that the unparalleled prosperity of the whole Union, unequalled as it is, in the history of civilized man, may not be intercepted, or paralized in any of its parts.

Believing that the prosperity and independence of this Republic, mainly depend upon the general peace and harmony which ought to exist among the several States, and that all should ever keep in view the adopted maxim, "united we stand, divided we fall," we feel it a duty, therefore, as American citizens, to cling, with pertinacity, to the Constitution of the United States, and to the preservation of the Union of the States. We cannot, therefore, view with indifference, much less can we lend our aid to any measure which is calculated to disturb the integrity of that Union.

Resolved, therefore, by the General Assembly of the State of Ohio, That we view with the deepest regret the unhappy movements, and apparent determination of the late Convention of the people of South Carolina, to Nullify the Laws of the General Government, made in conformity to the Constitution of the United States.

Resolved, That the Federal Union exists in a solemn compact, entered into by the voluntary consent of the people of the United States, and of each and every State, and that, therefore, no State can claim the right to secede from, or violate that compact, and however grievous may be the supposed or real burthens of a State, the only legitimate remedy is in the wise and faithful exercise of the elective franchise, and the solemn responsibility of the public agents.

Resolved, That the doctrine, that a State has the power to Nullify a Law of the General Government, is revolutionary in its character, and is, in its nature, calculated to overthrow the great Temple of American Liberty. Such a course cannot absolve that allegiance which the people of this Union, owe to the supremacy of the laws.

Resolved, That in levying and collecting duties, imposts and excises, whilst the general good should be the primary object, a special regard ought to be had to the end, that the interest and prosperity of every section of the country, should be equally consulted, and its burthens proportionably distributed.

Resolved, That the first object of the American people, should be, to cherish the most ardent attachment to the Constitution and Laws of this Union; and as a first and paramount object of a free people, we should use every honorable means to preserve the honor and integrity of the Union.

Resolved, That the Governor be requested to transmit copies of the foregoing preamble and resolutions to the President of the United States, and to the Executives of the several States.

DAVID T. DISNEY,
Speaker of the House of Representatives.

SAMUEL R. MILLER,
Speaker of the Senate.

February 25th, 1833.

RESOLVES

In relation to a call of a Convention to amend the Constitution of the United States.

Resolved, by the General Assembly of the State of Ohio, That in the opinion of this General Assembly, it is inexpedient, at the present time, to apply to the Congress of the United States, for a call of a Convention of the people to amend the Constitution of the United States, or to call a Convention of the States to consider and define questions of disputed powers, which may have arisen between any State of this Confederacy and the General Government.

Resolved further, That His Excellency the Governor be, and he is hereby requested to transmit copies of the foregoing resolution to each of the Executives of the several States of this Union, for the consideration of the Legislatures thereof.

DAVID T. DISNEY,
Speaker of the House of Representatives.

SAMUEL R. MILLER.
Speaker of the Senate.

February 25th, 1833.

RESOLVES

Relating to the President's Proclamation and Message.

Resolved by the General Assembly of the State of Ohio, That this Legislature do cordially approve of the exposition of the principles of the Constitution of the United States, touching the pernicious doctrines of nullification and secession, set forth in the Proclamation of the President of the United States, of the tenth of December last, and in his late Message to Congress, and that this Legislature do also feel the strongest assurance that the principles contained in that exposition, will be firmly sustained by the people of Ohio.

Resolved, That the Governor be requested to forward a copy of the foregoing resolution to the President of the United States, to the Executive of each of the United States, and to each of our Senators and Representatives in Congress.

DAVID T. DISNEY,
Speaker of the House of Representatives.

SAMUEL R. MILLER,
Speaker of the Senate.

February 25th, 1833.

SECRETARY OF STATE'S OFFICE,
COLUMBUS, OHIO, Feb. 26, 1833.

I hereby certify, that the foregoing Resolutions are true copies of the original rolls now on file in this office.

MOSES H. KIRBY,
Secretary of State.

RESOLVES

LEGISLATURE

INDIANA.

RESOLVES

Relative to the Proceedings of a late Convention of South Carolina, and to the President's Proclamation in relation thereto.

WHEREAS, An unusual and alarming excitement prevails in the State of South Carolina, on the subject of the Tariff Laws, awakened, as is believed, by a mistaken view of their constitutionality, and by exaggerated representations of their unequal operation ; and whereas, heretical and dangerous doctrines have sprung up under the name of Nullification, in which the constitutional right in a state, to render nugatory and resist the laws of the United States, and to secede from the Union, is boldly assumed ; and whereas, a Convention, delegated from a portion of the citizens of that State, has recently passed an Ordinance, a copy of which, and of the report of a Committee of said Convention thereon, and of Addresses to the people of the several States and of South Carolina, transmitted by order of the said Convention, through the Governor of that State to the Governor of Indiana, avowedly for the information of this Legislature, are now before the same ; and whereas, we, the Representatives of the People of Indiana, view the doctrines contained in those documents, as carrying with them internal evidence of their impracticability, absurdity, and treasonable tendency ; and whereas, we regard the said Ordinance as prescribing to, and attempting to enforce upon the people of South Carolina, " a course of conduct, in violation of their duty as citizens of the United States, contrary to the laws of their country, subversive of its Constitution, and as having for its object the destruction of the Union," and as a necessary consequence, the prostration of our liberties : Therefore,

Resolved, by the General Assembly of the State of Indiana, that we deeply deplore the political heresies, and threatened disorganization, recently promulgated by a portion of our brethren of South Carolina.

Resolved, That we cordially concur in the persuasive appeals of our venerable Chief Magistrate, to the people of South Carolina, to pause ere it be too late to save themselves from ruin.

Resolved, That the sentiment, " our Union must be preserved," meets with a hearty response from the people of Indiana, bound as they are, by interest and honor, to that confederacy into which they voluntarily entered, and from which they will never willingly be severed.

Resolved, That we regard the present juncture of our national affairs, as involving the preservation of our liberties, and as scarcely inferior in importance to that in which they were achieved.

Resolved, That as regards this important question, all minor differences should be forgotten ;—that devotion to party should be lost in devotion to country, and that the great contest among Americans, should be, as to the means best calculated to prevent the temple of our Union from crumbling into ruins.

Resolved, That the constitutional doctrines advanced, and views of policy embraced in the President's Proclamation on the present difficulties in South Carolina,—the patriotic spirit pervading that able document, and the prompt and decisive manner in which he has rebuked the pernicious doctrines, and unjustifiable course, recently adopted by a portion of the citizens of that State, command our entire approbation, and have crowned with new laurels the " Defender of his Country."

Resolved, That at the present alarming and eventful crisis, we conceive it to be a solemn and paramount duty of the people of the different States to express through their Representatives, a firm and unwavering determination, to protect "the Ark of our political safety" from the hand of violence, and to pledge their support in furtherance of the laudable resolution of the National Executive, " to take care that the Republic receive no detriment."

Resolved, That the Governor of this State be requested to transmit a copy of the foregoing Preamble and Joint Resolutions, to the President of the United States, and also, a copy to each of our Senators and Representatives in Congress, to be laid before that body, and one to the Governor of each State in the Union.

JOHN W. DAVIS,

Speaker of the House of Representatives.

DAVID WALLACE,

President of the Senate.

Approved 9th January, 1833.

N. NOBLE.

RESOLVES

OF THE

LEGISLATURE

OF

ALABAMA.

REPORT

Of the Select Committee of the House of Representatives, to
whom was referred so much of the Message of the Governor,
as relates to the Tariff, to the principle of protection and to
the doctrine of Nullification.

THE Select Committee to whom was referred so much of the
Message of the Governor, as relates to the Tariff, to the principle of protection and to the doctrine of Nullification, have had
the same under consideration, and have instructed me to report
a preamble and resolutions, which they respectfully submit to
the House for its adoption.

Your Committee deeply impressed with the present alarming
crisis in our history, have given to the subject that profound consideration, which its paramount importance so justly demands.

So much has been said and written on the subject submitted
to them, that they may be said to be exhausted, and they will
therefore submit a very few remarks prefatory to the resolutions, which they recommend to the adoption of the House.

In a country of such vast extent as the United States, embracing such a variety of soil, climate and products, and inhabit-
ed by a people, whose pursuits are as various as the climate under which they live ; any attempt on the part of the Government
to force manufactures into existence, by governmental bounties,
must of necessity operate unequally, and therefore be unjust.

If it be a truth, not now to be questioned, that no Government can justly take from one portion of its citizens a part of
their property, to benefit another, it is more especially unjust in
a country like ours, composed of different States, who are united in one common bond, only for the purpose of providing for
the common defence, of promoting the general welfare, and securing the blessings of liberty to themselves and posterity. For
these purposes, this Union was formed, and it cannot be sup-

posed, that those who consented to it, intended by implication and construction to confer on the General Government powers destructive of their happiness and best interest. Laws having their operation, and professing to derive their authority from the Constitution under which we live, being opposed to the true interest of every section of the republic and unjust in their operation on the Southern States, even if sustained by the letter of the Constitution, are contrary to its spirit and at war with the general scope and tenor of that instrument.

It cannot be believed that if the framers of the Constitution had assigned the exercise of such a power, as the right to create and protect domestic manufactures, by a system of high duties, that it would have been left to inference or implication ; its framers therefore could not have intended that such a power should be exercised. This reasoning is founded on, and these results drawn from the instrument itself; but in addition thereto, contemporaneous history informs us, that in the Convention which framed the Constitution, it was proposed in various modes to give that power to Congress, and refused.

It is the exercise of this power, which a large majority of the South believe to be against the spirit of the Constitution, and no inconsiderable number, contrary to its express letter, which has driven them to consider their Government as foreign to their interests, and alien to their feelings. Instead of looking up to it with pride and veneration, as the world's last hope, and as the favorite resort of freedom, no inconsiderable portion of the South have begun to estimate its value ; and to contemplate even disunion itself, as an evil less formidable than submission to the exactions of the Government.

And now at this fearful crisis, when one of our co-States has assumed the alarming attitude of declaring an act of Congress void within her limits, and the note of preparation is sounded to sustain this attitude by force, what shall Alabama do ? Our answer is never despair of our country. We believe that there is a vital energy, a living principle inherent in our institutions, and a sense of justice residing in the bosoms of our fellow citizens, which when properly appealed to, must succeed. We concede that our Northern brethren believe that they are acting within the pale of the Constitution ; but can it be believed, that they will by insisting on the obnoxious duties, peril the Union of these States, and make shipwreck of the last hope of mankind? Can any pecuniary benefit compensate for results like these? If blood be shed in this unhallowed contest, a wound will be inflicted, which may never be healed, to confidence will succeed distrust, mutual recriminations, and mutual interest, and the choicest blessings of Heaven, by madness and folly of man, will be converted into the most deadly poison.

Deeply impressed with these views, we recommend the adoption of the following resolutions, which we are satisfied embody the opinions of our constituents, and in their name propose to our co-States a Federal Convention.

RESOLVES.

Be it Resolved by the Senate and House of Representatives of the State of Alabama in General Assembly convened, That we consider the present Tariff of duties, unequal, unjust, oppressive and against the spirit, true intent and meaning of the Constitution ; that if persevered in, its inevitable tendency will be to alienate the affections of the people of the Southern States from the General Government.

And be it further Resolved, That we do not consider the Tariff of 1832, as fastening upon the country the principle of protection, but that we receive it as the harbinger of better times, as a pledge that Congress will at no distant period, abandon the principle of protection altogether, and reduce the duties on imports to the actual wants of the Government, levying those duties on such articles as will operate most equally on all sections of the Union.

And be it further Resolved, That Nullification, which some of our Southern brethren recommend as the Constitutional remedy for the evils under which we labor, is unsound in theory and dangerous in practice, that as a remedy it is unconstitutional and essentially revolutionary, leading in its consequences to anarchy and civil discord, and finally to the dissolution of the Union.

And be it further Resolved, That we earnestly intreat the people of this State, not to distrust the justice of the General Government, and to rest satisfied, though long delayed, it will certainly be accorded to them. And above all things, to avoid those dangerous and unconstitutional remedies proposed for their imitation and adoption, no matter how specious their exterior, which may lead to bloodshed and disunion, and will certainly end in anarchy and civil discord. And at the same time we would most solemnly adjure the Congress of the United States, in the name of our common country to abandon the exercise of those dubious and constructive powers, claimed under the Constitution, the assertion of which has produced jealousy, excitement and dissatisfaction to the Government, and if persevered in, will in all human probability dissolve this Union. By this means, and by this alone, can we be prevented from fulfilling our high destinies, and our onward march to greatness be arrested.

And be it further Resolved, That as we have now for the first time in the history of our country, presented to us the appalling spectacle of one of the States of this Union, arraying herself against the General Government, and declaring sundry acts of Congress void and of no effect within her limits; presenting to Congress the alternative of repealing the obnoxious laws or permitting her secession from the Union, and preparing by an armed force to sustain the position she has assumed, and as we cannot silently look on and witness the failure of the high raised hopes and just expectations of those patriots who cemented our liberty with their blood : Therefore, as a last resort, we recommend to our co-States the calling of a Federal Convention, to meet in the City of Washington on the first of March, 1834, or at such other time and place as may be agreed on, which shall be authorized to devise and recommend such plan, which will satisfy the discontents of the South, either by an explicit denial of the right of Congress to protect domestic industry by duties on imports laid for protection, or by defining and restricting the power aforesaid, within certain prescribed limits, and making such other amendments and alterations in the Constitution as time and experience have discovered to be necessary.

Resolved, That the Governor be desired to transmit a copy of the foregoing resolutions to the President of the United States, and to the Executive of each of the States, with a request that the same may be communicated to the Legislature thereof.

Resolved further, That the Governor furnish a copy of said resolutions to each of the Senators and Representatives of this State, in the Congress of the United States.

Approved, January 12, 1833.

RECOMMENDATIONS

Of the General Assembly of the State of Alabama to the President of the United States, to the State of South Carolina, and to the different States.

THE General Assembly of the State of Alabama have received and considered with absorbing interest, the late Ordinance of South Carolina, with the Address to the co-States accompanying the same, together with the Proclamation of the President of the United States, consequent thereon. The attitude assumed by the State of South Carolina and the Government of the United States through its Chief Magistrate, forbodes a crisis which threatens the peace of society and the harmony of the Union, and which should be deplored by every one who loves his country and liberty. The existence of our Constitution and the integrity of the Union, require the instant exertion of that patriotism, forbearance and virtue, which have hitherto characterised the history of our Government. Omitting, on this occasion, to enter into the causes which have produced the present afflicting posture between one State and the Federal Government; this General Assembly now affectionately and solemnly appeals to the Congress of the United States, and to the State of South Carolina, for that forbearance, patriotism and virtue, which alone can restore, by mutual sacrifice of opinion, harmony, peace and prosperity to our common country. The only bonds of our Union, and the sole preservatives of rational and constitutional liberty, are a strict adherence on the part of the constituted authorities, to the principles of our Government—the affection of the people for that Government, and a firm persuasion of the equality and justice of its administration, aided by a spirit of forbearance on the part of those States who may differ from the opinion of the majority.

To this end the General Assembly of Alabama recommend to the Congress of the United States, a speedy modification of the

Tariff Laws, in such manner as to equalise their burthens, and cause only so much revenue to be collected as will be necessary to pay the expenses of the Government, in its constitutional and economical administration. This Assembly further recommends to the Congress of the United States, as she has already done to her co-States, the call of a Federal Convention, to propose such amendments to our Federal Constitution, as may seem necessary and proper, to restrain the Congress of the United States from exerting the taxing power, for the substantive protection of domestic manufactures. This Assembly further earnestly recommends to the State of South Carolina, to suspend the operation of her late Ordinance, that the unfortunate collision of powers between that State and the Government of the United States, may be amicably adjusted in such manner as not to impair the rights and powers granted to the General Government, or retained and reserved to the States, or the people by the Constitution. This General Assembly further urgently recommends to the State of South Carolina to abstain from the use of military power, in enforcing her Ordinance, or in resisting the execution of the revenue laws of the United States. And this General Assembly, with equal earnestness, recommends to the Government of the United States, to exercise moderation, and to employ only such means as are peaceful and usual to execute the laws of the Union. The General Assembly of this State further recommends to her co-States, to concur with this State in the foregoing recommendations.

Resolved, That the Executive of this State be requested to transmit copies of the foregoing recommendations, to the Executive authorities of each of the United States : to the President of the United States, and to our Senators and Representatives in Congress, with instructions to lay the same before the Congress of the United States.

Approved, January 12, 1833.

RESOLVES

OF THE

LEGISLATURE

OF

MISSISSIPPI.

REPORT.

The select Committee to which was referred " so much of the Governor's Message as relates to the Resolutions from the States of Louisiana, Maine, New Hampshire, and Pennsylvania, with the accompanying documents," beg leave to report:

That they have had them under consideration, and would recommend, in regard to the Resolution first named, the adoption of the following Resolutions :

In relation to the Resolutions from the States of Maine, New Hampshire, and Pennsylvania, and that portion of the Message which points to their consideration, your Committee would express the belief that the sentiments of a majority of the people of this State, in regard to the subjects to which they relate, are in accordance with those expressed by the General Assembly in the year 1829, declaring the Tariff law of 1828, so far as it contemplated a system of protection, carried beyond the manufacture of such articles as are necessary to the national defence, to be " contrary to the spirit of the Constitution of the United States, impolitic and oppressive in its operation on the southern States, and should be resisted by all constitutional means." But fearful lest false inferences should be drawn from this expression of public opinion—inferences, calculated to induce a belief that this State is prepared to advocate and uphold the disorganizing doctrines, recently promulgated in South Carolina, your Committee deem it their duty to speak plainly, and to undeceive their sister States in this respect. We are opposed to Nullification. We regard it as a heresy, fatal to the existence of the Union. "It is resistance to law by force—it is disunion by force—it is civil war." Your Committee are constrained to express the opinion, that the State of South Carolina has acted with a reckless precipitancy, (originating, we would willingly believe, in delusion,) well calculated to detract from her former high character for wisdom in council, purity of patriotism, and a solicitous regard for the preservation of those fundamental principles, on which alone rest the peace, the prosperity and permanency of the Union. Your Committee deeply deplore the alarming crisis in our national affairs; they regret it the more as proceeding from the unwarrantable attitude assumed by a sister of the South, whose best interests are identified with our own. In the spirit of brethren of the same family, we would invoke them to pause—to hearken attentively to the paternal, yet ominous, warning of the Executive of the Union. We would conjure them to await patiently the gradual progress of public opinion; and to rely, with patriotic confidence, on the ultimate decision of the talented statesmen and pure patriots in the Congress of the United States. But they would also loudly proclaim, that this State owes a duty to the Union, above all minor considerations. That she prizes that Union less than liberty alone. That we heartily accord in the general political sentiments of the President of the United States, as expressed in his recent Proclamation; and that we stand firmly resolved, at whatever sacrifice of feeling, in all events, and at every hazard, to sustain him in enforcing the paramount laws of the land, and preserving the integrity of the Union—that Union, whose value we will never stop to calculate—holding it, as our fathers held it, precious above all price. Your Committee would therefore recommend the adoption of the following resolutions:

RESOLVES.

1. *Be it resolved by the Legislature of the State of Mississippi*, That, in the language of the father of his country, we will " indignantly frown upon the first dawning of every attempt to alienate any portion of our country from the rest, or to enfeeble the ties which link together its various parts."

2. *Resolved*, That the doctrine of Nullification is contrary to the letter and spirit of the Constitution, and in direct conflict with the welfare, safety and independence of every State in the Union ; and to no one of them would its consequences be more deeply disastrous, more ruinous, than to the State of Mississippi —that State in which are concentrated our dearest interests— around which cling our most tender ties—the fair land of our nativity or adoption—the haven of our hopes, the home of our hearts.

3. *Resolved*, That we will, with heart and hand, sustain the President of the United States, in the full exercise of his legitimate powers, to restore peace and harmony to our distracted country, and to maintain, unsullied and unimpaired, the honor, the independence and integrity of the Union.

4. *Resolved*, That the Governor of the State be, and he is hereby required to transmit a copy of the last Resolutions, with the preamble, to our Senators and Representatives in Congress, also to the Governors of the different States, with a request that the same may be laid before their respective Legislatures.

DAVID PEMBLE,
Speaker of the House of Representatives.

CHARLES LYNCH,
President of the Senate.

RESOLVES

OF THE

LEGISLATURES

OF

SOUTH CAROLINA AND GEORGIA,

PROPOSING A

CONVENTION OF THE STATES.

☞ The following Resolves of the Legislatures of South Carolina and Georgia, with those of the Legislature of Massachusetts, consequent upon them, though not directly embraced by the terms of the order under which the present volume has been published, are so closely connected with the general subject of the late political controversies, that it has been thought expedient to include them. It appears from a letter of the Governor of Georgia, subsequently received by the Governor of this Commonwealth, and which is also published, that the document transmitted and certified by the Governor of Georgia, as Resolves of the Legislature of that State, was in fact, a mere report, which was not adopted. The Resolves which were really passed, are now published from the printed volume of the Laws of Georgia.

State of South Carolina.

In the Senate, 13th December, 1832.

The Committee on Federal Relations, to whom was referred that portion of the Governor's Message, No. 3, which relates to the call of a Convention of the States, respectfully report the following

PREAMBLE AND RESOLUTIONS:

Whereas, serious causes of discontent do exist among the States of this Union, from the exercise, by Congress, of powers not conferred or contemplated, by the sovereign parties to the Compact—therefore,

Resolved, That it is expedient that a Convention of the States be called as early as practicable, to consider and determine such questions of disputed power, as have arisen between the States of this confederacy and the General Government.

Resolved, That the Governor be requested to transmit copies of this Preamble and Resolutions to the Governors of the several States, with a request that the same be laid before the Legislatures of their respective States, and also to our Senators and Representatives in Congress, to be by them laid before Congress for consideration.

Resolved, That the Senate do agree.

Ordered to the House of Representatives for concurrence.

In the Senate, 19th December, 1832.

The House of Representatives returned, with their concurrence, the Report of the Committee on Federal Relations, on that portion of the Governor's Message, No. 3, which relates to the call of a Convention of the States.

A true copy from the Journals.

JACOB WARLEY, *Clerk of the Senate.*

State of Georgia.

FOR as much as throughout the United States, there exist many controversies growing out of the conflicting interests which have arisen among the people, since the adoption of the Federal Constitution; out of the cases in which Congress claims the right to act under constructive or implied powers; out of the disposition, shown by Congress, too frequently to act under assumed powers, and out of the rights of jurisdiction, either claimed or exercised by the Supreme Court—all of which tend directly to diminish the affection of the people for their own government, to produce discontent, to repress patriotism, to excite jealousies, to engender discord, and finally to bring about the event, of all other, most deeply to be deplored, and most anxiously to be guarded against, viz: a dissolution of our happy Union, and a severance of these States into hostile communities, each regarding and acting towards each other with the bitterest enmity.

And the experience of the past having clearly proved, that the Constitution of the United States needs amendment in the following particulars:

1. That the powers delegated to the General Government, and the rights reserved to the States or to the people, may be more distinctly defined.

2. That the power of coercion by the General Government over the States, and the right of a State to resist an unconstitutional act of Congress, may be determined.

3. That the principle involved in a Tariff for the direct protection of domestic industry, may be settled.

4. That a system of Federal taxation may be established, which shall be equal in its operation upon the whole people, and in all sections of the country.

5. That the jurisdiction and process of the Supreme Court, may be clearly and unequivocally settled.

6. That a tribunal of last resort may be organized to settle disputes between the General Government and the States.

7. That the power of chartering a Bank and of granting incorporations, may be expressly given to, or withheld from Congress.

8. That the practice of appropriating money for works of Internal Improvement, may be either sanctioned by an express delegation of power, or restrained by express inhibition.

9. That it may be prescribed, what disposition shall be made of the surplus revenue, when such revenue is found to be on hand.

10. That the right to, and the mode of disposition of the public lands of the United States, may be settled.

11. That the election of President and Vice President may be secured, in all cases, to the people.

12. That their tenure of office may be limited to one term.

13. That the rights of the Indians may be definitely settled.

Be it therefore Resolved by the Senate and House of Representatives of the State of Georgia, in General Assembly met, and acting for the people thereof, That the State of Georgia, in conformity with the Fifth Article of the Federal Constitution, hereby makes application to the Congress of the United States, for the call of a Convention of the people, to amend the Constitution aforesaid, in the particulars herein enumerated, and in such others as the people of the other States may deem needful of amendment.

Resolved further, That His Excellency the Governor be, and he is hereby requested to transmit copies of this document to the other States of the Union, and to our Senators and Representatives in Congress.

Agreed to, 12th December, 1832.

Attest,   ASBURY HULL, *Speaker.*

Robert W. Carnes, *Clerk.*

In Senate, 20th December, 1832.

Concurred in.

Attest,   THOMAS STOCKS, *President.*

Iverson L. Harris, *Secretary.*

Approved, 22d December, 1832.

WILSON LUMPKIN, *Governor.*

RESOLVES

OF THE

LEGISLATURE

OF

MASSACHUSETTS.

Commonwealth of Massachusetts.

House of Representatives, January 16th, 1833.

Ordered, That the Resolutions of the Legislature of Georgia, proposing a Convention of the People of the United States, for the Amendment in various respects of the Constitution, and so much of the Governor's Special Message as relates thereto, be referred to

> Messrs. CUSHING, of Newburyport,
> SHAW, of Lanesborough,
> WHITE, of Boston,

with such as the Senate may join.

Sent up for concurrence.

> L. S. CUSHING, *Clerk.*

In Senate, January 17, 1833.

Read, and referred to Messsrs. BLAKE and WELLS, in concurrence.

> CHARLES CALHOUN, *Clerk.*

Commonwealth of Massachusetts.

In Senate, February, 1833.

The Special Joint Committee, to whom was referred, among other things, that portion of His Excellency the Governor's Message, relating to the subject of the Preamble and Resolutions of the Legislature of South Carolina, proposing that a " Convention of the States should be called, as early as practicable, to consider and determine such questions of disputed power as have arisen between the States of this confederacy and the General Government," have had the same under consideration, and respectfully submit the following

REPORT IN PART:

Upon the first presentment of the Resolutions in question, taken in connection with the matter contained in the Preamble, with which they are introduced, your Committee were considerably at a loss to determine what should be regarded as being their precise scope and object. The question occurred to them, whether it was the intention of the Legislature of South Carolina to invite a Convention of the States, with a view to certain specific amendments of the Constitution of the General Government, in conformity with the provisions in the fifth article of that instrument, or to assume the novel and extraordinary ground that such a Convention was necessary or expedient, for the purpose, merely, of considering, and determining, in their sovereign capacity, certain questions of disputed power, which are supposed to exist between that State more particularly, and the Government of the Union.

With reference to this point, the Committee were naturally led, in the first place, to a consideration of the very unusual manner (in case an amendment of the Constitution, in conformity with the article alluded to, were alone contemplated,) in which the proposition is submitted to the Legislature of Massachusetts.

Since the first organization of the Federal Government, it has, as the Committee believe, been the uniform practice of the Legislature of a State, whenever it has proposed to bring about any amendment or change in the Constitution of that Government by a Convention of the States, to specify, in their application to other States, for co-operation and support in such a measure, the precise points wherein the existing provisions of the system were supposed to be doubtful or insufficient, and the nature and extent of the correction proposed to be applied. This form of application, which, whether prescribed or not by the terms of the article before referred to, would seem to be such as the nature of the case requires, appears, nevertheless, to have been not inadvertently, but studiously avoided by the Legislature of South Carolina on the present occasion.

In another particular, the novelty of the proposition now submitted to this Legislature, not as respects its form only, but its matter and substance, is not less conspicuous. It is not proposed that a Convention should be called, with a view to any particular amendment, or even, in general terms, to a revision of the Constitution of the General Government, but that it should take upon itself, when assembled, in a manner wholly unknown in any existing provision of the Federal Compact, the office of umpire, and sit in judgment on certain disputes which are alleged to exist between a State or States, and the nation. It is believed by your Committee, that, with the exception of one solitary case of an analogous description, to which they may hereafter have occasion to advert, for another purpose, but which, considering the time of its occurrence, and the fate that awaited it, they can hardly suppose would be relied upon as affording the authority of a precedent, the proposition now submitted is entirely unexampled in the history of this Government.

It is, at any rate, most manifest, that, if assented to by the States, it would necessarily be attended with the most fatal consequences to the Union. If the principle be sanctioned that, whenever a single member of this confederacy, conceiving itself aggrieved by any, even a questionable measure of the General Government, shall be permitted, first, to resist the measure, and then to summon a Convention of the whole, in order to consider and determine the matter in dispute, it is easy to foresee what utter degradation of all the regular authorities of the Government, what scenes of anarchy and disorder throughout the land must inevitably and speedily ensue. But it appears to your Committee, that the proposition, in itself, is not more extraordinary than is the sweeping assertion with which it is prefaced, and which seems, indeed, to constitute the only grounds upon which it is predicated. In the Preamble to the Resolutions in question, it is declared " that serious causes of discontent do exist among the States of this Union, from the exercise by Congress of powers not conferred or contemplated by the sovereign parties to the compact." The Committee will not trust themselves to express, in terms such as their feelings might prompt them to employ on the occasion, the surprise, as well as the regret they have experienced, at meeting with a solemn, deliberate announcement like this, from the Legislative body of a respectable member of this Union. Nor will they stop to consider how far, under almost any imaginable circumstances, it is consistent with that courtesy and comity, to say nothing of respect and confidence, which the constituted authorities of the different States have hitherto been accustomed to manifest in their intercourse with one another, and with the several departments of the General Government. In the view of your Committee, the position here assumed, for it is unaccompanied by any reserve or qualification whatsoever, amounts in fact to nothing less than this, that both branches of the legislative department of this nation, including of course the chief executive, who must have sanctioned their proceedings, have manifestly been guilty of a dereliction of duty, a palpable abuse of power, while in the pretended exercise of their official functions.

An imputation of so grave and serious a nature, is not indeed in so many words pronounced against them, but as much as this is clearly implied by the whole tenor of the document alluded to. If, according to the naked assertion of the Preamble, which

is wholly unaccompanied by any allowance for a possible error
of judgment, the Congress of the United States have, on any occasion, been found to have exercised "powers not conferred
nor even contemplated by the parties to the Federal Compact,"
the inference would seem to follow of course, for all acts of a
legislative body must be supposed to have been the result of deliberation, that the outrage was perpetrated knowingly, intentionally. Indeed, the Committee have been reluctantly led to
the conclusion, especially when taking into view the present
communication from the Legislature of South Carolina, in connection with the extraordinary measures antecedently adopted,
and still maintained by a majority of the people of that State,
in their Convention, and in their halls of legislation, that it was,
in reality, their deliberate intention to pronounce a sentence
not less serious and severe than that before supposed, against
the legislative authorities of the General Government. It is, as
your Committee, from a due consideration of all the circumstances of the case, are constrained to believe, principally, with
a view to the confirmation or the reversal of this sentence, that
the invitation is now given to Massachusetts, to unite in sum-
moning a Convention of the States. In this connection, it may
be useful to notice, very briefly, the grounds on which, not the
leading politicians only, but the high functionaries in the Government of South Carolina, have attempted to justify the extraordinary proceedings that have been adverted to. It has been
promulgated as one of the first and fundamental principles in
their new theory of the Federal Government, that not one jot or
tittle of the sovereignty of any State was surrendered or compromised, in any manner, at the formation of the Union. That
a State has a right of course to be its own interpreter of the
laws of the General Government, and to be the judge in the last
resort of their validity. That, whenever a State, in its sovereign
capacity, shall be pleased to pronounce that the Congress of the
United States have, in regard to any of their enactments, transcended the authority delegated to them by the Constitution, all
such acts must thenceforth, so far at least as concerns the citizens of such State, be considered as utterly void and ineffectual.
Furthermore, it is contended, that a declaration, of the kind
above mentioned, is not only binding upon all within the juris-

diction of the disaffected State, but conclusive also, for the time being at least, against all the authorities of the General Government. From this novel and most extravagant doctrine, it results as a consequence, that an act of the highest legislative authority of this nation, whatever may be its scope or object, or however urgent in reference either to the foreign or internal affairs of the whole people may have been the cause of its adoption, must, when thus brought into question, remain as it were in abeyance, at the commandment of a single State. In other words, that the vast and complicated machinery of the National Government shall be made to stand still, until a grand Convention of twenty-four independent, contending sovereignties, if so many should be pleased to assemble on the occasion, shall have considered and determined the question of its validity.

Such, in substance, appears to be the theory of reform which has recently been promulgated, and is still maintained by the constituted authorities of South Carolina ; and your Committee is constrained to believe that it is, with reference to this system, and to a consummation of the very extraordinary course of procedure therein contemplated, that the proposition for a Convention of the States is now submitted to this Legislature. The Committee conceive that it would be a very useless appropriation of time, especially as the whole subject matter involved in the late extraordinary proceedings of South Carolina is already entirely familiar to the community, were they to proceed any further, on a course of reasoning, in order to demonstrate the utter fallacy and impracticability of the doctrines here adverted to ; or to dwell longer in contemplating the consequences in which, should they be sustained, they must naturally and necessarily involve the peace and safety of the Union. Their tendency, it is conceived, is quite too obvious to require, or even to admit of argument or illustration. They manifestly go to resolve at once our present glorious system of National Government into its original elements, and would leave, not for the present generation, but for posterity, the fearful, if not utterly hopeless task, of building some frail and miserable fabric upon its ruins.

In fine, your Committee are unanimously of the opinion, that, upon any such grounds, or for any such reasons as those which are set forth in the said Preamble and Resolutions, according to the construction thus given to them, it would be wholly inconsistent with the honor and the dignity of this Commonwealth, to accede to the call of a Convention of the States, for the purposes therein specified.

But, secondly, in case your Committee have been so unfortunate, in regard to the before mentioned particulars, as to have misinterpreted the import and intent of the communication from the Legislature of South Carolina; if, contrary to the construction now assumed, its real intention was to invite the co-operation of Massachusetts in the call of a Convention of the States, with a view to some legitimate amendment of the Constitution, in conformity with the existing provisions of the instrument, the Committee are, nevertheless, entirely agreed in the opinion, that there are, in truth and in fact, no such causes existing, as would justify, even for such a purpose, (especially during the present irritable state of feeling among the people of several States of the Union) a resort to a measure so unusual and extraordinary. Unless some one or two discontented States in this Union, should, by reason of their pre-eminence in virtue and patriotism, be considered as justly entitled to the distinguishing appellation of "the States of this Union," the Committee cannot assent to the position which is laid down in the sweeping language of the Preamble to the Resolutions from South Carolina, that there are, in fact, existing serious causes, or any just causes whatever, whether serious or trivial, of discontent among "the States of this Union"; much less are the Committee prepared to sanction the yet more extravagant assertion, that if discontents of any kind, or to any extent, do, in fact exist, "they have arisen from the exercise, by Congress, of powers not conferred, or contemplated, by the sovereign parties to the Federal Compact."

It is indeed true, that within the period of the last two or three years, one of the States of this Union has seen fit to proclaim aloud, throughout the land, her displeasure on account of certain prominent measures of the General Government.

She has been pleased to assign, as the cause of the discontent, that the highest legislative authority of the nation had assumed to itself the exercise of unwarrantable and exorbitant power ; and, on this ground, has, at length, placed herself in the attitude of open defiance of the Constitution and the laws of the land.

It is not less true, however, that whatever of sympathy or commiseration may have been expressed or felt, by any, for the errors and delusion of a much beloved, but wayward associate in the political family, not a single other State in this Union is united with her in sentiment, either as to the legal grounds of her complaint, or the propriety of the measures to which she has seen fit to resort for redress. On the contrary, in relation to both the one and the other, the voice of nearly the whole people, in their primary assemblages, in their halls of legislation, and every where throughout the land, has been heard, in a tone not of expostulation only, but of severe censure and reproof, to pronounce its decision against her.

In the opinion of your Committee, a Convention of the States cannot now be necessary to consider the validity of that decision, or to add any new provisions to those already existing in the Federal Compact, with the view of preventing a recurrence of similar discontents among the States, in future.

It is now nearly half a century since the present admirable system of Government first came from the hands of the illustrious statesmen and patriots by whom it was framed. Its theory, conceived as it would now seem to have been, almost by the power of superhuman intelligence, has been found, in experiment, in its wonderful adaptation to all the various and complicated concerns of this great and growing nation, not only to have equalled, but greatly to have transcended, the most sanguine hopes and expectations of the country.

In peace and in war, throughout all the trials and vicissitudes to which the nations, as well as individuals, in this imperfect state of being are necessarily subjected, its original principles, as they were at first established and understood by the people, have, to this day, remained without essential change or variation —unpolluted, undisturbed. Indeed, the members of the Committee are solemnly impressed with the conviction, that next to the superintending agency of a wise and beneficent Providence, which seems from the first, to have watched over the destinies of this much favored people, it is to this same system of civil Government, and to the mild, but firm and undeviating manner in which its principles have, for the most part, been maintained and administered, that we are chiefly indebted for the general, nay, almost universal prosperity which is now seen and felt in every part of this wide spread nation. It is this, as they verily believe, which, under the smiles of Heaven, has been the means of elevating these States from their once confused and imbecile condition, to that distinguished station which they now occupy among the proudest and most powerful nations of the world.

In the Constitution of a Government framed with such wisdom, which has been thus tried and proved, and found to have been attended with such happy results, it surely would not be the part of prudence or good policy to attempt, on any light occasion, or indeed in any case but one of the most imperious and urgent necessity, a fundamental change of any kind. It is the opinion of your Committee, that in the complaints lately put forth by the State of South Carolina, there is nothing, when their real causes are fairly and fully investigated, that can be supposed to amount to the presentment of an exigency of this latter description.

Nor do the Committee believe that a revision of the Federal Constitution, by a Convention of the States, would at this time be useful, much less that it can be necessary, as has of late been sometimes alleged, or pretended, with a view to some more clear and exact definition than is to be found in the existing provisions of that instrument, in relation either to the legitimate boundaries of jurisdiction between the General and the State Governments, or to any of the powers or immunities which these high parties respectively have hitherto been accustomed to claim or enjoy.

It was not unforeseen by the illustrious framers of the Federal compact, nor by the intelligent people who adopted it, that, in the very nature of things, such "questions of disputed power," (to use the language of the South Carolina resolutions,) would be likely to arise in the course of its operation. They were doubtless well aware also, that it was not in the power of any human wisdom or forecast, or indeed of any thing less than the intelligence which belongs alone to the Omniscient, to devise a system of Government for a nation like this, that should be forever exempt from such doubts and exceptions as the ingenuity or ambition of men might suggest, especially in times of party zeal or excitement. Differences of this kind in political opinion, and the collisions which sometimes spring from them, should be regarded as the natural, perhaps necessary incidents of all free institutions; as constituting in fact that portion of alloy which, by the ordination of Providence, seems to have been mingled with all our best comforts and blessings, and without which we could not have been permitted to enjoy the blessing of civil liberty, which is more precious in our estimation than all others.

But it is believed that the testimony of all history will demonstrate that such difficulties have been of less frequent occurrence, and attended with much less serious consequences in this, than in any other Government partaking in any degree of the republican form, which has existed on the face of the earth. It was, at any rate, precisely with a reference to these natural and necessary consequences of the freedom of all our political institutions, that the grand conservative principle, which is found in the Judiciary department, was deeply implanted in the system; that a high tribunal was appointed to stand, as it were, by the very tenure of its office, as well as by the peculiarity of its attributes in other respects, separate and distinct from all other departments of the Government. That to this tribunal was confided the great business of interpreting the Constitution and the laws, and of performing the high office of arbiter, in the last resort, of all questions " of disputed power" that might arise in the course of their administration. It is, in the opinion of the Committee, no more than a tribute justly due to the character and conduct of this distinguished tribunal, as well as to the wisdom and forecast of the illustrious statesmen who provided for its organization, to pronounce that it has hitherto fulfilled most faithfully and effectually, the great purposes of its appointment.

It must be admitted, indeed, that, in the course of a series of years, during which the system has been in operation, a few isolated instances of insubordination, not only among considerable masses of citizens, but extending, even, to the constituted authorities of whole States, have been known to exist, which seemed, at first, too mighty to be controlled by the mild, and peaceable operation of the principle alluded to ; but, happily, for the peace, and honor of the country, the Constitution and the laws have hitherto in all such cases, eventually triumphed. The Committee, here, feel a degree of pride as well as pleasure, from having an opportunity to unite their humble voice with that of a late distinguished Commentator, who had, perhaps, as much to do, as any other mortal, now living or dead, in the original formation and subsequent administration of our present system of government, in the declaration that, " with few exceptions, the course of the Judiciary has, hitherto, been sanctioned by the predominant sense of the nation."

If, in relation to this particular branch of the subject, any thing further were wanting in confirmation of the opinions which are entertained by every member of the Committee, they would beg leave to invoke to their aid, and indeed to adopt as their own, the sentiments that were once expressed by the Authorities of another leading State of this Union in a case corresponding, essentially, in its character, and in fact almost entirely analogous, in its circumstances, to that which is now presented for consideration.

The Committee, here, allude to the proceedings of the Legislature of Virginia, some thirty years ago, when a proposition was submitted to them by the Government of a neighboring State, then the largest, and most influential member of the confederacy, for an amendment of the Constitution of the United States, by providing for " the appointment of an impartial tribunal to decide disputes between the State, and Federal Judiciary ;" in other words, a tribunal, in relation to which, the one now established by the Constitution, should become, a mere Subordinate and Dependent. It would be foreign from the purpose of the present inquiry, and serve only to revive the remembrance of scenes, which, for the honor of the country, should rather be permitted to pass silently to oblivion, and, if possible, be obliterated from the history of this government, were the Committee to attempt a detail of the reasons, or rather, pretexts, which were urged as the grounds of this extraordinary, and, at the time, wholly unprecedented proposal, on the part of the great State that has been alluded to.

It is sufficient for us to know, that it was a case in which the highest Authorities of one of the States of this Union were seen in hostile array, on the very verge of open insurrection, against the Judicial power of the nation ; and which, but for a returning consciousness of error and delusion, on the one side, and a firm, undeviating perseverance in the execution of its high duties, on the other, must inevitably have involved the country in all the complicated horrors of civil war.

But, happily for the nation, the pretensions and the project of the disaffected State received no countenance from the State of Virginia. Her response, on the occasion, was precisely such as might reasonably have been anticipated from the intelligence and pure patriotism of such men as are known to have presided, at that day, in the councils of that much distinguished Commonwealth.

"It was, among other things, unanimously resolved by both Branches of their Legislature, that, in their opinion, there was a Tribunal, already provided by the Constitution of the United States, to wit, the Supreme Court, more eminently qualified, from their habits and duties, from the mode of their selection, and from the tenure of their office, to decide the disputes aforesaid, in an enlightened and impartial manner, than any other Tribunal which could be erected."

Such, to the very letter, was the magnanimous declaration of Virginia, when, by reason of an unpopular Judicial decision, (in the celebrated Olmstead case of Pennsylvania) she was invited to co-operate in an attempt to break up the existing foundations of the Judiciary Department of our Government. The example thus presented to us, is worthy of all praise, and of imitation ; and it surely is of not the less authority, from the circumstance of being holden up to us, by a member of this Union, which, whatever may at any time have been said, or thought of its political character, in other respects, has, it is believed, never been suspected of any deficiency of zeal, or devotedness to the cause of State rights, or the protection of its own dignity and sovereignty.

The Committee will not attempt, by any further commentary of their own, to give to this precedent, additional strength or weight.

In fine, upon a mature, and deliberate consideration of the whole subject submitted to them, the Committee have unanimously, agreed to recommend to this Legislature, the adoption of the following Resolves.

For the Committee.

GEORGE BLAKE.

RESOLVES.

WHEREAS, the Governor of the State of South Carolina did, by his communication, under date of the fifth day of January last past, transmit to His Excellency the Governor of this Commonwealth, copies of a certain preamble, and resolutions connected therewith, recently passed by both branches of the Legislature of the said first mentioned State, with a request that the same might be laid before the Legislature of this Commonwealth ; in which said preamble and resolutions, it is set forth that " serious causes of discontent do exist among the States of this Union, from the exercise, by Congress, of powers not conferred or contemplated by the sovereign parties to the compact; and resolving, therefore, that it is expedient that a Convention of the States be called, as early as practicable, to consider and determine such questions of disputed power as have arisen between the States of this Confederacy and the General Government."

AND WHEREAS, His Excellency the Governor of this Commonwealth hath, in pursuance of the said request, submitted to the consideration of this Legislature, the preamble and resolutions aforesaid : Therefore

1. *Resolved, by the Senate and House of Representatives of the Commonwealth of Massachusetts, in General Court assembled,* That the Legislature of this Commonwealth do not recognize the existence, at this time, of any serious causes of discontent, among the States generally, of this Union, or in any one of them ; much less, can they admit that, if any such discontents do, in fact, exist, they have arisen from the exercise by Congress of powers not conferred or contemplated by the sovereign parties to the compact, as is asserted in the before mentioned communication from the Legislature of South Carolina.

2. *Resolved,* That there is, already existing, under the Constitution of the United States, a proper and competent tribunal, namely, the Supreme Court of the United States, who are invested with sufficient power and authority; who are eminently

qualified, and to whom it constitutionally belongs, to consider and determine " the questions of disputed power," and all other matters of controversy which are referred to in the said preamble and resolutions : Therefore

3. *Resolved*, That the Legislature of this Commonwealth do not accede to the proposition of calling a Convention of the States for the purposes therein expressed, or for any other purpose whatsoever.

4. *Resolved*, That His Excellency the Governor, be requested to transmit a copy of these resolves, together with the report which accompanies them, to the President of the United States, the Governors of all the States, and to each of the Senators and Representatives of this Commonwealth in Congress.

IN SENATE, March 16, 1833.

Read twice and passed. Sent down for concurrence.

B. T. PICKMAN, *President*.

HOUSE OF REPRESENTATIVES, March 18, 1833.

Read twice and passed in concurrence.

W. B. CALHOUN, *Speaker*.

March 18, 1833.

Approved.

LEVI LINCOLN.

Commonwealth of Massachusetts.

The Joint Select Committee, appointed to consider the Resolutions of the Legislature of Georgia, proposing a Convention of the People of the United States, for the Amendment, in various respects, of the Constitution, and also so much of the Governor's Special Message as relates thereto, have attended to the duty assigned them, and ask leave to submit the following

REPORT :

The Resolutions of the State of Georgia propose to the other States of the Union the call of a Convention of the people, in conformity with the provisions of the fifth article of the Constitution, for the purpose of defining and making certain that instrument in regard to certain questions of disputed power, and for the purpose of altering it in other respects, wherein it needs amendment, in the opinion of the Legislature of Georgia. In the preamble to their resolutions, they premise that " throughout the United States there exist many controversies, growing out of the conflicting interests which have arisen among the people since the adoption of the Federal Constitution,—out of the cases in which Congress claims the right to act under constructive or implied powers,—out of the disposition, shown by Congress, too frequently to act under assumed powers,—and out of the rights of jurisdiction, either claimed or exercised by the Supreme Court,"—all of which controversies, they allege have a tendency to produce discontent and disaffection among the citizens of the United States, and ultimately to bring about a dissolution of the Union ; and upon these premises they conclude that experience has " clearly proved" the Constitution to need amendment in thirteen distinct particulars, which they proceed to set forth specifically, as the basis of their Resolutions. Your Committee propose briefly to remark upon the several portions of the Preamble to the Resolutions, and in so doing they will have explained the grounds of the Resolves, which they offer to the consideration of the Senate and House of Representatives.

Your Committee do not pretend to deny, that " controversies" exist in some parts of the Union, " growing out of the conflicting interests, which have arisen among the people since the adoption of the Federal Constitution." Such controversies, and such sources of controversy, are inseparable from the very existence of political society, and belong to the practical operation of every system of government in every country. They are not such as any modifications of the present Constitution could remove, or any prescribed form of fundamental law prevent. Of course, whatever may be the extent, nature, degree, or tendency of controversies of this description, they do not seem to your Committee to afford any argument in favor of the call of a Convention.

And whatever controversies may have arisen out of " the cases, in which Congress claims the right to act under constructive or implied powers," your Committee conceive that still less can such cases be admitted to render the call of a Convention necessary or expedient. Prior to the time when the people of the United States adopted the Constitution, they possessed, either in themselves individually, or in their respective state governments, all the powers of sovereignty. That Constitution consists in part of a specification of powers, whereof the people saw fit to divest themselves or the States, in order to concede them to the government of the United States ; and it is manifest that, according to the settled principles of constitutional jurisprudence, the Union cannot rightly claim any powers, other than such as are bestowed upon it by the Constitution. What those powers are, and what their extent, are in themselves essentially questions of *construction*, that is, of the legal meaning and effect of the terms of the instrument. Whether it shall be construed liberally, or whether it shall be construed strictly,— or whether neither liberally nor strictly, if there be any middle course,—still at any rate it must be construed in some way; and the force of any grant, in respect of the powers conveyed by it either expressly or impliedly, is and must forever continue to be a question of construction. That construction is a process of definition, dependant upon the same rules of law, philology, and common sense, which settle the construction of other instruments; and if any doubts arise thereon, the Constitution itself provides for the mode by which such doubts are to be removed, namely, by means of the Supreme Court of the United States. To assemble a Convention for the purpose of making such construction, would not only be contrary to the tenor of the Constitution itself, but would serve to defeat its own object, because every definition or explanation, which a Convention should undertake to give concerning questions which now exist, would of necessity furnish the materials of new questions, just as difficult to decide as the old ones, and just as much requiring the interposition of a Convention. Your Committee are of opinion that the Constitution, as it stands, is a model of clear, exact, intelligible specification and limitation, admirable for the distinctness of its language, remarkable as well for legal precision of expression, as for the profound political wisdom which characterizes it; and they have no hopes that in these respects it could be improved as a whole by the labors of a new Convention

Your Committee, with all due respect for the Legislature of Georgia, feel bound to say they are not conscious that Congress has frequently shewn a disposition " to act under assumed powers"—provided the Legislature of Georgia understand by those words what alone the Committee can understand by them,— powers not conferred by the Constitution. Congress acts on the people through the medium of legislation, and it cannot so act without the concurrence of the Executive; and the rules of conduct which Congress and the Executive conjointly prescribe in the form of laws, are subject to the revision of the Judiciary, by whom their constitutionality, and of course their validity, is to be judged. Your Committee deem this mode of redress amply sufficient, in the ordinary course of affairs, to protect the people against the actual exercise of usurped powers;

and they are wholly at a loss to perceive how a Convention could govern and control the disposition of any future Congress.

The Supreme Court, in the judgment of your Committee, neither claims nor exercises ' any rights of jurisdiction' not vested in it by the Constitution. They are persuaded, on the contrary, from careful observation of the judgments of that august tribunal, that it has ever manifested a becoming diffidence of its own powers, a disposition to act strictly within the prescribed boundaries of its constitutional functions, and a conscientious deference for the reserved rights of the States.

Your Committee are constrained to say thus much in reference to the premises laid down by the Legislature of Georgia, because the Committee cannot admit them to be sound, in any view of which they seem to be justly susceptible, as alleged inducements to the call of a Convention, or even as any genuine or adequate causes of such discontent among the people, as should menace the safety of the Union. And while the Committee deny that these general consideratious afford any motives to constitutional action, they equally deny that past ' experience' proves the necessity of altering the Constitution in the manner proposed by the State of Georgia.

The Legislature of Georgia seeks ' amendment' of the Constitution,—

' First, That the powers delegated to the General Government, and the rights reserved to the States or to the people, may be more distinctly defined.'

The Committee have already remarked upon this point, which is purely a matter of judicial construction, not of fundamental legislation by the agency of a Convention.

' Secondly, That the power of coercion by the General Government over the States, and the right of a State to resist an unconstitutional act of Congress, may be determined.'

Your Committee conceive that these points are ' determined' already by the Constitution. The people of the several States have bestowed certain specified powers upon the General Government, and all the citizens of the Union, whether acting individually as men, or collectively through the intervention of the constituted authorities of a State, are alike bound to yield obedience to the General Government within the limits prescribed by the Constitution. If Congress, or the Executive, overleap those limits, the Judiciary affords the means of immediate redress ; and the people, in the exercise of their functions as electors, can provide new depositaries of the legislative and executive power ; and if these remedies fail, and the public abuse and usurpation be of adequate magnitude to warrant recurrence to ultimate means of relief, there remains the right of revolution and of armed resistance. These principles, sufficiently clear in themselves, have already been acted upon by the Legislature in their decision upon the proceedings in South Carolina, and do not require any further elucidation; and your Committee will only add that this subject of amendment, like the preceding, is also matter of judicial definition, not of constitutional organization.

'Thirdly, That the principle involved in a tariff for the direct protection of domestic industry may be settled.'

Your Committee have only to refer, on this point, to the opinions heretofore expressed by the Legislature upon the constitutionality of protective tariff regulations, and to add that this also is a question of definition or construction.

'Fourthly, That a system of federal taxation may be established, which shall be equal in its operation upon the whole people, and in all sections of the country.'

Your Committee, knowing that Congress has power to lay and collect taxes, duties, imposts, and excises, do not perceive any cause, in the history of the country or the nature of the subject, for taking away that authority ; and they are not aware of any useful object to be attained by subjecting this part of the Constitution to revision by a Convention.

'Fifthly, That the jurisdiction and process of the Supreme Court may be clearly and unequivocally settled.'

Your Committee are of opinion that the jurisdiction of the Supreme Court, extending to all cases in law and equity arising under the Constitution, laws, and treaties of the Union, and to various other classes of cases described in the Constitution, is therein defined with comprehensive precision, so far as it can be defined by means of language. Its process is matter of legislation, within the powers of Congress, and there is no need of the action of a Convention upon that point. And although an amendment of the Constitution might grant new powers to the

Supreme Court, or abstract from it powers which it now possesses, the Committee do not perceive how its jurisdiction could be
any more 'clearly and unequivocally settled' by a Convention.

'Sixthly, That a tribunal of last resort may be organized to
settle disputes between the General Government and the States.'

Your Committee conceive such an object to be entirely impracticable ; and moreover, to be quite incompatible with the
principles or the healthful action of the Constitution. The authority of the United States, under the Constitution, attaches
to individuals, not to States ; and a Convention could neither
cure nor prevent such 'disputes,' unless it should totally change
the whole theory of the Government, and interpose the authority
of the States between individuals and the Union. The great
distinction between our Constitution and the fundamental system of other federal governments is, that the latter were sovereignties over sovereignties, and that they legislated for political
communities, and thus whenever either of the members of those
confederacies chose to disobey the commands of their general
government, either a civil war or a dissolution of the confederacy
ensued ; whereas the power of the United States acts upon private individuals, and thus holds the constitutional, as well as the
physical means, to compel the obedience of the citizens of any
refractory State. Your Committee regard this as one of the most
beautiful and essential features of that admirable charter ; as the
great object, in fact, which our forefathers sought to secure in
substituting the present Constitution in place of the old articles
of confederation,—and as among the last of its provisions, which
we ought to be willing to abandon or jeopardize.

'Seventhly, That the power of chartering a bank, and of
granting incorporations, may be expressly given to or withheld
from Congress.'

Your Committee cannot think it of any consequence now to
introduce a clause into the Constitution, to the effect of expressly authorizing Congress to establish a bank or other corporation.
The power of Congress is incontrovertibly settled in the point
of general power, by the repeated action of Congress and of the
Executive on the subject, and by adjudications of the Supreme
Court. Of course, the power of chartering a bank is to be
deemed and taken as a part of the Constitution, just as much

as if it had been expressly specified. No practical object could be answered by a Convention, in respect of this, unless to prohibit the establishment of a bank by Congress, which your Committee cannot recommend, impressed as they are with a strong sense of the utility and importance of a National Bank, to every portion of the Union.

'Eighthly, That the practice of appropriating money for works of internal improvement, may be either sanctioned by an express delegation of power, or restrained by express inhibition.'

If the Constitution were now to be framed, your Committee will not deny that it might be expedient to insert in it an explicit provision upon this vexed question. They are aware that grave differences of opinion have obtained among the most distinguished statesmen of the country, as to the power of Congress to make appropriations of money for objects of internal improvement, so called, within the limits of any of the States. Under the power to establish post roads, to regulate commerce, and to raise moneys to provide for the general welfare, Congress has repeatedly authorized the execution, at the charge of the United States, in part or in whole, of public works of this description; and whatever questions have been, or may hereafter be raised, concerning the extent of this power, your Committee believe that the opinions and practice of the two Houses of Congress and the Executive, in their discussion and action upon the subject, will ere long have provided a safe construction of the Constitution in this respect, as they have done in others, where doubt once existed as to the meaning of that instrument. However this may be, your Committee do not think it is a matter which demands the call of a Convention; and that if the Constitution needs amendment in that particular, it should be provided by means of Congress, under the provisions in the fifth article of the Constitution.

'Ninthly, That it may be prescribed, what disposition shall be made of the surplus revenue, when such revenue is found to be on hand.'

'Tenthly, That the right to, and the mode of disposition of the public lands of the United States, may be settled.'

Your Committee are not aware that any serious constitutional difficulty exists in relation to these two subjects, which they deem to be mere questions of public policy and expediency, entirely within the competency of Congress.

' Eleventhly, That the election of President and Vice President may be secured, in all cases, to the people.'

' Twelfthly, That their tenure of office may be limited to one term.'

Whatever considerations there may be in favor of an amendment of the Constitution in these particulars, and your Committee admit that the expediency of a change in the second of them rests upon highly plausible grounds, yet the mode of amendment through the agency of Congress, pointed out by the Constitution, seems to them to be fully competent to effect such an amendment, whenever it shall be the will and desire of a decided majority of the people of the United States.

' Lastly, that the rights of the Indians may be definitely settled.'

Your Committee believe this to be purely a subject of judicial construction under the Constitution, laws, and treaties of the United States; that the Supreme Court is competent to settle any questions appertaining to it, which do exist, or which may hereafter exist; and that, of course, it offers no exigency requiring the call of a Convention.

In fine, the specific objects of amendment proposed by the State of Georgia, are of two kinds :—first, things wherein the true intendment of certain clauses of the Constitution may have been deemed questionable, which your Committee regard as the proper subject matter of judicial construction or definition, in the last resort of constitutional, as distinguished from extra constitutional modes of procedure, and of course as not fitting objects of a Convention ; and, secondly, things wherein specific alterations of, or additions to the Constitution may have been deemed expedient, which your Committee regard as belonging to the competency of Congress, and by no means of such vital consequence as to justify the extraordinary step of a Convention of the people of the United States.

Having thus adverted to the reasons on which the Legislature of Georgia found their proposition for the call of a Convention, and also to the specific objects of amendment which they propound for investigation, your Committee have only to add, in conclusion, that they conceive the meeting of a Convention of the people, for the purpose of revising the Constitution, in these or any other respects, to be a remedy required only by pressing emergencies of national exigency ; and they apprehend that, under any subsisting state of public feeling, its tendency would be to create new questions of difficulty, and to augment the differences of opinion in regard to old ones, and thus to weaken rather than confirm the power of the Union. The Legislature of Georgia have alleged various subjects of fundamental law as requiring the agency of a Convention, being such as the peculiar views or position of the State of Georgia have suggested to her Legislature. It would be easy for your Committee to swell the number of subjects equally suitable for the consideration of a Convention with those under discussion, derived from the views and position of this Commonwealth ; and some of the latter class of subjects involve questions of public right, of national expediency, of constitutional organization, quite as important in themselves, and quite as dear to the convictions of the people of Massachusetts, as any of the former class can possibly be to the people of Georgia. But your Committee are content with the Constitution in the form they have received it from their fathers, regarding it as a monument of comprehension and sagacity, which the labors of a Convention might perhaps improve in some points, but which they would be more likely to unsettle and overturn, without possessing the capacity or the power to raise upon its ruins another equally noble fabric of political wisdom to supply its place. Whilst entertaining, therefore, all proper respect for the opinions of the Legislature of Georgia, and while solicitous to treat that State with deference as a coequal member of the Union, your Committee, in view of the whole matter, recommend to the Legislature the adoption of the following Resolves.

For the Committee,

CALEB CUSHING.

RESOLVES.

Whereas, the Governor of the State of Georgia did, by his communication under date of the twenty-eighth day of December last, transmit to His Excellency the Governor of the Commonwealth, copies of a certain Preamble and Resolutions connected therewith, recently adopted by the Legislature of said State of Georgia, and His Excellency did, by his Special Message of the sixteenth of January last, communicate the same to the Legislature of this Commonwealth :—

And whereas, in said Preamble and Resolutions it is set forth that, for certain reasons therein alleged, the State of Georgia doth make application to the Congress of the United States for the call of a Convention of the People to amend the Constitution in sundry particulars, enumerated in said Preamble, and in such others as the People may consider needful :—

And whereas, the specified subjects of amendment are either matters of definition or construction merely, arising on the face of the Constitution, as to which the meaning of the Constitution is already, or may hereafter be, satisfactorily ascertained under the Constitution, and by means provided therein, and which matters do not properly come within the functions of a Convention ; or else matters of amendment suitable for the consideration of Congress, under the Fifth Article of the Constitution, and not of such vital moment as to require the call of a Convention :—Therefore,

1. *Resolved*, That the Legislature of this Commonwealth do not concur in the proposition of the State of Georgia, inviting a Convention of the People of the United States for the purpose of amending the Constitution.

2. *Resolved*, That His Excellency the Governor be requested to transmit a copy of these Resolves, together with the Report which accompanies them, to the President of the United States, to the Governors of all the States, and to each of the Senators and Representatives of this Commonwealth in Congress.

EXECUTIVE DEPARTMENT, GA.

MILLEDGEVILLE, JUNE 7, 1833.

SIR,—

IN transmitting to you, the Acts of the General Assembly of this State, passed at its last session, I beg leave to correct an error, which occurred through the inadvertence of the press, and a want of proper scrutiny at this Department, in regard to a resolution, transmitted to you on the 28th of December last, and purporting to have been approved on the 22d of said month. The resolution forwarded to you, was rejected by the Legislature, and a substitute adopted (which you will find in the printed laws, pages 49 and 50.)

The official signatures of the officers of both branches of the General Assembly, and that of the Governor, were improperly placed by the printer, to the resolutions heretofore forwarded to you, and forwarded from this Department without detecting the error.

I have the honor to be, respectfully,

Your Obedient Servant,

WILSON LUMPKIN.

His Excellency the Governor of Massachusetts.

State of Georgia.

RESOLVES.

WHEREAS, The Tariff Law of the last session of Congress has not satisfied the just expectation of the people of the Southern States : *whereas*, the recent attempt to provide a remedy for the evils which we suffer from the protective system, by a State Convention, not only will probably be abortive, but is likely, if persisted in, materially to disturb the public harmony, and lessen the moral force of the State: and, *whereas*, the resolutions adopted by the delegates of a minority of the people, and which are about to be submitted to the whole State for ratification, are in several respects of a most objectionable character, it becomes the duty of those who are the unquestionable representatives of the people of Georgia, to interpose for the purpose of tranquillizing the public mind, and concentrating the public will, by the recommendation of a course of policy, which, they trust, will obtain the general approbation of the community. Therefore,

Resolved, That if a Southern Convention be desirable, it is expedient for the State of Georgia, to invite the States of Virginia, North Carolina, South Carolina, Alabama, Tennessee, and Mississippi, to concur with her in electing Delegates to a Convention, which shall take into consideration the Tariff system of the General Government, and devise and recommend the most effectual and proper mode of obtaining relief from the evils of that system.

Resolved, That in order to ascertain the sense of the people of Georgia, on this subject, the following plan of a Southern

Convention, be submitted to them, and that their votes on the
same be received at the appointed time and places of voting for
county officers in the several counties of this State, on the first
Monday in January next; that no person be allowed to vote on
this matter, who is not entitled to vote for members of the General Assembly; that the vote be expressed by endorsing on the
ticket the words " Southern Convention," or " No Southern
Convention ;" and that a regular list be kept of the votes so en-
dorsed, and transmitted to the Executive Department, by the
officers presiding at the elections.

PLAN OF A SOUTHERN CONVENTION.

ART. 1. The State of Georgia invites the States of Virginia,
North Carolina, South Carolina, Alabama, Tennessee, and Mississippi, to concur with her in electing Delegates to a Convention, which shall take into consideration the Tariff system of the
General Government, and devise and recommend the most effectual and proper mode of obtaining relief from the evils of that
system.

ART. 2. She proposes that each invited State, shall send to
the Convention, a number of Delegates equal to the number of
Senators and Representatives to which such State is entitled in
the Congress of the United States.

ART. 3. The Convention shall not take place, unless (five)
States of the six, which it is proposed to invite, assent to the
proposal.

ART. 4. The time and place of assembling the proposed Convention, shall be arranged and determined by correspondence
among those who shall be duly authorized by the States assent-
ing to this plan.

ART. 5. The Governor of this State, is authorized and desired
to communicate the invitation and proposals contained in the
four preceding articles to the Governors of the other States
above mentioned, with a request that they be made known to
the people of those States respectively. He is also authorized
and desired to arrange by correspondence, the time and place
of assembling the proposed Convention, conformably to the provision of the fourth article.

ART. 6. When the time and place for the meeting of said Convention, are determined, the Governor of this State is authorized and desired to issue his proclamation, with timely notice, for an election of eleven delegates by general ticket, to represent the State in said Convention; the election to be regulated by the same principles as those which govern the election of members of Congress. It is also desired and expected, that the Legislature of this State will make such provision as may be necessary for carrying more completely and readily into effect, the above plan, if it should be adopted as proposed.

ART. 7. If the delegates assembled in a Southern Convention, according to the above plan, shall agree on a course of proceeding which they recommend to the States represented, the Governor of this State is authorized and desired to issue a proclamation, with timely notice, for an election of delegates to a State Convention, declaring the time and place at which it shall assemble. Such Convention shall consist of delegates from every County, equal in number to that of its members in the House of Representatives of this State, and the elections for said delegates shall be regulated by the same principles, and authenticated by the same forms as elections for members of the General Assembly. To the State Convention thus elected, the recommendations of the Southern Convention shall be submitted. If the same are approved by the State Convention, they shall then be referred to the people for final ratification, in such manner as may be prescribed by said Convention; and if they are ratified by the majority of those persons entitled to vote for members of the General Assembly, the State Convention shall proclaim that the said recommendations being regularly adopted, express the will of the people of Georgia ; and shall also provide the mode of giving permanent and authentic record to such ratification.

Resolved, That if the above plan of a Southern Convention is adopted by the votes of a majority of the citizens of this State, given in the manner therein described, it will be the right and duty of the different functionaries of the State Government, to afford all necessary aid in facilitating its execution.

Resolved, That we earnestly advise our fellow-citizens, not to give their votes on the resolutions of the Convention recently adjourned, as therein proposed. That Convention manifestly consisted of delegates from a minority of the people ; yet they submit their acts for ratification to the whole people, according to a form contrived by themselves, through the agency of persons appointed by themselves, while they themselves remain final judges of the ratification proposed. To sanction such a procedure, would open a door for the grossest imposition, would establish an alarming precedent for usurping the rights of the majority, and might alternately [ultimately] expose us to all the horrors of discord and anarchy.

Resolved, That while we would provide a corrective for the possible continuance of those evils, of which we have so much reason to complain, we still hope that the regular operations of the General Government will supercede the necessity of any extraordinary measures on the part of the Southern people, and that we recognize the happiest augury of better things, in the growing certainty of the re-election of that illustrious patriot, Andrew Jackson.

Resolved, That we abhor the doctrine of Nullification as neither a peaceful, nor a constitutional remedy, but, on the contrary, as tending to civil commotion and disunion ; and while we deplore the rash and revolutionary measures, recently adopted by a Convention of the people of South Carolina, we deem it a paramount duty to warn our fellow citizens against the danger of adopting her mischievous policy.

Agreed to, November 29, 1832.

ASBURY HULL, *Speaker.*

Attest, ROBERT W. CARNES, *Clerk.*

In SENATE, concurred in, December 12, 1832.

THOMAS STOKES, *President.*

Attest, IVERSON L. HARRIS, *Secretary.*

Approved, December 14, 1832.

WILSON LUMPKIN, *Governor.*

RESOLVES

OF THE

LEGISLATURE

OF

MISSISSIPPI.

RESOLVES.

The Committee to which was referred the communication of the Executive, transmitting to this House a resolution of the Senate and House of Representatives of the State of Georgia, " making application to the Congress of the United States, in conformity with the fifth article of the Federal Constitution, for the call of a Convention of the people to amend the Constitution aforesaid, in the particulars therein enumerated, and in such others as the people of the other States deem needful of amendment", beg leave to

REPORT:

That, deeply impressed with the momentous importance of the subject referred to them, they have bestowed on it their most deliberate consideration. They are proud to avow the sincere and sacred reverence, which they, in common with a vast majority of their fellow citizens entertain for the Federal Constitution, the great charter of our national liberties, our independence and union. Framed as it was originally, by a Convention of the people of the United States, and sanctioned afterwards by the people of the respective States, in their highest sovereign capacity, we should, it would seem, await the existence of the most urgent and palpable necessity of amendment ere we proceed to provide for any important alteration in a system of government presented to us under such imposing circumstances. But when to these circumstances is added the recollection of the great, the good, the pure and gifted statesmen by whom it was framed, the all embracing spirit of conciliation and patriotism in which it originated, and by which it was perfected—the signal and glorious triumphs which under it have attended the eagle of our star-spangled banner on the land and on the deep—the high and wide spread national character which it has enabled us to attain—the unexampled rapidity of our march under its fortunate auspices to national glory, power, prosperity and happiness—the marked and all pervading influence which it has exerted in liberalizing the forms of government throughout the civilized world, by conferring on mankind a knowledge of their rights, and a determination and courage to maintain and defend them ;—when to all these glorious results, it is added, that the paternal voice of Him who was first in war, first in peace, and still is first in the hearts of his countrymen, employed its latest accents in inculcating a deep and solemn veneration for this Constitution and the Union ;—your Committee would do injustice to their feelings, were they to suppress the avowal that they seem to themselves to be treading upon holy ground, and that nothing short of the most palpable necessity could induce them to recommend the adoption of any measures which, however well designed, might ultimately endanger the existence or mar the symetry and beauty of this most perfect monument of uninspired wisdom.

Your Committee, however, cannot refrain from expressing, that they believe that a wild and latitudinarian construction has been placed upon the Constitution of the United States, by many in our Government, and which they believe to be well calculated, by the exercise of such unlimited construction, to be productive of discontent, sectional injustice, and even oppression itself. Your Committee believe that the Congress of the United States have no right to exercise any powers other than those which are expressly delegated, and those incidental powers which arise under that express grant; and would gladly see those ambiguities which are contained in that instrument, which has been justly styled the " charter of the liberties of the American people," at the proper time so amended as to set at rest those disputed powers which have agitated our happy Government for a series of years; but the turbulent spirit of the times, and the numberless sectional influences, which under almost every variety of form and shape and intensity, pervade and agitate the great divisions of our country, would, in the opinion of your Committee, render it imprudent to concur in the application contained in the resolutions of the State of Georgia at the present critical period of our national affairs ; while the citizens of the Union are subjected to those adverse influences, it would seem more than madness to expect that calm deliberation—that mutual spirit of concession and conciliation, that broad patriotism in which alone it originated, and which should inform, direct and animate the proceedings of any body of men who may be called together to alter or amend it.   Under the Constitution as it exists, we enjoy a freedom of laws, of order, of security and peace, and we enjoy it to an extent hitherto unexampled in the records of the world.   Freedom, Americans always will possess. Her image is stamped so deeply upon our hearts, that like the form of Phidias on the shield of his Minerva, it can be obliterated by the annihilation alone of the substance on which it is impressed.   But an unsuccessful attempt to render the Constitution more congenial to the wishes of those States which are most anxious for its amendment—the angry warmth and excitement which would attend the struggle, and the malignant passions it would engender, might change this peaceful freedom, (which is our pride and boast,) into a freedom of fraternal wars, of bloodshed and desolation.

If a Convention were called for the purpose of defining with more precision those parts of the Constitution which are considered indefinite, and prohibiting the exercise of those powers which being considered doubtful, have constituted the groundwork of those violent party divisions which distract our country, your Committee believe that it would be productive of results wholly foreign to the wishes of those who are most anxious for the call.   A Convention assembled at this time, they have every reason to believe, would affirm these very powers which are so obnoxious to a majority of the citizens of the southern sections of the Union.   The constitutionality of a Tariff of protection has been affirmed by eighteen of the twenty-four States; the larger States all being in favor of the affirmation.   Now it should be recollected that the power of the smaller States is greater in Congress than it would be in a Convention of the States, called upon any plan of representation which we could reasonably expect would be adopted ; under the most favorable circumstances the co-ordinate power held by us in the Senate, would be merged in the mass of the popular representation of the larger States. For a redress of the grievances, therefore which are assigned as the causes for the call, prudence would seem to dictate a reliance on the equity and patriotism of the National Legislature, and more especially a reliance on the progressive influence, the intelligence and virtue of the people of the Union.

In accordance with these suggestions, your Committee would recommend the adoption of the following resolution :

Be it resolved by the Legislature of the State of Mississippi, That this State does not conceive it expedient to concur in the resolution of the State of Georgia, " making application to the Congress of the United States for the call of a Convention of the people to amend the Federal Constitution in the particulars therein enumerated, and in such others as the people of the other States may deem needful of amendment."

Be it further resolved, That His Excellency the Governor be requested to transmit a copy of this Resolution to the Executive of the State of Georgia, and of each of the other States of the Union.

DAVID PEMBLE,
Speaker of the House of Representatives.

CHARLES LYNCH,
President of the Senate.

☞ The following Documents were received at too late a period, to be inserted in their proper places.

RESOLVES

OF THE

LEGISLATURE

OF

CONNECTICUT.

RESOLVES.

At a General Assembly of the State of Connecticut, holden at Hartford, in said State, on the first Wednesday of May, in the year of our Lord one thousand eight hundred and thirty-three.

Upon the Report of the Joint Committee, to whom had been referred so much of the Message of His Excellency the Governor, as relates to the several communications from the Executive Departments of the States of Maine, New Hampshire, Massachusetts, New York, New Jersey, Pennsylvania, Delaware, Virginia, South Carolina, North Carolina, Georgia, Ohio, Indiana, Illinois, and Mississippi, on the subject of the Tariff Laws, Internal Improvements, and Amendments of the Constitution of the United States :

Resolved by this Assembly, That the Congress of the United States are authorized by the Constitution, to pass acts for the levying and collecting of duties on imposts, and thereby to raise a revenue sufficient for all the exigencies of the Government; that in forming a Tariff of such duties, it is just and constitutional that the interests of our own manufactures should be regarded, and due encouragement and protection thereby given to them; that such acts, when approved by the President, are binding on all the States, and on all the people of every State, and that no State has power to nullify, or the right to resist the execution of the same.

Resolved, That it is the imperious duty of the President of the United States, to see that such laws are carried into execution; and that in the constitutional discharge of this duty, he is entitled to and ought to receive the aid and support of every citizen of the Union.

Resolved, That this Assembly do most fully approve the essential principles and the determination avowed by the President, in his Proclamation of the 10th of December, 1832, and in his subsequent Message to Congress; and that this Assembly, and the people of this State, will cordially and faithfully co-operate with him in carrying the same into effect.

Resolved, That the members of this Assembly cherish a sincere regard and affection for the citizens of the State of South Carolina, as well as for all their brethren of this great confederated family; and that they shall ever remember with gratitude and pride the many and brilliant services rendered by that distinguished State, in the struggle for independence.

Resolved, That much would be hazarded, and nothing valuable could be gained, by an attempt, at the present time, and in the present state of the Union, to amend the Constitution of the United States; and, therefore, this Assembly do not concur in the proposition of the State of Georgia, inviting a Convention of the people for that purpose.

Resolved, That the Secretary of this State cause thirty copies of the foregoing Resolutions to be printed; and that His Excellency the Governor of this State be requested to transmit one copy thereof to the President of the United States, and a similar copy thereof to the Governor of each State and Territory of the Union.

A true copy of record,

Examined and certified by

THOMAS DAY, *Secretary.*

RESOLVES

OF THE

LEGISLATURE

OF

MARYLAND.

RESOLVES.

By the House of Delegates, Feb. 9, 1833.

The Joint Committee, to whom was referred the Ordinance and other Documents, transmitted us by the Governor of South Carolina, and that part of our late Governor's Message, relating thereto, have given the subject that attention which its serious import demands, and report the following :

Resolved by the General Assembly of Maryland, That in expressing our opinion upon the Ordinance of Nullification, and the recent proceedings of South Carolina, it is our duty to declare our opinions firmly on the principles assailed, and to expostulate mildly and affectionately with her.

Resolved, That we hold these principles to be incontrovertible, that the Government of the United States was adopted by the people of the different States, and established " in order to form a more perfect union, establish justice, ensure domestic tranquillity, provide for the common defence, promote the general welfare, and secure the blessings of liberty to ourselves and our posterity ;" that it possesses all the powers necessary for the purposes for which it was instituted ; that it is irreconcileable with the objects and purposes for which the Constitution was adopted, to suppose that it contains in itself the principles of its own destruction, or has failed to endue the Government, created by it, with the essential power of self-preservation.

That it is not in the power of any one State to annul an act of the General Government, as void or unconstitutional.

That the power of deciding controversies among the different States, or between the General Government and a State, is reposed in the Federal Judiciary, and that it is an act of usurpation for any State to arrogate to herself jurisdiction in such cases.

That the Supreme Court is the only tribunal, having conclusive jurisdiction in cases involving the constitutionality of the acts of the General Government.

That whenever a State is aggrieved by the Constitutional acts of the General Government, the fifth article of the Constitution prescribes the remedy, declaring that " the Congress, whenever two-thirds of both Houses shall deem it necessary, shall propose amendments to this Constitution, or on the application of the Legislatures of two-thirds of the several States, shall call a Convention for proposing amendments, which, in either case, shall be valid to all intents and purposes, as part of this Constitution, when ratified by the Legislatures of three-fourths of the several States, or by Conventions, in three-fourths thereof, as the one or the other mode of ratification may be proposed by Congress."

That the right to annul a law of the General Government, assumed by one State, is "incompatible with the existence of the Union, contradicted expressly by the letter of the Constitution, unauthorized by its spirit, inconsistent with every principle on which it was founded, and destructive of the great object for which it was formed."

That our fellow citizens of South Carolina, who remain faithful to the Constitution and laws of the United States, are entitled to the protection of the General Government, both for their property and their persons.

That if any State, regardless of the constitutional remedies which are afforded for every grievance and oppression, should attempt to withdraw from the Union, it is the right and duty of the General Government, to protect itself, and the other States, from the fatal consequences of any such attempt.

Further Resolved, That the Ordinance of Nullification of South Carolina, is calculated to mislead her citizens from the true character of the Federal Government, and the just allegiance, which they owe to that Government.

Resolved, That this State is ardently attached to the Union— that it does not desire any additional powers to be conferred on the General Government, but wishes every delegated power to be exerted that has a tendency to strengthen the bonds that unite us, and to fortify the hope that the Union will be perpetual.

Resolved, That this State does not recognize the power in any State, to nullify a law of Congress, nor to secede from the Union, and that it will sustain the General Government in the exercise of every constitutional means to preserve unimpaired the integrity of the United States.

Resolved, That our mutual interests and general welfare impel us to guard with care, the integrity of the Constitution, and to appeal in the most solemn and affectionate manner to the other States, and particularly to South Carolina, to reciprocate with this State, its well founded attachment to the Union, and to oppose, with becoming firmness, every infraction of those great and fundamental principles of the Constitution, which form the only basis on which our happy institutions can with safety repose.

Resolved, That we deeply deplore the excitement which has prompted our sister State of South Carolina to the attitude of defiance, which she now exhibits ; that however extravagant her irritation may be deemed, or impatient her proceedings, we will not renounce the hope that a calmer feeling will yet enable her to see the dreadful consequences of repelling the laws of the Union. That, conspicuous and persevering as her valor was in achieving the great results which gave birth to our Union, she will yet remember the glory of her early toils, and will offer up, in the sanctuary of the Union, her Ordinance and her consequent laws, a patriotic sacrifice to the cause of American liberty and union.

Resolved, That the Tariff Laws of 1828, and of 1832, are within the Legitimate exercise of the constitutional powers of Congress, but we will acquiesce with pleasure, in any modification of those laws, which the wisdom of Congress may devise for allaying the excitement on that subject, in the Southern portion of our country, which shall reduce the amount of revenue to the necessary expenditures of the Government, and at the same time sufficiently guard those great interests which have grown up under the system of protection.

Resolved, That the following words from Washington's Farewell Address, should at all times, but particularly at the present

alarming crisis, be impressed upon the heart of every American :
" The unity of Government, which constitutes you one people,
is also now dear to you, it is justly so, for it is a main pillar of
the edifice of your real independence ; the support of your
tranquillity at home, your peace abroad ; of your safety, of your
prosperity, of that very liberty which you so highly prize."

" It is of infinite moment that you should properly estimate
the immense value of your National Union to your collective
and individual happiness, that you should cherish a cordial, habitual and immoveable attachment to it ; accustoming yourselves
to think and speak of it as the palladium of your political safety
and prosperity, watching for its preservation with jealous anxiety, discountenancing whatever may suggest even a suspicion
that it can, in any event be abandoned, and indignantly frown-
ing upon the first dawning of every attempt to alienate any portion of our country from the rest, or to enfeeble the sacred ties
which now link together the various parts."

Resolved, That the Governor be requested to transmit a copy
of the above Resolutions to the President of the United States,
to the Executives of the several States, and to each of our Senators and Representatives in Congress.

By order,

G. G. BREWER, *Clerk.*

By the Senate, Feb. 26, 1833.

Read and assented to.

JOS. H. NICHOLSON, *Clerk.*

JOURNAL

OF THE

CONVENTION

OF

THE PEOPLE

OF

SOUTH CAROLINA,

WHICH

ASSEMBLED AT COLUMBIA, ON THE 19TH NOVEMBER, 1832,
AND AGAIN ON THE 11TH MARCH, 1833.

JOURNAL.

MONDAY, November 19, 1832.

PURSUANT to an Act of the Legislature of the State of South Carolina, entitled " An Act to provide for the calling of a Convention of the People of this State," passed on the 26th of October, 1832, the Delegates of the several Election Districts of this State, assembled in the Hall of Representatives, in the Town of Columbia, on this day at twelve o'clock.

On motion of Gen. J. B. EARLE, the Hon. STEPHEN D. MILLER, of Claremont, was called to the Chair, and Mr. A. BURT, of Abbeville, appointed Secretary.

The credentials of the following individuals were then exhibited, and their names enrolled as Members of the Convention.

From Greenville.

B. F. Perry, Thomas P. Brockman, Silas R. Whitten.

From Spartenburg.

John S. Rowland, J. S. Richardson, J. B. O'Neal, James Crook.

From Laurens.

Archibald Young, William Arnold, John S. James, A. Fuller, Robert Long.

From Abbeville.

George M'Duffie, John Lipscomb, John Logan, A. Bowie, Samuel L. Watt, A. Burt.

From York.

Benjamin Chambers, I. A. Campbell, James A. Black, James Moore, John L. Miller.

From Marlborough.
Benjamin Rogers, Nicholas Ware.

From Union.
J. S. Sims, Thomas Ray, A. Lancaster, John Littlejohn, George Douglas.

From Kershaw.
Everard Cureton, Chapman Levy, John Chesnut, C. J. Shannon.

From Chesterfield.
P. Phillips, James R. Ervin, Alfred M. Lowry.

From Darlington.
William H. Cannon, S. B. Wilkins, Robert Ervin.

From Marion.
A. L. Gregg, Thomas Harllee, William Evans.

From Williamsburg.
T. D. Singleton, Sen., William Waties, P. G. Gourdin.

From Clarendon.
John P. Richardson, Richard J. Manning, N. R. Burgess.

From Claremont.
Stephen D. Miller, John B. Miller, James G. Spann, Stephen Lacoste.

From All Saints.
Peter Vaught.

From Prince George, Winyaw.
Philip Tidyman, Allard H. Belin.

From Saint Peter's.
J. Hamilton, Jr., A. J. Lawton, John S. Maner.

From Saint Luke's.
A. Huguenin, T. E. Screven, James Mongin Smith.

From Saint Helena.

R. W. Barnwell, Charles G. Capers.

From Saint James, Goose Creek.

Isaac Bradwell, Jr., G. H. Smith.

From Saint Thomas and Saint Dennis.

Francis D. Quash, John L. Nowell.

From Saint John's, Berkley.

Peter Gailliard, Jr., William Porcher.

From Saint John's, Colleton.

William M. Murray.

From Chester.

R. G. Mills, John Douglas, Thomas B. Woodward, Thomas G. Blewett, William Stringfellow.

From Fairfield.

William Harper, D. H. Means, Edward G. Palmer, John B. McCall, William Smith.

From Richland.

Pierce M. Butler, William C. Clifton, Sterling C. Williamson, Sen., James Adams, John G. Brown.

From Saint Philip's and Saint Michael's.

James Hamilton Sen., Richard B. Baker, Sen., Robert J. Turnbull, S. L. Simons, John Magrath, Charles Parker, Barnard E. Bee, Elias Vanderhorst, Peter J. Shand, Nathaniel Heyward, Robert Y. Hayne, C. J. Colcock, John Ball, John L. Wilson, James Lynah, C. C. Pinckney, Philip Cohen.

From Christ Church.

Jacob Bond I'On, James Anderson.

From Saint James', Santee.

Samuel Cordes.

From Saint Stephen's.

W. Dubose, Theodore L. Gourdin.

From Saint Matthew's.

R. P. McCord, T. J. Goodwyn.

From Saint Andrew's.

Benjamin Adams, John Rivers.

From Saint Paul's.

F. Y. Legare, Thomas W. Boone.

From Saint Bartholomew's.

W. C. Pinckney, F. H. Elmore, Isham Walker.

From Prince William's.

Wm. Williams, Thomas H. Colcock, J. B. Ulmer.

From Orange.

Edmund J. Felder, Donald Rowe.

From Barnwell.

Jennings O'Bannon, Stephen Smith, L. M. Ayer, J. G. Brown.

From Lexington.

West Caughman, Jacob H. King, Edwin J. Scott.

From Edgefield.

James Spann, John Key, John Bauskett, Abner Whatley, John S. Jeter, R. G. Mays, F. H. Wardlaw.

From Pendleton.

R. Anderson, Thomas Harrison, J. B. Earle, Thomas Pinckney, J. T. Whitefield, Francis Burt, Jr., F. W. Symmes, Bailey Barton.

From Newberry.

Job Johnston, George W. Glenn, John Counts, John K. Griffin, John Hatton.

From Lancaster.

Samuel R. Gibson.

On motion of Judge Harper, the Convention now proceeded to the election of a President. Colonels Pinckney, of Pendleton, and Butler, of Richland, and Mr. Black, of York, having been appointed a Committee to count the votes, reported that His Excellency James Hamilton, Jr., Governor and Commander in Chief in and over the State, has been duly elected President of the Convention.

On motion of Judge Harper, a Committee was appointed to inform Governor Hamilton of his election, and to conduct him to the chair. The Committee consisted of the Hon. Robert Y. Hayne, the Hon. George McDuffie, and the Hon. R. W. Barnwell. The President, in a short address, returned his grateful acknowledgments for the honor conferred, and entered upon the duties of his station.

Col. Butler now moved that the Convention should go into the election of a Clerk, which being agreed to, Judge Colcock nominated Mr. Isaac W. Hayne. Messrs. Elmore, Cohen, and Barton, were appointed a Committee to count the votes.

While the Committee had retired, Judge Harper moved that the Messenger and Door Keeper of the House of Representatives, should be appointed Messenger and Door Keeper of the Convention, which was agreed to ; and on motion of the Hon. John L. Wilson, Mr. A. S. Johnston was appointed Printer.

Col. Elmore, on the part of the Committee appointed to count the votes for Clerk, now reported Isaac W. Hayne, Esq., duly elected Clerk of the Convention.

On motion of Col. I'On, a Committee was appointed to draft and report rules for the regulation of the Convention during its further session. The Committee consisted of Col. I'On, Col. Thomas Pinckney, and the Hon. J. B. O'Neal.

On motion of Judge Colcock, it was ordered that Clergymen should be invited to open the proceedings of each day with prayer.

Judge Colcock, then introduced the following Resolution :

" *Resolved*, That the Act ' to provide for the calling of a Convention of the People of this State,' be referred to a Select Committee, to consist of twenty-one members, and to be nominated by the President, with instructions to consider and report thereon, and especially as to the measures proper to be adopted by this Convention, in reference to 'the violations of the Constitution of the United States, in the enactment by Congress, on divers occasions, of laws laying duties and imposts for the purpose of encouraging and protecting domestic manufactures, and for other unwarrantable purposes.' "

This Resolution having been considered and adopted, Gen. Hayne moved that the Convention stand adjourned until 10 o'clock to-morrow, in order that time might be allowed the President for the selection of the Committee, which being agreed to, the Convention adjourned accordingly.

ISAAC W. HAYNE,
Clerk of the Convention.

TUESDAY, November 20, 1832.

The Convention met according to adjournment. After a prayer from the Rev. Mr. Ray, the Journal of the proceedings of the day previous was read. The following gentlemen then appeared and enrolled their names as members of the Convention : Henry Middleton, from Greenville, Minor Clinton, from Lancaster, M. Jacobs, from St. Helena.

Col. I'On, on the part of the Committee to draft Rules for the regulation of the Convention, then made the following Report, to wit :

RULES FOR THE CONVENTION.

The Committee appointed to draft Rules for the government of the Convention in its deliberations, beg leave to submit the following :

1. The President and one hundred and twelve members shall be a quorum to transact business.

2. If any member shall break the Convention, or absent himself without leave, he shall be sent for at his own expense, and be subject to the censure of the Convention.

3. No member shall speak more than twice to the same point, without leave of the Convention.

4. Each member, when speaking, shall address himself to the chair, standing, and uncovered, at his place.

5. If two members rise to speak nearly at the same time, the President shall decide which was first up.

6. Every member, when speaking, shall adhere to the point before the Convention, and shall not be interrupted unless he departs from it, when he may be called to order.

7. When a question of order arises, it shall be determined by the President in the first instance, but any member may appeal from his determination, to the Convention.

8. When a motion is made and seconded, it shall, if required by a member, be reduced to writing, and delivered in at the table.

9. When a question is put by the President, and the Convention divides, the Clerk shall, at the request of any seven members present, take down and enter on the Journals, the names of all those members who vote for and against the question, and have them published and printed in any Gazette of the State.

10. When the President desires to be heard, the members shall take their seats, and keep order whilst he is speaking.

11. When a motion is made for adjournment, and seconded, no question shall be debated until the Convention have decided on that motion.

J. B. I'ON,
Chairman of the Committee.

The Report having been adopted, Col. I'On moved that two hundred and fifty copies should be printed for the use of the members, which was agreed to.

Joseph L. Stephens and Alfred Huger appeared, and enrolled their names as Delegates from St. John's, Colleton, and Spartanburg.

The President, under the Resolution of the day previous, now appointed the following gentlemen to constitute the Select Committee of twenty-one, to consider and report upon the Act of the Legislature, entitled " An Act to provide for the calling of a Convention of the People of this State," to wit :

Hon. Charles J. Colcock,

Gen. J. B. Earle,	Hon. Robert Y. Hayne,
Hon. J. B. O'Neal,	Hon. S. D. Miller,
Col. W. C. Pinckney,	Hon. Geo. McDuffie,
Chancellor Johnston,	R. J. Turnbull, Esq.,
Hon. J. K. Griffin,	Hon. R. W. Barnwell,
Benjamin Rogers, Esq.,	J. R. Ervin, Esq.,
Col. J. Bond I'On,	Col. P. M. Butler,
T. D. Singleton, Esq.,	Col. John Bauskett,
James A. Black, Esq.,	Hon. R. J. Manning,
Hon. William Harper,	Hon. Henry Middleton.

J. A. Keith, of Prince George, Winyaw, appeared, and enrolled his name.

On motion of Judge Colcock. the Convention then adjourned until one o'clock to-morrow.

ISAAC W. HAYNE,
Clerk of the Convention.

WEDNESDAY, November 21, 1832.

The Convention met according to adjournment, and the proceedings were opened with a prayer from the Rev. Mr. Ray.

The roll being called, the following gentlemen answered to their names, viz :—B. Adams, James Adams, Ayer, J. Anderson, Robert Anderson, Arnold, Baker, Ball, Bee, Boone, Barnwell, Bradwell, Blewett, Butler, J. G. Brown, *Richland*, J. G. Brown, *Barnwell*, Bauskett, A. Burt, Francis Burt, Jr., Barton, Brockman, Bowie, Burgess, Belin, Cohen, Cordes, Thomas H. Colcock, Capers, Clifton, Caughman, Counts, Crooke, Chambers, Campbell, Cureton, Chesnut, Cannon, Clinton, Dubose, Dawson, John Douglas, George Douglas, Elmore, Earle, James R. Ervin, Robert Ervin, William Evans, Felder, Fuller, T. L. Gourdin, P. G.

Gourdin, Goodwyn, Gailliard, Griffin, Glenn, Gibson, J. Hamilton, Sen., Heyward, Harper, Hatton, Harllee, Huguenin, Alfred Huger, l'On, Jeter, Johnston, James, Jacobs, Keith, Key, Levy, Lowry, Lacoste, Lynah, Legare, Lawton, Long, Lipscomb, Logan, Littlejohn, Lancaster, Magrath, Manning, Maner, Murray, Mills, Means, Moore, John L. Miller, Stephen D. Miller, John B. Miller, McCord, Middleton, Nowell, O'Neale, O'Bannon, P. Phillips, Parker, Porcher, Palmer, Perry, C. C. Pinckney, Thomas Pinckney, Quash, John P. Richardson, Rivers, Rowe, Rowland, Rogers, Ray, James G. Spann, James Spann, Simons, Shand, James M. Smith, G. H. Smith, William Smith, Stephen Smith, Stringfellow, Scott, Symmes, Sims, Shannon, Singleton, Stevens, Screven, Turnbull, Tyler, Tidyman, Ulmer, Vaught, Vanderhorst, Wilson, Walker, Williams, Woodward, Williamson, Wardlaw, Whatley, Whitefield, Whitten, Watt, Waties, Wilkins, Ware, Warren, Young.

The Journal of the day previous having been read, this was announced by the President as the proper time for presenting Reports from Committees.

Gen. J. B. Earle, of the Select Committee, to which was referred the consideration of the Act of the Legislature, providing for the call of a Convention, in the absence of the Chairman, stated, on the part of the Committee, that they had not found it practicable to prepare a Report for to-day, and moved that further time should be allowed them; which was agreed to.

Mr. A. M. Lowry, from Chesterfield, then introduced the following Resolution, viz:

" *Resolved*, That the tenth section of the first article of the Constitution of this State, be altered and made to read as follows:

" Senators and Members of the House of Representatives, shall be chosen on the second Monday in October next, and on the same days in every year thereafter, in such manner, and at such time as are herein directed. And shall meet on the fourth Monday in November, annually, at Columbia, (which shall remain the seat of Government until otherwise determined by the concurrence of two-thirds of both branches of the whole Representation,) unless the casualties of war, or contagious disorders should render it unsafe to meet there; in either of which cases, the Governor or Commander in Chief for the time being, may, by Proclamation, appoint a more secure and convenient place of meeting."

The question of consideration being put by the President, the Convention refused to consider this Resolution.

Benjamin A. Markley, from St. Philip's and St. Michael's, and J. Walter Philips, from All Saints, appeared and enrolled their names as members of the Convention. The Convention then adjourned until to-morrow at one o'clock.

ISAAC W. HAYNE,

Clerk of the Convention.

====

THURSDAY, November, 22, 1832.

The Convention met according to adjournment, and the proceedings were opened with a prayer by the Rev. Mr. Ware.

The roll being called, the following gentlemen answered to their names, viz :—B. Adams, James Adams, Ayer, J. Anderson, Robert Anderson, Arnold, Baker, Ball, Bee, Boone, Barnwell, Bradwell, Blewett, Butler, J. G. Brown, *Richland*, J. G. Brown, *Barnwell*, Bauskett, A. Burt, Francis Burt, Barton, Brockman, Bowie, Black, Burgess, Belin, Cohen, Cordes, Thomas H. Colcock, C. J. Colcock, Capers, Clifton, Caughman, Counts, Crooke, Chambers, Campbell, Cureton, Chesnut, Cannon, Clinton, Dubose, Dawson, John Douglas, Geo. Douglas, Elmore, Earle, James R. Ervin, Robert Ervin, Wm. Evans, Felder, Fuller, T. L. Gourdin, P. G. Gourdin, Goodwyn, Gailliard, Griffin, Glenn, Gibson, Gregg, James Hamilton, Sen., Hayne, Heyward, Harper, Harrison, Hatton, Harllee, Huguenin, Alfred Huger, I'On, Jeter, Johnston, James, Jacobs, Keith, Key, King, Levy, Lowry, Lacoste, Legare, Lawton, Long, Lipscomb, Logan, Littlejohn, Lancaster, Magrath, Markley, Manning, Maner, Murray, Mills, McCall, Means, Mays, Moore, J. L. Miller, S. D. Miller, John B. Miller, McCord, Nowell, O'Neale, O'Bannon, P. Phillips, J. W. Phillips, Parker, Porcher, Palmer, Perry, C. C. Pinckney, W. C. Pinckney, Thomas Pinckney, Quash, J. P. Richardson, J. S. Richardson, Rivers, Rowe, Rowland, Rogers, Ray, J. G. Spann, James Spann, Simons, Shand, J. M. Smith, G. H. Smith, Wm. Smith, Stephen Smith, Stringfellow, Scott, Symmes, Sims, Shannon, Singleton, Stevens, Screven, Turnbull, Tyler, Tidyman, Ulmer, Vaught, Vanderhorst, Wilson, Walker, Williams, Woodward, Whitefield, Whitten, Watt, Waties, Wilkins, Ware, Whatley, Young.

The Journal of the day previous having been read, Samuel Warren, from St. James, Santee, and D. E. Huger, from Kingston, appeared and enrolled their names as members of the Convention.

Judge Colcock, from the Select Committee of twenty-one, informed the Convention that the Committee was ready to report, and moved that the reading of the Report should be dispensed with, and that it should lie on the table, and be ordered to be printed. Judge O'Neal moved to amend this motion, so as to make this Report the order of the day for Saturday. To this Judge Colcock objected, and obtained leave to withdraw his motion, upon which Judge O'Neal withdrew his amendment. Judge Colcock then called to his assistance Gen. Hayne, one of the Committee, by whom the Report was read to the Convention. An Ordinance, accompanying the Report, was then read by the Chairman.

At the motion of Col. Barnwell, the Report and Ordinance were ordered to lie on the table, be printed, and made the order of the day for to-morrow.

Mr. Wilson moved to amend this motion, by specifying the number of copies to be printed, and proposed five thousand, which Col. Pinckney, of St. Bartholomew's, moved to amend, by inserting ten thousand instead of five ; but on the suggestion of Judge Harper, that it would be best to defer the printing of a larger number of copies than were needed for the use of the Convention, until the Report should be finally adopted, the amendments were withdrawn.

The following Resolution was then introduced by the Hon. Henry Middleton, a Delegate from Greenville, to wit :

" *Whereas*, the Sovereignty of the State of South Carolina, resides in the aggregate body of freemen, inhabiting the territory; and, consequently, all just legislation can be alone founded upon the collective will of a majority of that body. *And, whereas,* the supreme will of this body of freemen can only be collected either by an actual vote of the majority taken in primary assemblies, or by the election of Delegates, chosen in numbers, proportionate to the number of free white men, in each District and Parish of the State, so as to constitute an equal and adequate representation of the people thereof. *And, whereas,* the Convention now actually here assembled, under the recommendation of the Legislature, is apportioned on a compound ratio of population and of property, which may be, and probably is, an equitable apportionment for the purposes of taxation and municipal regulations; but is by no means adequate or competent, to the exercise of the highest attributes of sovereignty, by reason of the want of a full and equal representation of the people, a defect which cannot be remedied by any enactment of the Legislature. *And, whereas,* any act amounting to an exercise of sovereignty, on the part of the portion of the people, here convened at this time, might be considered as a manifest and palpable usurpation of power, possessed alone by the whole people ; therefore,

" *Resolved,* That this Convention, deeming itself incompetent, for the reasons above assigned, to wield the sovereign authority of the people it unequally represents, doth remand to the Legislature, the high matters referred, by the Act of the 25th October last, with a recommendation to the said Legislature, that they reconsider, at their next stated meeting, the whole question ; and if, according to the constitutional provision, two-thirds of both branches shall agree so to do, then, and in that case to recommit the said subject matter to a Convention, wherein the representation of the people shall be full and complete, and which will be thereby competent to determine such questions of sovereign right, as they may see fit to consider as affecting the interest of the State of South Carolina, her dignity and honor."

The Hon. George M'Duffie moved the question of consideration. Judge Huger requested the withdrawal of the motion, that the Resolution might be freely discussed ; but the question being insisted on, and put by the President, the Convention refused to consider the Resolution.

Col. Anderson, of Pendleton, submitted to the Convention a Memorial from sundry citizens of Pendleton District, praying that the Constitution might be so amended as to make two Election Districts of the two Judicial Districts into which Pendleton is divided. The question of consideration being moved by Judge Harper, the Convention refused to consider the Memorial.

On motion of Gen. Hayne, it was then ordered that the Select Committee of twenty-one have leave to sit again, and the Convention adjourned until twelve o'clock to-morrow.

ISAAC W. HAYNE,
Clerk of the Convention.

———

FRIDAY, November 23, 1832.

The Convention met according to adjournment; and after a prayer from the Rev. Mr. Goulding, the roll was called, and the following gentlemen answered to their names, viz:—B. Adams, James Adams, Ayer, James Anderson, R. Anderson, Arnold, Baker, Ball, Bee, Boone, Bradwell, Blewett, Butler, J. G. Brown, *Richland*, J. G. Brown, *Barnwell*, Bauskett, A. Burt, Francis Burt, Jr., Barton, Brockman, Bowie, Black, Burgess, Cohen, Cordes, T. H. Colcock, C. J. Colcock, Capers, Clifton, Caughman, Counts, Crooke, Chambers, Campbell, Cureton, Chesnut, Cannon, Clinton, Dubose, Dawson, John Douglas, Geo. Douglas, Elmore, Earle, J. R. Ervin, Robert Ervin, Wm. Evans, Felder, Fuller, T. L. Gourdin, P. G. Gourdin, Goodwyn, Gailliard, Griffin, Glenn, Gibson, Gregg, J. Hamilton, Sen., Hayne, Heyward, Harper, Harrison, Hatton, Harllee, Huguenin, Alfred Huger, I'On, Jeter, Johnston, James, Jacobs, Keith, Key, King, Levy, Lowry, Lacoste, Legare, Lawton, Long, Lipscomb, Logan, Littlejohn, Lancaster, Magrath, Manning, Maner, Murray, Mills, McCall, Means, Mays, Moore, J. L. Miller, S. D. Miller,

John B. Miller, McCord, Nowell, O'Neale, O'Bannon, P. Phillips, J. W. Phillips, Parker, Porcher, Palmer, Perry, C. C. Pinckney, Wm. C. Pinckney, Thomas Pinckney, Quash, J. P. Richardson, J. S. Richardson, Rivers, Rowe, Rowland, Rogers, Ray, J. G. Spann, James Spann, Simons, Shand, J. M. Smith, G. H. Smith, Wm. Smith, Stephen Smith, Stringfellow, Scott, Symmes, Sims, Shannon, Singleton, Stevens, Screven, Turnbull, Tyler, Tidyman, Ulmer, Vanderhorst, Wilson Walker, Williams, Woodward, Williamson, Wardlaw, Whatley, Whitten, Watt, Waties, Wilkins, Ware, Warren, Young.

The Journal of the previous day having been read, the Hon. R. W. Barnwell, offered the following Resolution, which was agreed to, viz:

"*Resolved*, That the President of the Senate, and Speaker of the House of Representatives, be invited to take seats upon the floor in the Chamber in which the Convention is now assembled."

Judge Colcock, from the Committee of twenty-one, made a further Report to the Convention, consisting of an Address to the People of the State, which having been read by Robert J. Turnbull, Esq., on motion of Judge Colcock, it was ordered to lie on the table and to be printed.

Mr. Samuel R. Gibson, a Delegate from Lancaster, presented a Memorial from a portion of the citizens of that District, praying an alteration of the Constitution as to the basis of representation in the State Legislature.

Mr. S. D. Miller moved that the Memorial be laid on the table.

Mr. McDuffie moved the question of consideration.

The President deciding the first motion to be first in order, the question was taken, and the Memorial ordered to be laid on the table.

The Hon. J. L. Wilson then introduced the following Resolution, viz:

"*Whereas*, the Convention of the People of the State of South Carolina, having learned with deep and unfeigned regret, the death of Charles Carroll, of Carrollton, the last surviving signer of the Declaration of Independence, and lately the only living link that connected us with that important event—as a testimony of respect to the memory of the deceased,

" *Resolved*, That the members of this Convention wear crape on the left arm, for the space of thirty days."

This Resolution having been adopted by the unanimous vote of the Convention, it was ordered to be so entered on the Journal of the proceedings.

The Ordinance, which was made the order of the day, was now taken up for consideration. The Ordinance having been read by the Clerk, Col. Wilson moved that it should be read again, clause by clause; but at the suggestion of Judge Colcock, that further time for consideration was desirable, the motion was withdrawn.

Judge Colcock then moved that the consideration of the Ordinance should be made the order of the day for to-morrow, and that the Convention should stand adjourned until 11 o'clock on that day, which being agreed to, the Convention adjourned accordingly.

ISAAC W. HAYNE,
Clerk of the Convention.

———

SATURDAY, November 24, 1832.

The Convention met according to adjournment, and the proceedings were opened with a prayer by the Rev. Mr. Freeman.

A Parchment Roll was then exhibited, on which, at the President's request, the members enrolled their names, with the respective Election Districts which had delegated them, which was ordered to be deposited with the Records of the Convention. The following gentlemen were found to be present :

From Greenville.

B. F. Perry, Thomas P. Brockman, Silas R. Whitten, Henry Middleton.

From Spartanburg.

John S. Rowland, J. S. Richardson, J. B. O'Neal, James Crooke, Alfred Huger, J. P. Evans.

From Laurens.

Archibald Young, William Arnold, John S. James, A. Fuller, Robert Long.

From Abbeville.

George M'Duffie, John Lipscomb, John Logan, A. Bowie, Samuel L. Watt, A. Burt.

From York.

Benjamin Chambers, I. A. Campbell, James A. Black, James Moore, John L. Miller.

From Marlborough.

Benjamin Rogers, Nicholas Ware.

From Union.

J. S. Sims, Thomas Ray, A. Lancaster, John Littlejohn, George Douglas.

From Kershaw.

Everard Cureton, Chapman Levy, John Chesnut, C. J. Shannon.

From Chesterfield.

P. Phillips, James R. Ervin, Alfred M. Lowry.

From Darlington.

William H. Cannon, S. B. Wilkins, Robert Ervin.

From Marion.

A. L. Gregg, Thomas Harllee, William Evans.

From Williamsburg.

T. D. Singleton, Sr., William Waties, P. G. Gourdin.

From Clarendon.

John P. Richardson, Richard J. Manning, W. R. Burgess.

From Claremont.

Stephen D. Miller, John B. Miller, James G. Spann, Stephen Lacoste.

From All Saints.

Peter Vaught, J. Walter Phillips.

From Prince George, Winyaw.

Philip Tidyman, Allard H. Belin, J. A. Keith.

From Saint Peter's.

J. Hamilton, Jr., A. J. Lawton, John S. Maner.

From Saint Luke's.

A. Huguenin, T. E. Screven, James Mongin Smith.

From Saint Helena.

R. W. Barnwell, Charles G. Capers, M. Jacobs.

From Saint James, Goose Creek.

Isaac Bradwell, Jr., G. H. Smith.

From Saint Thomas and Saint Dennis.

Francis D. Quash, John L. Nowell.

From Saint John's, Berkley.

Peter Gailliard, Jr., William Porcher, J. H. Dawson.

From Saint John's, Colleton.

William M. Murray, Joseph L. Stevens.

From Chester.

R. G. Mills, John Douglas, Thomas B. Woodward, Thomas G. Blewett, William Stringfellow.

From Fairfield.

William Harper, D. H. Means, Edward G. Palmer, John B. McCall, William Smith.

From Richland.

Pierce M. Butler, William C. Clifton, Sterling C. Williamson, Senr., James Adams, John G. Brown.

From Saint Philip's and Saint Michael's.

James Hamilton Senr., Richard B. Baker, Senr., Robert J. Turnbull, S. L. Simons, John Magrath, Charles Parker, Barnard E. Bee, Elias Vanderhorst, Peter J. Shand, Nathaniel Heyward, Robert Y. Hayne, C. J. Colcock, John Ball, John L. Wilson, James Lynah, C. C. Pinckney, Philip Cohen, B. A. Markley.

From Christ Church.

Jacob Bond I'On, James Anderson.

From Saint James's, Santee.

Samuel Cordes, Samuel Warren.

From Saint Stephen's.

W. Dubose, Theodore L. Gourdin.

From Saint Matthew's.

R. P. McCord, T. J. Goodwyn.

From Saint Andrew's.

Benjamin Adams, John Rivers.

From Saint Paul's.

F. Y. Legare, Thomas W. Boone.

From Saint Bartholomew's.

W. C. Pinckney, F. H. Elmore, Isham Walker.

From Prince William's.

Wm. Williams, Thomas H. Colcock, J. B. Ulmer.

From Orange.

Edmund J. Felder, Donald Rowe, Elisha Tyler.

From Barnwell.

Jennings O'Bannon, Stephen Smith, L. M. Ayer, J. G. Brown.

From Lexington.

West Caughman, Jacob H. King, Edwin J. Scott.

From Edgefield.

James Spann, John Key, John Bauskett, Abner Whatley, John S. Jeter, R. G. Mays, F. H. Wardlaw.

From Pendleton.

R. Anderson, Thomas Harrison, J. B. Earle, Thomas Pinckney, J. T. Whitefield, Francis Burt, Jr., F. W. Symmes, Bailey Barton.

From Newberry.

Job Johnston, George W. Glenn, John Counts, John K. Griffin, John Hatton.

From Lancaster.

Samuel R. Gibson, Miner Clinton.

From Kingston.

D. E. Huger.

The Journal of the day previous having been read, on motion of Chancellor Johnston, a correction of the Journal was ordered, and made accordingly.

Judge Colcock, on the part of the Select Committee of twenty-one, announced that the Committee were ready with a further Report, consisting of an Address to the People of the United States. This Address having been read by the Hon. George McDuffie, was, on motion of Mr. Turnbull, adopted by the Convention.

The Ordinance which had been made the special order of the day, was now taken up for consideration. Having been read by the Clerk, Judge Colcock moved so to amend it as to exempt the members of the Legislature from the oath required of the civil and military officers of the State, which amendment was adopted.

Mr. Turnbull moved to amend the title of the Ordinance, by

striking out the words " provide for arresting the operation of," and substituting the word " Nullify," so that when amended it should read, " An Ordinance to Nullify certain Acts of the Congress," &c. This amendment was likewise adopted.

The question was then taken on the adoption of the Ordinance thus amended. Seven members having risen for the Ayes and Noes, they were taken accordingly, and found to be as follows :

AYES—B. Adams, James Adams, Ayer, James Anderson, Robert Anderson, Arnold, Baker, Ball, Bee, Boone, Barnwell, Bradwell, Blewett, Butler, J. G. Brown, John G. Brown, Bauskett, A. Burt, F. Burt, Barton, Bowie, Black, Belin, Cohen, Cordes, T. H. Colcock, C. J. Colcock, Capers, Clifton, Caughman, Counts, Chambers, Campbell, Dubose, Dawson, J. Douglas, G. Douglas, Elmore, Earle, W. Evans, Felder, Fuller, T. L. Gourdin, P. G. Gourdin, Goodwyn, Gailliard, Griffin, Glenn, Gregg, J. Hamilton, Sen., Heyward, Hayne, Harper, Harrison, Hatton, Harllee, Huguenin, l'On, Jeter, Johnston, James, Jacobs, Keith, Key, King, Lacoste, Legare, Lawton, Long, Lipscomb, Logan, Littlejohn, Lancaster, Magrath, Markley, Maner, Murray, Mills, McCall, Means, Mays, McDuffie, Moore, J. L. Miller, S. D. Miller, J. B. Miller, McCord, Nowell, O'Bannon, J. W. Phillips, Parker, Porcher, Palmer, C. C. Pinckney, W. C. Pinckney, T. Pinckney, Quash, Rivers, Rowe, Rogers, Ray, J. G. Spann, J. Spann, Simons, Shand, J. M. Smith, W. Smith, S. Smith, G. H. Smith, Stringfellow, Scott, Symmes, Sims, Singleton, Stevens, Screven, Turnbull, Tyler, Tidyman, Ulmer, Vaught, Vanderhorst, Wilson, Walker, Williams, Woodward, Williamson, Wardlaw, Whatley, Whitefield, Watt, Ware, Waties, Warren, and Young.

His Excellency James Hamilton, Jr., President of the Convention, claimed his privilege of voting as a Delegate from St. Peter's, and gave it in the affirmative, making, in all, one hundred and thirty-six—Ayes.

NOES—Brockman, Burgess, Crooke, Cureton, Chestnut, Cannon, Clinton, J. R. Ervin, R. Ervin, J. P. Evans, Gibson, Alfred Huger, D. E. Huger, Levy, Lowry, Manning, Middleton, O'Neale, P. Phillips, Perry, John P. Richardson, J. S. Richardson, Rowland, Shannon, Whitten, and Wilkins.—Making, in all, twenty-six—Noes.

One member absent from sickness—five not yet enrolled.

The Ordinance was consequently adopted, by a majority of the members present of 109, and a majority of 103 of the whole number of Delegates elected by the people.

On motion of Mr. M'Duffie, the Report accompanying the Ordinance was taken up for consideration, and the reading being dispensed with, was adopted by the Convention.

Mr. M'Duffie then moved the consideration of the Address to the People of this State, reported by the Select Committee of twenty-one, which being agreed to, and the reading being dispensed with, the Address was adopted by the Convention.

On motion of Chancellor Johnston, a reconsideration of the Address was granted.

Mr. Turnbull then moved to amend the Address, by striking out in the 19th paragraph, the words " with a full confidence that other divisions of the Confederacy will nobly follow and sustain us." He explained, that the State wished to be understood, notwithstanding her hopes that she would be sustained by other members of the Confederacy, as relying not on them, but on herself alone. The amendment was agreed to without opposition, and the Address so amended, adopted by the Convention.

Col. W. C. Pinckney, of St. Bartholomew's, introduced the following Resolution, which was concurred in by the Convention, to wit :

" *Resolved*, That twenty thousand copies of the Report, the Addresses, and the Ordinance, (as adopted) be printed ; and that for each of the members of the Convention, thirty copies in separate sheets, shall be immediately printed—that ten thousand copies, with the Ordinance annexed to the Report, in pamphlet form, be separately printed for distribution ; and that the remaining five thousand be bound up with the proceedings of the Convention, the whole of which shall be published under the direction of a Committee to be appointed by the President, for that purpose ;—that the documents thus ordered to be printed, be distributed under the direction of the President. And it shall be the duty of the Clerk, under the direction of the Committee, to assist in superintending the printing, and to make such distribution as the President shall direct.—That he carry on the necessary correspondence, and cause a record of all the proceedings of the Convention to be made, and deposited in the Secretary of State's Office, in Columbia ; and to perform such other duties in reference to the business of the Convention, as may be prescribed by the President; and that during his continuance in office, he shall receive the same compensation as the Clerk of the House of Representatives."

Judge Harper, of Fairfield, and Cols. Brown and Clifton, of Richland, were appointed a Committee under this Resolution.

On motion of the Hon. John Lynde Wilson, a Committee was appointed to engross the Ordinance as adopted, and to superintend its signature, by such members as might wish to affix their names to it.

Messrs. Wilson and C. C. Pinckney, were appointed the Committee.

Col. Wilson then moved a recess until 5 o'clock, P. M., that the Engrossing Committee might have time to perform that service. The motion was carried, and the Convention adjourned accordingly.

ISAAC W. HAYNE,

Clerk of the Convention.

SATURDAY, November 24—5 o'clock, P. M.

The Convention met according to adjournment. The Journal of the morning's proceedings having been read, Mr. Wilson, on the part of the Engrossing Committee, made the following Report to wit :

" The Engrossing Committee, to whom was confided the care of the Ordinance of this Convention, for engrossing and enrolment, have performed that duty, and caused the great Seal of the State to be attached thereto.

"Your Committee have so engrossed the Ordinance, as to

admit the signatures of all the members of the Convention, a ratification observed by those who proclaimed our Independence. Your Committee suggest the propriety of submitting to the Patriots of '76, yet abiding with us, and laboring in one common cause, for the continuance of our liberties, the first lines for their signatures."

JOHN L. WILSON, Chairman.

This Report was was unanimously adopted.

The Report of the Select Committee accompanying the Ordinance, as adopted by the Convention, and the Ordinance, as finally ratified, are as follows, to wit:

[For the Report and Ordinance, see pages 1 and 28.]

Of the signatures to the Ordinance, the seven first, are according to the Resolution, the signatures of those Delegates who bore arms in the war of the Revolution. The signatures of the other Delegates approving, were taken alphabetically, with the exception of R. Barnwell Smith, Esq., who, though prevented by sickness from taking his seat in the Convention, was, by a Resolution of the Convention, permitted to sign the Ordinance, and record his approval of the proceedings.

The Address to the People of the State, read by Robert J. Turnbull, Esq., as adopted by the Convention, is as follows, to wit:

[For the Address, see p. 37.]

The Address to the People of the United States, as read by the Hon. George McDuffie, and adopted by the Convention, is as follows, to wit:

[For the Address, see page 59.]

The Report and Ordinance, with the two Addresses, as given above, having been adopted by the Convention, the Convention then, on motion of Dr. Tidyman, went into a Committee of the whole, Col. I'On being called to the Chair. Dr. Tidyman offered the following Resolution:

" *Resolved,* That the thanks of the members of this Convention be given to the President, for the very able, dignified and impartial manner with which he has presided over their deliberations, and for the zeal and fidelity with which he has disdischarged the duties of his office."

The Resolution having been unanimously adopted, the Committee rose, and reported it to the Convention, as so adopted.

Gen. Hayne then offered the following Resolution, which was adopted by the Convention, to wit :

" *Resolved,* That copies of the Ordinance just adopted by this Convention, with the Report thereon, and the Addresses to the People of the several States, and of this State, be transmitted, by the Governor, to the President of the United States, to be, by him, submitted to Congress ; and also to the Governors of the several States, for the information of their respective Legislatures."

Judge Harper offered the following Resolution, to wit :

" *Resolved,* That when this Convention adjourns, it shall adjourn to meet at this place, at such time as the President shall appoint, who is authorized, if in his opinion the public exigencies shall require, by notice under his hand, duly published, to assemble the Convention at any time before the 12th of November next ; and that he appoint a Committee, a majority of whom, or the survivors or survivor of such majority, in case of the death or disqualification of the President, shall have like authority to assemble the Convention, and appoint a time for its meeting."

This Resolution was adopted, and the Hon. William Harper, of Fairfield, the Hon. Robert Y. Hayne, of Charleston, and Messrs. Benjamin Rodgers, of Marlborough, Thomas Harrison, of Pendleton, and John S. Maner, of Saint Peter's, were appointed the Committee.

On motion of Chancellor Johnston, the following Resolution was adopted, to wit :

" *Resolved,* That the President be authorized to draw his warrant or warrants on the Treasury, for the contingent expenses of this Convention."

Mr. Turnbull moved the following, which was likewise adopted, to wit :

" *Resolved,* That the President of this Convention be requested to transmit to the Legislature, a copy of the Ordinance just passed by this Convention, together with copies also of the Report of the Committee of twenty-one, and of the Addresses to the People of this State, and the People of the United States."

Chancellor Johnston offered the following Resolution, which was concurred in by the Convention, to wit :

" *Resolved,* That any Delegate shall be at liberty hereafter to sign the Ordinance adopted by the Convention, and record his approbation of the proceedings thereof."

The Hon. Robert W. Barnwell then moved the following, to wit :

Whereas, It is the duty of a people at all times to acknowledge their dependence upon God, and more especially to commit themselves to his keeping, when they have adopted measures of deep import to their future welfare and security."

" *Be it resolved,* That we, the Delegates of South Carolina, assembled in Convention, do recommend to our fellow citizens of the State, to observe Thursday, the 31st day of January, 1833, as a day of solemn fasting, humiliation and prayer, imploring the Almighty to bestow his blessing upon the proceedings of this body, that they may eventuate in the promotion of his glory, and in restoring and perpetuating the liberty and prosperity of our native State."

This Resolution was unanimously adopted, and ordered to be so entered on the Journal of the Convention.

The President then rose and asked, " Has any member any further proposal to bring before this Convention ?"

None being offered, the President held up the Ordinance, and said, " I do announce that this Ordinance has been adopted and ratified by the good people of the State of South Carolina, assembled in their highest sovereign capacity."

The President then addressed the Convention, in a short

speech. In concluding it, he requested the Rev. Mr. Ware to ask the Divine blessing upon the proceedings of the Assembly.

After prayer by that reverend gentleman, Col. I'On moved an adjournment.

The motion was carried. Whereupon the President pronounced the Convention adjourned, until it should be again assembled according to the provisions of Judge Harper's Resolution.

ISAAC WILLIAM HAYNE,
Clerk of the Convention.

SECOND SESSION.

MONDAY, March 11, 1833.

PURSUANT to a Proclamation of the President of the Convention, issued on the 13th day of February, one thousand eight hundred and thirty-three, the Convention of the people of South Carolina re-assembled in the Hall of the House of Representatives, in the Town of Columbia, on this day, at meridian.

The proceedings were opened by a prayer from the Rev. Mr. Ware; after which the roll was called, and the following members answered to their names, viz:—James Adams, Ayer, J. Anderson, Robert Anderson, Arnold, Baker, Ball, Bee, Boone, Blewett, Butler, J. G. Brown, *Richland*, J. G. Brown, *Barnwell*, Bauskett, F. Burt, Black, Belin, Cohen, Cordes, Thos. H. Colcock, C. J. Colcock, Capers, Clifton, Caughman, Counts, Crooke, Chambers, Campbell, Cureton, Chesnut, Clinton, Dubose, Dawson, John Douglas, George Douglas, Elmore, Earle, J. R. Ervin, William Evans, J. P. Evans, Felder, T. L. Gourdin, P. G. Gourdin, Goodwyn, Gailliard, Griffin, Glenn, Gibson, Gregg, Hayne, Heyward, Harper, Harrison, Hatton, Harllee, Huguenin, I'On, Jeter, Johnston, James, Keith, Key, King, Levy, Lowry, Lacoste, Legare, Lawton, Long, Logan, Littlejohn, Lancaster, Magrath, Maner, Murray, Mills, McCall, Means, Mays, McDuffie, Moore, J. L. Miller, S. D. Miller, John B. Miller, McCord, Nowell, O'Neale, O'Bannon, P. Phillips, J. W. Phillips, Porcher, Palmer, Perry, C. C. Pinckney, William C. Pinckney, Thomas Pinckney, Quash, Rowland, Rivers, Rowe, Rogers, Ray, J. G. Spann, James Spann, Simons, Shand, J. M. Smith, G. H. Smith, Wm. Smith, Stephen Smith, Stringfellow,

Scott, Symmes, Sims, Shannon, Singleton, Stevens, Turnbull, Tyler, Tidyman, Ulmer, Wilson, Walker, Williams, Woodward, Whitten, Watt, Waties, Wilkins, Ware, Warren, Williamson, Wardlaw, Whatley, Young.

The President then addressed the Convention, explaining to them the objects for which they had been convoked. In concluding, he announced, that as he had been chosen to preside over this body, as Governor of the State, and as another now filled that station, he would, after submitting to the Convention the documents which had induced him to call them together at this time, resign his office into their hands. The following documents were then read by the Clerk, to wit:

[I.]

Letter from the Governor of the State, to the President of the Convention.

EXECUTIVE DEPARTMENT, }
COLUMBIA, March 11, 1833. }

To JAMES HAMILTON, JUN. ESQ.,

President of the Convention of the People of South Carolina.

SIR,—I herewith transmit you a letter which I have received from the Hon. Benjamin Watkins Leigh, Commissioner from the State of Virginia, which, together with the correspondence in relation to Mr. Leigh's Mission, and the Resolutions of Virginia, of which he is the bearer, you are requested to lay before the Assembly over which you preside.

I am very respectfully,

Your obedient servant,

ROBERT Y. HAYNE.

COLUMBIA, March 11th, 1833.

SIR,—

Having, at our first interview, presented you the Resolutions of the General Assembly of Virginia, of the 26th January last, on the subject of Federal Relations, I have now to request your Excellency to lay these Resolutions before the Convention of the People of South Carolina, which, at my instance, has been re-assembled for the purpose of considering them.

The General Assembly of Virginia has expressed, in its own language, its sentiments concerning the unhappy controversy between the State of South Carolina and the Federal Government, and its motives, its views and object, in making this intercession. In these respects, therefore, the Commissioner it has thought proper to depute to South Carolina, can have nothing to add, and nothing even to explain. The duty presented to him is simple and precise. He is instructed to communicate the Preamble and Resolutions to the proper authorities of this State, and " to give them such direction as in his judgment may be best calculated to promote the objects which the Legislature of Virginia has in view ;" and this part of his duty he has already, by the prompt and cordial compliance of those authorities, had the happiness to accomplish, to the entire satisfaction (as he has reason to believe) of the Legislature of Virginia. And he is further instructed and " authorized to express to the public authorities and people of this, our sister State, the sincere good will of the Legislature, and people of Virginia, towards their sister State, and their anxious solicitude that the kind and respectful representations they have addressed to her, may lead to an accommodation of the differences between this State and the General Government."

Virginia is animated with an ardent and devoted attachment to the Union of the States, and to the rights of the several States that compose the Union ; and if similarity of situation and of interests naturally induce her to sympathize, with peculiar sensibility, in whatever affects the prosperity and happiness of South Carolina, and the other Southern States, she knows how

to reconcile this sentiment with her affection and duty towards
each and every other State, severally, and towards the United
States. She is most solicitous to maintain and preserve our
present institutions, which, though they partake of imperfection,
from which no human institutions can ever be exempt, and notwithstanding some instances of mal-administration or error, to
which all governments are liable, are yet, as she confidently believes, the happiest frame of polity that is now or ever has been
enjoyed by any people ;—to maintain and preserve the whole,
and every part of these institutions, in full vigor and purity ; to
uphold the Union, and the States ; to maintain the Federal
Government in all its just powers, administered, according to
the pure principles of the Constitution, without the least depart-
ure from the limitations prescribed by the compact, fairly understood, and the State Governments, in all their rights and authority, as absolutely necessary to the good government and happiness of their respective citizens. Consolidation and disunion
are alike abhorrent from her affections and her judgment—the
one involving, at the least, a forfeiture of the manifold advantages and blessings so long and so generally felt and acknowledged to have been derived from the Union ; and the other having an apparent, perhaps inevitable, tendency to military despotism. And she is apprehensive, for reasons too obvious to
need particular mention, that in case any differences between
the Federal Government and the States, shall ever be brought
to the arbitrament of force, the result, let it be what it may,
must effect such a change in our existing institutions as cannot
but be evil, since it would be a change from those forms of government, which we have experienced to be good, and under
which we have certainly been, in the main, free, prosperous,
contented and happy. Therefore, in the present controversy,
between the Federal Government and the State of South Carolina, she deprecates any resort to force by either, and is sanguine in the hope, that, with proper moderation and forbearance
on both sides, this controversy may be adjusted (as all our controversies hitherto have been) by the influence of truth, reason
and justice.

Virginia, remembering the history of South Carolina, her services in war and in peace, and her contributions of virtue and

intelligence to the common councils of the Union ; and knowing
well the generosity, the magnanimity, and the loyalty of her
character, entertained the most perfect confidence, that these
sentiments, so cherished by herself, would find a response in the
heart and understanding of every citizen of this State. And
that confidence induced her intercession on the present occasion. She has not presumed to dictate, or even to advise. She
has addressed her entreaty to the Congress of the United States,
to redress the grievance of which South Carolina complains.
And she has spoken to South Carolina also, as one sovereign
State, as one State of this Union, ought to speak to another.
She has earnestly, affectionately, and respectfully requested and
entreated South Carolina, " to rescind or suspend her late Ordinance, and to await the result of a combined and strenuous effort of the friends of Union and Peace, to effect an adjustment
and conciliation of all public differences now unhappily existing." She well hoped, that this State " would listen willingly
and respectfully to her voice ;" for she knew and felt that South
Carolina could not descend from the dignity, and would nowise
compromit the rights of her sovereignty, by yielding to the intercession of a sister State.

If, therefore, no other considerations could have been presented to the Convention of the people of South Carolina—if
no other motives for compliance could have been suggested,
than the intercession of Virginia, offered in the temper and
manner it has been, and the interests we all have in the Union,
the common attachment we feel for our tried republican institutions, the aversion from civil discord and commotion, and the
wise and just dread of changes of which no sagacity can foresee
the consequences,—it might have been hoped and expected,
that the Convention would rescind, or at least suspend for a
time, its late Ordinance.

But, in truth, the Convention comes now to a consideration
of this subject, under a state of circumstances, not anticipated
by Virginia when she interposed her good offices to promote a
peaceable adjustment of the controversy between this State and
the Federal Government. There has been made that " combined and strenuous effort of the friends of peace and union, to
effect an adjustment and conciliation" of this controversy—the

result of which South Carolina was requested and expected to await—and that effort, it is hoped, will prove successful. The recent Act of Congress, " to modify the Act of the 14th July, 1832, and all other Acts imposing duties on imports," is such a modification of the Tariff Laws as (I trust) will leave little room for hesitation on the part of the Convention of the People of South Carolina, as to the wisdom and propriety of rescinding its Ordinance.

Forbearing, therefore, to enter at large into the many and forcible considerations of justice and policy, which, independently of this measure of Congress, might, I humbly conceive, have sufficed to induce the Convention to suspend, if not to rescind the Ordinance, I shall rest in the hope, that the wisdom of the Convention will adopt, at once, the course which the dignity and patriotism of South Carolina, her attachment to the Union, so constantly expressed, and manifested by her deeds, her duty to herself and towards her sister States, and (I hope I may add, without presumption,) her respect for the intercession of Virginia, shall dictate to be proper ; and that that course will lead to a renewal of perfect harmony.

Sensible as I am, how little any effort of mine has or could have contributed to the result I now anticipate, I shall be well content with the honor of having been the bearer of the Resolutions of Virginia, and of a favorable answer to them—happy in being the humblest instrument of such a work.

I have the honor to be,

With profound respect,

Your most obedient servant,

B. W. LEIGH.

To His Excellency ROBERT Y. HAYNE, }
    Governor of South Carolina. }

[II.]

Letter from the Governor of Virginia, to the Governor of South Carolina.

VIRGINIA.

EXECUTIVE DEPARTMENT,
January 26, 1833.

To His Excellency ROBERT Y. HAYNE :

SIR,—This will be delivered to you by the Hon. Benjamin Watkins Leigh, a distinguished citizen of Virginia, who has been elected by the General Assembly, a Commissioner of this State, to the State of South Carolina, in conformity to a Preamble and Resolutions on the subject of Federal Relations, this day adopted by the General Assembly of Virginia. Mr. Leigh will make known to you any further views, that may be entertained, on the subject of the Preamble and Resolutions.

I have the honor to be,

With high consideration and respect,

Your Excellency's most obedient servant,

JOHN FLOYD.

[III.]

Certified Copy of the Preamble and Resolutions adopted by the Virginia Legislature, and transmitted, through their Commissioner, to the constituted Authorities of this State.

VIRGINIA, TO WIT:

I, JOHN FLOYD, Governor of the State aforesaid, do hereby certify and make known unto all whom it may concern, that George W. Munford, whose name is subscribed to the certificate to two documents hereunto annexed, marked A and B, is as he there styles himself, Clerk of the House of Delegates, and Keeper of the Rolls of Virginia, duly appointed and qualified according to law; and to all his official acts as such, full faith, credit and authority are had and ought to be given.

In testimony whereof, I have subscribed my name, and caused the great seal of the State to be affixed hereunto.

Done at the City of Richmond, the twenty-sixth [L. S.] day of January, in the year of our Lord, one thousand eight hundred and thirty-three, and of the Commonwealth the fifty-seventh.

JOHN FLOYD.

[By the Governor.]

Wm. H. Richardson, *Secretary*
of the Commonwealth, and Keeper of the Seal.

A

Whereas, The General Assembly of Virginia, actuated by a desire to preserve the peace and harmony of our common country,—relying upon the sense of justice of each and every State in the Union, as a sufficient pledge that their Representatives in Congress will so modify the Acts laying duties and imposts on the importation of foreign commodities, commonly called the Tariff Acts, that they will no longer furnish cause of complaint to the people of any particular State; believing, accordingly, that the People of South Carolina are mistaken, in supposing that Congress will yield them no relief from the pressure of those Acts, especially as the auspicious approach of the extinguishment of the Public Debt, affords a just ground for the indulgence of a contrary expectation; and confident that they are too strongly attached to the Union of the States, to resort to any proceedings which might dissolve or endanger it, whilst they have any fair hope of obtaining their object, by more regular and peaceful measures; persuaded, also, that they will listen willingly and respectfully to the voice of Virginia, earnestly and affectionately requesting and entreating them to rescind or sus-

pend their late Ordinance, and await the result of a combined
and strenuous effort of the friends of Union and Peace, to effect
an adjustment and reconciliation of all public differences now
unhappily existing ; regarding, moreover, an appeal to force, on
the part of the General Government, or on the part of the Government of South Carolina, as a measure which nothing but extreme necessity could justify or excuse in either ; but apprehensive, at the same time, that if the present state of things is
allowed to continue, acts of violence will occur, which may lead
to consequences that all would deplore—cannot but deem it a
solemn duty to interpose, and mediate between the high contending parties, by the declaration of their opinions and wishes,
which they trust that they both will consider and respect :
Therefore,

*Resolved, by the General Assembly, in the name and on behalf of
the people of Virginia,* That the competent Authorities of South
Carolina be, and they are, hereby, earnestly and respectfully
requested and entreated to rescind the Ordinance of the late
Convention of that State, entitled " An Ordinance to Nullify
certain Acts of the Congress of the United States, purporting to
be laws, laying duties and imposts on the importation of foreign
commodities ;" or, at least to suspend its operation until the
close of the first session of the next Congress.

Resolved, That the Congress of the United States be, and
they are, hereby, earnestly and respectfully requested and entreated, so to modify the Acts laying duties and imposts on the
importation of foreign commodities, commonly called the Tariff
Acts, as to effect a gradual but speedy reduction of the resulting Revenue of the General Government, to the standard of the
necessary and proper expenditures for the support thereof.

Resolved, That the people of Virginia expect, and, in the
opinion of the General Assembly, the people of the other States
have a right to expect, that the General Government and the
Government of South Carolina, and all persons acting under the
authority of either, will carefully abstain from any and all acts,
whatever, which may be calculated to disturb the tranquillity of
the country, or endanger the existence of the Union.

And, *whereas*, considering the opinions which have been advanced and maintained by the Convention of South Carolina, in its late Ordinance and Addresses, on the one hand, and by the President of the United States, in his Proclamation, bearing date the tenth day of December, one thousand eight hundred and thirty-two, on the other, the General Assembly deem it due to themselves, and the people whom they represent, to declare and make known their own views in relation to some of the important and interesting questions which these papers present: Therefore,

Resolved, by the General Assembly, That they continue to regard the doctrines of State Sovereignty and State Rights, as set forth in the Resolutions of 1798, and sustained by the Report thereon, of 1799, as a true interpretation of the Constitution of the United States, and of the powers therein given to the General Government; but that they do not consider them as sanctioning the proceedings of South Carolina, indicated in her said Ordinance; nor as countenancing all the principles assumed by the President in his said Proclamation, many of which are in direct conflict with them.

Resolved, That this House will, by joint vote with the Senate, proceed, on this day, to elect a Commissioner, whose duty it shall be to proceed immediately to South Carolina, and communicate the foregoing Preamble and Resolutions to the Governor of that State, with a request that they be communicated to the Legislature of that State, or any Convention of its citizens, or give them such other direction as, in his judgment, may be best calculated to promote the objects which this Commonwealth has in view; and that the said Commissioner be authorized to express to the public authorities and people of our sister State, in such manner as he may deem most expedient, our sincere good will to our sister State, and our anxious solicitude that the kind and respectful recommendations we have addressed to her may lead to an accommodation of all the differences between that State and the General Government.

Resolved, That the Governor of the Commonwealth be, and he is, hereby, requested to communicate the foregoing Preamble and Resolutions to the President of the United States, to the

Governors of the other States, and to our Senators and Representatives in Congress.

Agreed to by the House, the twenty-sixth day of January, one thousand eight hundred and thirty-three.

GEORGE W. MUNFORD,

Clerk of the House of Delegates, and
Keeper of the Rolls of Virginia.

B.

IN THE HOUSE OF DELEGATES, Jan. 26, 1833.

The House of Delegates have, this day, by joint vote with the Senate, elected Benjamin Watkins Leigh, Esq., a Commissioner of this State to the State of South Carolina, in conformity to a Preamble and Resolutions upon the subject of Federal Relations, also adopted to-day.

GEGRGE W. MUNFORD,

Clerk of the House of Delegates, and
Keeper of the Rolls of Virginia.

[IV.]

Correspondence between the Commissioner of Virginia, and the Constituted Authorities of this State.

LETTER No. 1.

CHARLESTON, February 5, 1833.

SIR,—

When I had the honor, yesterday, of laying before your Excellency, the Resolutions of the General Assembly of Virginia,

of the 26th January last, and called your attention particularly
to the Resolution of the General Assembly, in the name and on
behalf of the people of Virginia, that the competent authorities
of South Carolina be, and are hereby earnestly and respectfully
requested and entreated to rescind the Ordinance of the State
Convention of that State, entitled " An Ordinance to Nullify
certain Acts of the Congress of the United States, purporting to
be laws, laying duties and imposts on the importation of foreign
commodities ;" or, at least, to suspend its operation until the
close of the first session of the next Congress, you informed me,
that the only authority competent to comply with that request,
or even to consider it, is the Convention of the people of South
Carolina, which made the Ordinance, and the power of re-as-
sembling the Convention is vested in the President of that body.

I have now, therefore, to request your Excellency to communicate the Resolutions of the General Assembly of Virginia, and
this letter also, to the President of the Convention ; confidently
hoping that that officer will not refuse or hesitate to re-assemble
the Convention, in order that the Resolutions of the General
Assembly may be submitted to it, and that the Convention may
consider, whether, and how far the earnest and respectful request and entreaty of the General Assembly shall and ought to
be complied with.

I have the honor to be, &c. &c.,

B. W. LEIGH.

To His Excellency ROBERT Y. HAYNE, }
      Governor of South Carolina. }

LETTER No. 2.

EXECUTIVE DEPARTMENT, }
CHARLESTON, Feb. 6, 1833. }

SIR,—

I have had the honor to receive your letter of the 5th instant,
and in compliance with the request therein contained, commu-

nicated its contents, together with the Resolutions of the Legislature of Virginia, of which you are the bearer, to Gen. James Hamilton, Jun., the President of the Convention. I have now the pleasure of inclosing you his answer, by which you will perceive, that in compliance with the request conveyed through you, he will promptly re-assemble the Convention, to whom the Resolutions adopted by the Legislature of Virginia, will be submitted, and by whom they will doubtless receive the most friendly and respectful consideration. In giving you this information, it is due to the interest manifested by Virginia, in the existing controversy between South Carolina and the Federal Government, to state that as soon as it came to be understood that the Legislature of Virginia had taken up the subject in a spirit of friendly interposition, and that a bill for the modification of the Tariff was actually before Congress, it was determined, by the common consent of our fellow-citizens, that no case should be made under our Ordinance until after the adjournment of the present Congress. The propriety of a still further suspension, can, of course, only be determined by the Convention itself. With regard to the solicitude expressed by the Legislature of Virginia, that there should be " no appeal to force," on " the part of either the General Government, or the Government of South Carolina, in the controversy now unhappily existing between them," and that " the General Government and the Government of South Carolina, and all persons acting under the authority of either, should carefully abstain from any and all acts, whatever, which may be calculated to disturb the tranquillity of the country, or endanger the existence of the Union ;" it is proper that I should distinctly and emphatically state, that no design now exists, or ever has existed, on the part of the Government of South Carolina, or any portion of the people, to " appeal to force," unless that measure should be rendered indispensable in repelling unlawful violence.

I beg leave to assure you, and through you, the people of Virginia, and our other sister States, that no acts have been done, or are contemplated by South Carolina, her constituted authorities, or citizens, in reference to the present crisis, but such as are deemed measures of precaution. Her preparations are altogether defensive in their character ; and notwithstanding the concentration of large naval and military forces in this harbor, and the adoption of other measures on the part of the General Government, which may be considered as of a character threatening the peace and endangering the tranquillity and safety of the State, we shall continue to exercise the utmost possible forbearance, acting strictly on the defensive, firmly resolved to commit no act of violence, but prepared, as far as our means may extend, to resist aggression. Nothing, you may be assured, would give me, personally, and the people of South Carolina, more satisfaction than that the existing controversy should be happily adjusted, on just and liberal terms; and I beg you to be assured, that nothing can be further from our desire, than to disturb the tranquillity of the country, or endanger the existence of the Union.

Accept, Sir, for yourself,

The assurance of the high consideration

Of yours, respectfully and truly,

ROBERT Y. HAYNE.

To the Hon. B. W. LEIGH.

———

LETTER No. 3.

CHARLESTON, February 6, 1833.

SIR,—

I do myself the honor of acknowledging the receipt of your letter of the 5th, enclosing a copy of a communication you have received from Benjamin Watkins Leigh, Esq., Commissioner from the State of Virginia, covering certain Resolutions passed by the Legislature of that State, which that gentlemen has been deputed to convey to the Executive of this State.

In reply to the reference which you have made to me, as President of the Convention of the People of South Carolina, consequent on the application on the part of that gentleman, for the meeting of that body, I beg leave to communicate to him, through your Excellency, that, appreciating very highly, the kind disposition, and the patriotic solicitude, which have induced the highly respectable Commonwealth which he represents, to interpose her friendly and mediatorial offices in the unhappy controversy subsisting between the Federal Government and the State of South Carolina, I should do great injustice to those dispositions on her part, and, I am quite sure, to the feelings of the people of South Carolina, if I did not promptly comply with his wishes in reference to the proposed call.

You are, therefore, authorized to say to Mr. Leigh, that the Convention will be assembled with as much despatch as may be compatible with the public convenience, and with a due regard to those circumstances which best promise a full consideration and final decision, on the proposition of which he is the bearer.

I have the honor to remain,

With distinguished consideration and esteem,

Your Excellency's obedient servant,

JAMES HAMILTON, JR.,

President of the Convention of the People of South Carolina.

To His Excellency ROBERT Y. HAYNE.

Messrs. Geo. Sistrunk, from St. George's, R. Barnwell Smith, from St. Bartholomew's, Robert W. Gill, from Lancaster, Benjamin Gause, from Kingston, and James C. Coggeshall, from Prince George, Winyaw, now appeared for the first time, exhibited their credentials, enrolled their names, and took their seats as members of the Convention.

The Convention then proceeded to the election of a President. Messrs. Butler, Burt, and Quash, were appointed a Committtee to count the votes, and make known the result. The Committee reported His Excellency Robert Y. Hayne, Governor and Commander in Chief in and over the State, duly elected President of the Convention.

Chancellor Johnston and Col. Thomas Pinckney, were appointed a Committee to wait on the President elect, inform him of his election, and conduct him to the chair; which, having been done, Governor Hayne, after a short address, entered upon the duties of his station.

On motion of General Hamilton, the following Resolutions were adopted unanimously, to wit:

Resolved, That a Committee of three be appointed to wait on Benjamin Watkins Leigh, Esq., Commissioner of the Commonwealth of Virginia, and invite him to a seat within the bar of this Convention."

" *Resolved,* That this Convention will receive Mr. Leigh, standing and uncovered."

The Committee consisted of Gen. Earle, Col. I'On, and Mr. Heyward.

On motion of the Hon. C. J. Colcock, it was

" *Resolved,* That a Committee of twenty-one be appointed to take into consideration the communication of the Hon. Benjamin W. Leigh, Commissioner from the State of Virginia, and all other matters connected with the subject, and the course which should be pursued by the Convention, at the present important crisis of our political affairs."

The following gentlemen were named by the President, to constitute the Committee, viz:

Hon. C. J. Colcock,

Gen. J. B. Earle,	R. J. Turnbull, Esq.,
Hon. William Harper,	B. Rogers, Esq.,
Hon. J. B. O'Neal,	Hon. R. W. Barnwell,
Col. Wm. C. Pinckney,	Col. J. R. Ervin,
Hon. S. D. Miller,	Col. J. Bond I'On,
Chancellor Job Johnston,	T. D. Singleton, Esq.,
Hon. G. McDuffie,	Col. P. M. Butler,
Hon. R. J. Manning,	Jas. A. Black, Esq.,
Hon. J. K. Griffin,	Col. John Bauskett,

On motion of Judge Harper, it was ordered, that the correspondence between Mr. Leigh and Governor Hayne, should be printed for the use of the Convention; likewise the Acts of the late Congress, connected with the controversy between this State and the Federal Government.

On motion of Col. I'On, the members of Congress, and of the State Legislature, who might be present, were invited to a seat within the bar of the Convention.

On motion of Gen. Hamilton, the Convention now adjourned until to-morrow at one o'clock, P. M.

ISAAC W. HAYNE,

Clerk of the Convention.

—

TUESDAY, March 12, 1833.

The Convention met according to adjournment, at one o'clock, P. M., and the proceedings were opened by a prayer from the Rev. Mr. Ray.

The roll having been called, the President suggested that as this formality was an unnecessary consumption of the time of the Convention, and as there was no rule requiring its observance, it would, if no objections were made, be dispensed with for the future.

Messrs. John Lipscomb, of Abbeville, and J. T. Whitefield, of Pendleton, appeared and took their seats.

The President then announced the names of Gen. James Hamilton, Jun., and Samuel B. Wilkins, Esq. as completing the Select Committee of twenty-one ; these names being substituted for those of his Excellency R. Y. Hayne, now President of the Convention, and of the Hon. Henry Middleton, absent, who, with the gentlemen named yesterday, constituted the select Committee of the Convention, at its late session.

Judge Colcock, on the part of the Committee, stated that they were unable to report to-day, and obtained leave to sit again.

On motion of Gen. Hamilton, the following Resolution was adopted, to wit:

"*Resolved,* That a Committee of Accounts, to consist of three members, be raised, for the purpose of examining and reporting on the Accounts of this Convention, and what balance may stand to its credit in the Treasury, and what further sum may be necessary for defraying the expenses of its present session."

Messrs. Simons, Bauskett, and Chesnut, were appointed the Committee.

Mr. Turnbull moved that, until otherwise ordered, the Convention should adjourn from day to day to meet at twelve o'clock, meridian, which being agreed to, he moved that the Convention do now adjourn; which being likewise concurred in, the Convention adjourned accordingly.

ISAAC W. HAYNE,

Clerk of the Convention.

——

WEDNESDAY, March 13, 1833.

The Convention met pursuant to adjournment, at meridian to-day. The proceedings were opened by a prayer from the Rev. Mr. Wafford, and the Journal of yesterday read.

Messrs. A. Bowie and A. Burt, of Abbeville, M. Jacobs, of St. Helena, and Peter Vaught, of All Saints, appeared and took their seats.

The Hon. C. J. Colcock, from the Select Committee of twenty-one, reported to the Convention an Ordinance and an accompanying Report, on the subject of the Act of the late Congress of the United States, entitled " An Act to modify the Act of the 14th July, 1832, and all other Acts imposing duties on imports."

On motion of Mr. Wilson, these were ordered to be printed; and, on motion of Judge Colcock, made the order of the day for to-morrow.

Mr. Wilson, after a few explanatory remarks, introduced the following Resolution, to wit:

" *Resolved,* That a Committee be appointed to wait on our

Senators and Representatives lately in Congress, and now in the Town of Columbia, requesting them to give us genuine information relative to the late proceedings of the Federal Government towards South Carolina, in consequence of the Ordinance of Nullification, passed by the people of this State, in Convention in November last; and that the Committee report what arrangements may be made as to the manner and time of giving the information desired."

On motion of Judge Colcock, this Resolution was ordered to lie on the table. After a short interval, Mr. Wilson moved to take it up for immediate consideration. Gen. Hamilton moved to postpone it until to-morrow. After some slight debate, the vote was taken on the question of postponement, and the motion failed—Ayes, 66—Noes, 69. The Resolution was then adopted, and Mr. Wilson, Gen. Hamilton, and Chancellor Johnston, were appointed the Committee.

Mr. Wilson then introduced the following Resolutions, to wit :

" *Whereas*, A Convention of the People of the State has been called, to place the State of South Carolina upon its Sovereignty, and to consider of, and do such acts as may, in the opinion of this Convention, serve more effectually to perpetuate the same ; *and*, *whereas*, protection and allegiance are reciprocal duties, and a fundamental principle of all Governments ; be it, therefore,"

" *Resolved*, That it is expedient and proper, that the Constitution of this State, be so altered and amended, as to require every Elector, who may claim to exercise the elective franchise, in addition to the oath of qualification now prescribed, to take an oath of allegiance to the State of South Carolina ; and upon the refusal of any Elector to take such oath, the Managers of Elections shall not be permitted to receive his vote."

" *Resolved*, That it is expedient and proper, that all officers hereafter to be elected to any office of honor, profit or trust, civil or military, be required to take an oath of paramount allegiance to the State of South Carolina."

These Resolutions having been laid before the Convention, by the President, Mr. Turnbull stated that the Committee of twenty-one, already had the subjects to which they related, under consideration ; whereupon Mr. Wilson moved that they should be referred to that Committee, which was agreed to. Gen. Hamilton then moved that the gentleman who offered these Resolutions, should be added to the Committee, which being agreed to, the Hon. John L. Wilson was added to the Select Committee of twenty-one.

Gen. Earle then moved to adjourn, but withdrew the motion, in order that an earlier hour than the regular time of meeting might be fixed on for that purpose. On motion of Col. Elmore, it was ordered that when the Convention adjourned, it should adjourn to meet at 11 o'clock, A. M, to-morrow. Gen. Earle renewed his motion for immediate adjournment, which having been carried, the Convention adjourned accordingly.

ISAAC W. HAYNE,
Clerk of the Convention.

THURSDAY, March 14, 1833.

The Convention met to-day at 11 o'clock, A. M., pursuant to adjournment. The proceedings were opened with a prayer by the Rev. Mr. Keeney, and the Journal of yesterday read.

Judge Colcock, on the part of the Select Committee of twenty-one, stated that they were not prepared to make a further report to-day, and obtained leave to sit again.

The following Report was then presented by Mr. Wilson, to wit:

" The Committee appointed to wait upon our late Members and Senators in Congress from this State, now in Columbia, requesting them to give such genuine information as they may possess, in relation to the Acts of the Federal Government, growing out of the late Ordinance of Nullification, by the People of this State, in Convention, in November last, have performed the duty assigned them, and beg leave respectfully to

REPORT:

" That the gentlemen lately composing our Delegation in

Congress, now in Columbia, deem it unnecessary, as a body, to give any exposition of the Acts of Congress referred to, but that the views of those who are members of this Convention, on the subject, will be submitted to the Convention."

"J. L. WILSON, *Chairman.*"

The Report was, at the motion of Mr. Wilson, ordered to lie on the table.

The Convention then proceeded to the consideration of the Ordinance, which had been made the order of the day.

Judge Colcock moved that the Ordinance should be amended, by striking out, in the Preamble, the words, " as amounts, substantially, to an ultimate reduction of the duties to the Revenue standard, and that no higher duties shall be laid, than may be necessary to defray the economical expenditures of the Government," and inserting the following, to wit : " as will ultimately reduce them to the Revenue standard, and provides that no more Revenue shall be raised than may be necessary to defray the economical expenses of the Government." This amendment was adopted.

Mr. Wilson moved the following amendments, which were likewise adopted, to wit :—that after the word " Ordinance," should be inserted, " adopted by this Convention, on the 24th day of November, 1832,"—after the word " passed," to insert " by the General Assembly of this State,"—and again, after the word " passed," occurring the second time, the same words, to wit : " by the General Assembly of this State."

After some discussion upon the question of the adoption of the Ordinance, thus amended, in which the Hon. Stephen D. Miller, the Hon. R. W. Barnwell, R. Barnwell Smith, Esq., Gen. Hamilton, and Col. F. H. Elmore, took part, Gen. Hamilton moved to re-commit the Report and Ordinance to the Committee of twenty-one. Chancellor Johnston moved that the question should be separately taken on the Report and Ordinance. The President stated that, as the Report was not properly before the Convention, the question would be solely on the re-commitment of the Ordinance. Gen. Hamilton then withdrew his motion. After some further discussion, as to the adoption of the Ordinance, Mr. Bowie moved that its further considerration should be postponed until to-morrow. The vote by acclamation leaving the President in doubt, a division was called for, and the Ayes were found to be 57—the Noes, 83. The motion was consequently lost. Mr. Butler then moved to adjourn, which was also lost. On motion, a recess of two hours was taken by the Convention.

Four o'clock, P. M.

The Convention re-assembled. Mr. J. Walter Phillips moved that the Preamble to the Ordinance should be stricken out. This elicited a debate, in which Mr. Wilson, Mr. Phillips, Gen. Hamilton, and Mr. Whitefield, bore a part, when the question being taken, the motion was lost. Judge Colcock then moved that the further consideration of the Ordinance should be postponed, and that it should be made the order of the day for to-morrow, which was agreed to.

On motion of Mr. Butler, the Report was then taken up, and ordered to be re-committed to the Committee of twenty-one. The Convention then adjourned until 10 o'clock to-morrow.

ISAAC W. HAYNE,
Clerk of the Convention.

FRIDAY, March 15, 1833.

The Convention met to-day at 10 o'clock, pursuant to adjournment. After a prayer from the Rev. Mr. English, the Journal of yesterday was read.

The following Resolution was submitted by Mr. Wilson, to wit:

" *Resolved,* That the Librarian receive   dollars, for his attendance at the Legislative Library, during the last and present session of the Convention; and the President of the Convention be authorized to draw his warrant for the same."

On motion of Mr. Wilson, the blank was filled with the word " sixty," and the Resolution adopted.

Judge Colcock presented a Resolution, fixing Monday next, as the time for the adjournment of the present session of the Convention, which was, on motion of Mr. Spann, laid on the table.

Judge Colcock presented the Report, which was yesterday re-committed to the Committee of twenty-one.

Judge Harper, on the part of the same Committee, made a further report, consisting of a Report and Ordinance in relation to the Act of the late Congress, entitled " an Act further to provide for the collection of duties on imports."

Gen. Hamilton, on the part of the same Committee, made a third Report, on the subject of the mediation of Virginia.

On motion of Judge Colcock, the two last Reports were ordered to be printed, and made the order of the day for to-morrow.

The following Resolution was then introduced by Gen. Hamilton, to wit :

" *Resolved*, That whilst this Convention, as an offering to the peace and harmony of this Union, in a just regard to the interposition of the highly patriotic Commonwealth of Virginia, and with a proper deference to the united vote of the whole Southern States, in favour of the recent accommodation of the Tariff, has made the late modification of the Tariff, approved by Act of Congress, of the 2d March, 1833, the basis of the repeal of her Ordinance of the 24th November, 1832—yet this Convention owes it to itself, to the people they represent, and the posterity of that people, to declare that they do not, by reason of said repeal, acquiesce in the principle of the substantive power existing on the part of Congress, to protect domestic manufactures : and hence, on the final adjustment, in 1842, of the reductions, under the Act of 2d March, 1833, or at any previous period, should odious discriminations be instituted for the purpose of continuing in force the protective principle, South Carolina will feel herself free to resist such a violation of what she conceives to be the good faith of the Act of the 2nd March, 1833, by the interposition of her sovereignty, or in any other mode she may deem proper."

This resolution was also ordered to be printed, and made the special order of the day for tomorrow. R. Barnwell Smith, Esq. moved to append to it the following resolution, which was ordered accordingly, to wit:

" *Resolved*, That it is the opinion of this Convention, that the military preparations heretofore begun by the State, should be continued, and that effectual measures should be adopted and completed, for putting the State in a firm attitude of defence."

The Ordinance, which was made the order of the day, was then taken up for consideration.

On motion of Chancellor Johnston, it was agreed to re-consider the question as to the adoption of the Preamble to the Ordinance. Mr. J. Walter Phillips moved to strike it out. This was opposed by Mr. Turnbull, advocated by Mr. Phillips and Judge Richardson, and opposed by Mr. McDuffie, in reply.

Mr. Turnbull then moved to amend the Preamble, by substituting the words, " provided for," for the word " made," which was agreed to. The Ayes and Noes were then taken on striking out the Preamble, and were as follows:

AYES—Messrs. Brockman, Crooke, Chesnut, Cannon, Clinton, R. Ervin, J. P. Evans, Gibson, Gause, Gill, James, Lancaster, McCord, O'Neale, P. Phillips, J. W. Phillips, Perry, J. S. Richardson, Sistrunk, Whitten, Wilkins.—21.

NOES—Robert Y. Hayne, President, B. Adams, J. Adams, Ayer, J. Anderson, R. Anderson, Arnold, Baker, Ball, Bee, Boone, Barnwell, Bradwell, Blewett, Butler, John G. Brown, J. G. Brown, Bauskett, A. Burt, F. Burt, Barton, Bowie, Black, Belin, Cohen, Cordes, T. H. Colcock, C. J. Colcock, Capers, Clifton, Caughman, Counts, Chambers, Campbell, Cureton, Coggeshall, Dubose, Dawson, J. Douglas, G. Douglas, Elmore, Earle, J. R. Ervin, W. Evans, Felder, Fuller, T. L. Gourdin, P. G. Gourdin, Goodwyn, Gailliard, Griffin, Glenn, Gregg, J. Hamilton, Jr., Heyward, Harper, Harrison, Hatton, Harllee, Huguenin, I'On, Jeter, Johnston, Jacobs, Key, Keith, King, Levy, Lowry, Lacoste, Legare, Lawton, Long, Lipscomb, Logan, Littlejohn, Magrath, Maner, Murray, Mills, McCall, Means, Mays, McDuffie, Moore, J. L. Miller, S. D. Miller, J. B. Miller, Nowell, O'Bannon, Parker, Porcher, Palmer, C. C. Pinckney,

W. C. Pinckney, T. Pinckney, Quash, Rivers, Rowe, Rogers, Ray, J. G. Spann, J. Spann, Simons, Shand, J. M. Smith, G. H. Smith, W. Smith, S. Smith, R. B. Smith, Stringfellow, Scott, Symmes, Sims, Shannon, Singleton, Stevens, Turnbull, Tyler, Tidyman, Ulmer, Vaught, Vanderhorst, Wilson, Walker, Williams, Woodward, Williamson, Wardlaw, Whatley, Whitefield, Watt, Waties, Ware, Warren, Young.—136.

The question was then put as to the adoption of the Ordinance, and the Ayes and Noes being taken, were as follows:

AYES—Robert Y. Hayne, President, B. Adams, J. Adams, Ayer, J. Anderson, R. Anderson, Arnold, Baker, Ball, Bee, Boone, Barnwell, Bradwell, Blewett, Butler, John G. Brown, J. G. Brown, Bauskett, A. Burt, F. Burt, Barton, Brockman, Bowie, Black, Belin, Cohen, Cordes, T. H. Colcock, C. J. Colcock, Capers, Clifton, Caughman, Counts, Crooke, Chambers, Campbell, Cureton, Chesnut, Cannon, Clinton, Coggeshall, Dubose, Dawson, J. Douglas, G. Douglas, Elmore, Earle, J. R. Ervin, R. Ervin, W. Evans, J. P. Evans, Fuller, T. L. Gourdin, P. G. Gourdin, Gailliard, Griffin, Glenn, Gibson, Gregg, Gause, Gill, J. Hamilton, Jr., Heyward, Harper, Harrison, Hatton, Harllee, Huguenin, I'On, Jeter, Johnston, James, Jacobs, Keith, Key, King, Levy, Lowry, Lacoste, Legare, Lawton, Long, Lipscomb, Logan, Littlejohn, Lancaster, Magrath, Maner, Murray, Mills, McCall, Means, Mays, McDuffie, Moore, J. L. Miller, S. D. Miller, J. B. Miller, Nowell, O'Neale, O'Bannon, P. Phillips, Parker, Porcher, Palmer, Perry, C. C. Pinckney, W. C. Pinckney, T. Pinckney, Quash, J. S. Richardson, Rivers, Rowe, Rogers, Ray, J. G. Spann, J. Spann, Simons, Shand, S. Smith, J. M. Smith, G. H. Smith, W. Smith, R. B. Smith, Stringfellow, Scott, Symmes, Sims, Shannon, Singleton, Stevens, Sistrunk, Turnbull, Tyler, Tidyman, Ulmer, Vaught, Vanderhorst, Wilson, Walker, Williams, Woodward, Williamson, Wardlaw, Whatley, Whitefield, Whitten, Watt, Waties, Wilkins, Ware, Warren, Young.—153.

NOES—Felder, Goodwyn, McCord, J. W. Phillips.—4.

Absent—11.

Messrs. Whitten, Perry, Lipscomb, and J. R. Ervin, obtained

leave to be absent from the Convention, during the remainder of the session.

A motion was now made to adjourn, but having been lost, the Report accompanying the Ordinance just adopted, was taken up for consideration. The Report was read by the President, and the question put as to agreeing to the amendment reported by the Committee, recommending to strike out the words " and triumph," from the phrase " cause for congratulation and triumph," which passed in the affirmative.

A verbal amendment was moved by Col. Bauskett, and agreed to.

Mr. R. Barnwell Smith moved to lay the Report on the table, but withdrew the motion to give an opportunity for discussion. In this, the Hon. S. D. Miller, Judge Colcock, Mr. Smith, and Gen. Hamilton, took part. The question was then put, on the motion to lay the Report on the table, and the motion lost. The vote being taken on the adoption of the Report, it was adopted by the Convention.

It was then moved by Gen. Hamilton, to take up for consideration the Resolution fixing the time of adjournment. This elicited some debate, when Mr. Miller moved to adjourn until to-morrow, at ten o'clock, which having been agreed to, the Convention adjourned accordingly.

ISAAC W. HAYNE,
Clerk of the Convention.

———

SATURDAY, March 16, 1833.

The Convention met at ten o'clock, A. M., pursuant to adjournment. The proceedings were opened with a prayer by the Rev. Mr. Jackson, and the Journal of yesterday read. The following Report was presented by the Hon. J. L. Wilson, to wit :

" The Engrossing Committee, to which was referred the Ordinance passed yesterday, in Convention, for rescinding the

Ordinance of Nullification, adopted on the 24th of November last, beg leave to report the same as engrossed, and suggest the propriety of the same order of signature as was observed in the Ordinance of Nullification.

JOHN L. WILSON, Chairman."

On motion of Mr. Miller, it was ordered that the ratification should be according to the usual parliamentary form, viz : by the signatures, merely, of the President and Clerk. The Ordinance as engrossed, after having been read by the Chair, was so ratified, in the presence of the Convention.

A recess was then taken until twelve o'clock, M.

The Ordinance as ratified, and the accompanying Report, as adopted by the Convention, are as follows, to wit :

REPORT.

The Committee, to whom was referred the communication of the Hon. B. W. Leigh, Commissioner from the State of Virginia, and all other matters connected with the subject, and the course which should be pursued by the Convention, at the present important crisis of our political affairs, beg leave to

REPORT:

(IN PART,)

That they have had under consideration, the Act passed at the late session of Congress, to modify the " Act of the 14th July, 1832, and all other Acts imposing duties upon imports ;" and have duly deliberated on the course which it becomes the people of South Carolina to pursue at this interesting crisis in her political affairs. It is now upwards of ten years since the people and constituted authorities of this State, took ground against the Protecting System, as " unconstitutional, oppressive and unjust," and solemnly declared, in language which was then cordially responded to by the other Southern States, that it never could be submitted to " as the settled policy of the country." After remonstrating for years against this system in vain, and making every possible effort to produce a redress of the grievance, by invoking the protection of the Constitution, and by appealing to the justice of our brethren, we saw, during the session of Congress which ended in July last, a modification effected, avowedly as the final adjustment of the Tariff, to take effect after the complete extinguishment of the Public Debt, by which the Protecting System could only be considered as riveted upon the country forever. Believing that under these circumstances, there was no hope of any further reduction of the duties, from the ordinary action of the Federal Government, and convinced, that under the operation of this system, the labor and capital of the plantation States must be forever tributary to the manufacturing States, and that we should in effect, be reduced to a condition of colonial vassalage, South Carolina felt herself constrained, by a just regard for her own rights and interests, by her love of liberty and her devotion to the Constitution, to interpose in her sovereign capacity, for the purpose of arresting the progress of the evil, and maintaining, within her own limits, the authorities, rights and liberties, appertaining to her as a sovereign State. Ardently attached to the union of the States, the people of South Carolina were still more devoted to the rights of the States, without which the Union itself would cease to be a blessing ; and well convinced that the regulation of the whole labor and capital of this vast Confederacy by a great central Government, must lead inevitably to the total destruction of our free institutions, they did not hesitate to throw themselves fearlessly into the breach, to arrest the torrent of usurpation which was sweeping before it all that was truly valuable in our political system.

The effect of this interposition, if it has not equalled our wishes, has been beyond what existing circumstances would have authorized us to expect. The spectacle of a single State, unaided and alone, standing up for her rights,—influenced by no other motive than a sincere desire to maintain the public liberty, and bring about a salutary reform in the administration of the Government, has roused the attention of the whole country, and has caused many to pause and reflect, who have heretofore seemed madly bent on the consummation of a scheme of policy absolutely fatal to the liberty of the people, and the prosperity of a large portion of the Union. Though reviled and slandered by those whose pecuniary or political interests stood in the way of a satisfactory adjustment of the controversy—deserted by many to whom she had a right to look for succor and support, and threatened with violence from abroad, and convulsions within, South Carolina, conscious of the rectitude of her intentions, and the justice of her cause, has stood unmoved; firmly resolved to maintain her liberties, or perish in the conflict. The result has been a beneficial modification of the Tariff of 1832, even before the time appointed for that Act to go into effect, and within a few months after its enactment; accompanied by a provision for a gradual reduction of the duties to the revenue standard. Though the reduction provided for by the Bill which has just passed, is, neither in its amount. nor the time when it is to go into effect, such as the South had a right to require, yet such an approach has been made towards the true principles on which the duties on imports ought to be adjusted under our system, that the people of South Carolina are willing so far to yield to the measure, as to agree that their Ordinance shall henceforth be considered as having no force or effect. Unequal and oppressive as the system of raising revenue by duties upon imports, must be upon the agricultural States, which furnish more than two thirds of the domestic exports of the United States, yet South Carolina always has been, and sti'l is willing to make large sacrifices to the peace and harmony of the Union. Though she believes that the Protecting System is founded in the assumption of powers not granted by the Constitution of the Federal Government, yet she has never insisted on such an immediate reduction of the duties as should involve the manufacturers in ruin. That a reduction to the lowest amount necessary to supply the wants of the Government, might be safely effected in four or five years, cannot, in our estimation, admit of a reasonable doubt; still, in a great struggle for principles, South Carolina would disdain to cavil about a small amount of duties, and a few years more or less in effecting the adjustment, provided only she can secure substantial justice, and obtain a distinct recognition of the principles for which she has so long contended. Among the provisions of the new Bill, which recommend it to our acceptance, are the establishment of a system of *ad valorem* duties, and the entire abandonment of the specific duties, and the minimums ; tyrannical provisions, by which duties rated nominally at 25 per cent. were, in many cases, raised to upwards of 100 per cent ; and by which the coarse and cheap articles, used by the poor, were taxed much higher than the expensive articles used by the rich ; a regulation against which we have constantly protested in the most earnest terms, as unjust and odious. The reduction before the expiration of the present year, of one tenth part of the excess of the duties over 20 per cent., on all articles " exceeding 20 per cent. on the value thereof," (embracing the entire mass of the protected articles,) and a gradual reduction thereafter, on such articles, down to 20 per cent., (the duties upon which, under the Tariff of 1832, range from 30 to upwards of 100 per cent., and average upwards of 50 per cent.,) are great and manifest ameliorations of the system, to the benefits of which we cannot be insensible. But great as must be the advantages of these reductions, they are small in comparison with the distinct recognition, in the new Bill, of two great principles which we deem of inestimable value—that the duties shall be eventually brought down to the revenue standard, even if it should be found necessary to reduce the duties on the protected articles below 20 per cent., and that no more money shall be raised than shall be necessary to an economical administration of the Government.

These provisions embody great principles in reference to this subject, for which South Carolina has long and earnestly contended ; and if the pledge therein contained shall be fulfilled in good faith, they must in their operation, arrest the abuses which have grown out of the unauthorized appropriations of the public money. We should consider the reduction of the revenue to the amonnt " necessary to the economical administration of the government," as one of the happiest reforms which could possibly take place in the practical operation of our system ; as it would arrest the progress of corruption, limit the exercise of Executive patronage and power, restore the independence of the States, and put an end to all these questions of disputed power, against which we have constantly protested. It is this aspect of the question which has reconciled us to the provisions of the new Bill, (certainly not free from objections) which provide for the introduction of linens, silks, worsted, and a number of other articles, free of duty. The reduction of revenue which will thereby be effected, and the beneficial influence of a free trade, in several of these articles which are almost exclusively purchased by the agricultural staples of the Southern States, and which will furnish an advantageous exchange for these productions, to the amount of several millions of dollars annually, are considerations not to be overlooked. Nor can we be insensible to the benefit to be derived from the united efforts of the whole South, aided by other States having interests identified with our own, in bringing about the late adjustment of the Tariff; promising, we trust, for the future, that union of sentiment, and concert in action, which are necessary to secure the rights and interests of the Southern States. On the whole, in whatever aspect the question is contemplated, your Committee find, in the late modification of the Tariff, cause for congratulation. If we have not yet succeeded in the complete establishment of the great principles of free trade and constitutional liberty, such progress has been made towards the accomplishment of the former, as must serve to re-kindle our hopes, and to excite us to fresh exertions in the glorious work of reform in which we are engaged. Influenced by these views, the Committee is satisfied that it would not comport with the liberal feelings of the people of South Carolina, nor be consistent with the sincere desire by which they have always been animated, not only to live in harmony with their brethren, but to preserve the Union of the States, could they hesitate under existing circumstances, in recommending that the Ordinance of Nullification, and the acts of the Legislature consequent thereon, be henceforth held and deemed of no force and effect. And they recommend the following Ordinance.

AN ORDINANCE.

Whereas, the Congress of the United States, by an Act recently passed, has provided for such a reduction and modification of the duties upon foreign imports, as will ultimately reduce them to the Revenue Standard—and provides that no more Revenue shall be raised than may be necessary to defray the economical expenses of the Government.

It is, therefore, Ordained and Declared, That the Ordinance adopted by this Convention on the 24th day of November last, entitled " An Ordinance to Nullify certain acts of the Congress of the United States, purporting to be laws, laying duties on the importation of foreign commodities," and all acts passed by the General Assembly of this State, in pursuance thereof, be henceforth deemed and held to have no force or effect : *Provided,* That the Act entitled " An Act further to alter and amend the Militia laws of this State," passed by the General Assembly of this State on the 20th day of December, 1832, shall remain in force, until it shall be repealed or modified by the Legislature.

Done at Columbia, the fifteenth day of March, in the year of our Lord one thousand eight hundred and thirty-three, and in the fifty-seventh year of the Sovereignty and Independence of the United States of America.

ROBERT Y. HAYNE, Delegate from the Parishes of St. Philip and St. Michael, } *President of the Convention.*

ISAAC W. HAYNE, *Clerk.*

Twelve o'clock, M.

The Convention re-assembled. Mr. S. L. Simons, from the Committee on Accounts, presented the following Report, to wit :

" The Committee on Accounts, to whom was referred a Resolution, instructing them to examine and Report on the Accounts of this Convention, and what balance may stand to its credit in the Treasury, and what further sum may be necessary for defraying the expenses of its present session, beg leave to

REPORT:

" That they have carefully examined all the accounts which were contracted under the orders of the Convention, together with the pay roll of its Members and Officers, and find them correct in every particular. Of the sum of ten thousand dollars appropriated by the Legislature for the use of the Convention, eight thousand, three hundred and eighty-five dollars 53-100, have been disbursed ; and a balance of one thousand six hundred and fourteen dollars 47-100, remain to its credit in the Treasury. Taking the expenditures of the former as a guide for the wants of the present session, your Committee would respectfully recommend the adoption of the following resolution :

" *Resolved*, That the President of this Convention be authorized to issue his warrants on the Treasury, to the amount of ten thousand dollars, for the purpose of defraying the expenses of the present session, if so much be necessary.

S. L. SIMONS, *Chairman.*"

This Resolution was adopted by the Convention.

On motion of Mr. Spann, a Resolution was passed, inviting to a seat within the bar of the Convention, the Hon. Dixon H. Lewis, a Representative in Congress from the State of Alabama, now in Columbia.

The Report and Ordinance on the Force Bill, which had been made the order of the day, were then taken up. The Ordinance was announced by the President to be first in order. The Hon. R. W. Barnwell moved to strike out so much of the Ordinance as

reláfes to the requisition of an oath of allegiance. The following motions to amend having precedence, were first put and
adopted, to wìt : that the words " or appointed," should be added after the word " elected ;" the word " such" be inserted after
the word " any," in the first line of the last paragraph, and the
words " heretofore elected, or hereafter to be elected," be strick-
en out.

Mr. Barnwell's motion being now again before the Convention, on motion, it was ordered, that when the question should
be taken, it should be by Ayes and Noes. A discussion arose,
in which Judge O'Neale, Judge Harper, Mr. Turnbull, and Mr.
P. Phillips, took part. Mr. Wilson proposed to amend the Ordinance, by striking out, after the words " We further ordain," and
inserting the following, to wit : " That no person, who shall be
hereafter elected or appointed, or who has heretofore been elected, but who has not yet taken the oaths of office required at the
time of his election or appointment, 'to any office, civil or military, within this State, (members of the Legislature excepted)
shall enter on the execution of such office, or be in any respect
competent to discharge the duties thereof, until he shall have
taken, in addition to the oaths of office now required, at the
same time and in the same manner, that such oaths are required
to be taken, the following oath of allegiance.

" I declare myself a citizen of the Free and Sovereign State
of South Carolina ; I declare that my allegiance is due to the
said State, and hereby renounce and abjure all other allegiance,
incompatible therewith ; and I will be true and faithful to the
said State, so long as I continue a citizen thereof : So help me
God.

" *And it is further Ordained,* That if any officer heretofore
elected, shall refuse or neglect to take the aforesaid oath, within
the time that other oaths of office are required by law to be
taken, such office shall be considered as vacant, and the Governor
of the State shall proceed (except in the instance of Judges of
the State) to fill such vacancy by appointing an officer, to serve
until another officer shall be elected and qualified."

This amendment was ordered to be printed. The Convention
then took a recess of two hours.

The Convention re-assembled. Mr. Barnwell moved to lay the Ordinance upon the table, and to take up the Report and Resolutions relating to the Virginia Mediation, which was agreed to. Mr. Perry moved that the question should be taken separately on the Report and Resolutions, which was likewise agreed to. The Resolutions, being first in order, were considered and unanimously adopted, and were ordered to be so entered on the Journals. The Report was then taken up and adopted by the Convention.

The Report and Resolutions, as adopted, are as follows:

REPORT,

ON THE MEDIATION OF VIRGINIA.

The Committee to whom were referred the Resolutions of the General Assembly of Virginia, and the communication of Mr. Leigh to the Governor of the State of South Carolina, beg leave to

REPORT:

That, although circumstances have supervened, since the institution of this Commission on the part of the highly respected Commonwealth from which it proceeds, which have enabled this Convention to accomplish the object, which her Assembly so anxiously and patriotically had in view, we are nevertheless sensible of the friendly dispositions and sympathy, which induced the interposition of her good offices, at a moment when South Carolina, denounced by the Executive of the Federal Government, and threatened with the extremity of its vengeance, stood absolutely alone in the contest she was waging for the rights of the States and the Constitutional liberties of the Country.

To this interference and these friendly dispositions, South Carolina desires to respond, as a sister, sovereign, and independent Commonwealth, in a tone of candor, confidence and affection. Appreciating thus sensibly, both the motives and objects which influenced the General Assembly of Virginia, to despatch at a moment so interesting, her Commissioner to this State, whose mission, even if the recent modification of the Tariff had not been adopted, would have challenged her high respect and profound consideration, she cannot permit the occasion thus offered, to pass, without making a few declarations which she regards as due to herself and the public liberty of the Country.

In the first place, South Carolina desires to stand acquitted, and believes, on a calm and dispassionate reflection by her co-States, she must stand acquitted, of the charge of having acted with any undue precipitation, in the controversy hitherto pending with the General Government. For ten years she petitioned, protested and remonstrated, against that system of unjust and unconstitutional Legislation, which had equally received the reprobation of Virginia, before she resorted to her veto, to forbid its enforcement within her limits. In exercising this faculty of her sovereignty, she believed she rested on those doctrines which, in 1798 and 1799, had conferred on Virginia and her distinguished statesmen a renown so unfading. She now refers to this subject in no invidious spirit of controversy : but when Virginia asserted, in those memorable Resolutions of her General Assembly, " that she viewed the powers of the Federal Government as resulting from the compact to which the States are parties ; as limited by the plain sense and intention of the instrument constituting that compact; as no further valid than they are authorized by the grants enumerated in that compact ; and that, in case of a deliberate, palpable and dangerous exercise of other powers, not granted by the said compact, the States, who are parties thereto, have the right, and are in duty bound, to interpose for arresting the progress of the evil, and for maintaining within their respective limits the authorities, rights and liberties, appertaining to them"—we conceived she had done nothing more or less, than announce the remedy which South Carolina has resorted to, through her State interposition. It is moreover asserted, in the Report explanatory of those Resolutions, that this right is a Constitutional, and not a Revolutionary right; and by the whole context of the powerful argument embraced in that Report, the right itself stands forth as separate and independent of the ordinary remedies of procuring a redress for the ordinary abuses of the Federative Government.

When, therefore, the General Assembly of Virginia, in the recent Resolutions, borne by her Commissioner, which your Committee are now considering, declares " that she does not regard the Resolutions of 1798, and '99, as sanctioning the proceedings of South Carolina, as indicated in the Ordinance of her Convention," with all proper deference, South Carolina must, nevertheless, adhere, with an honest and abiding confidence, to her own construction. It is within the providence of God that great truths should be independent of the human agents that promulgate them. Once announced, they become the subjects and property of reason, to all men and in all time to come. Nor will South Carolina feel less confidence in the conservative character of her remedy, which she believes to be in perfect harmony with a true exposition of the doctrines of the Resolutions of 1798, by the recent testimony afforded of its efficacy, in a pacific accommodation of the late controversy with the Federal Government, although that Government has attempted to destroy the authority and efficiency of this remedy, by the contemporary passage of an act, perpetrating a worse and more aggravated outrage on the Constitution, which has again demanded the interposition of this Convention.

With this brief justification of the principles of South Carolina, your Committee take leave of the subject; assuring the ancient and distinguished Commonwealth, whose mission has been borne, by her Commissioner, with an ability, temper, and affection, entirely corresponding with her own dispositions, that in the struggles for liberty and right which we apprehend from the antagonist principles, now fearfully at work, between those who support a limited and economical system of Government, and those who favor a consolidated and extravagant one, which the States in a minority are destined to wage, she will find, in South Carolina, a faithful and devoted ally, in accomplishing the great work of Freedom and Union. If she cannot say, with Virginia, that consolidation and disunion are equivalent evils, because she believes, with their own Jefferson, that consolidation is the greatest of all political curses to which our Federative form of Government can have any possible tendency; she, nevertheless, affirms, and challenges the production of any event in her history to disprove the declaration, that she is devoted to the union of these States, on the very terms and conditions of that compact out of which the Union had its origin; and for these principles she is prepared to peril, at all times and under all circumstances, the lives and fortunes of her people.

Your Committee conclude, by recommending the adoption of the following Resolutions :

Resolved, unanimously, That the President of this Convention do communicate to the Governor of Virginia, with a copy of this Report and these Resolutions, our distinguished sense of the patriotic and friendly motives which actuated her General Assembly, in tendering her mediation, in the late controversy between the General Government and the State of South Carolina; with the assurance that her friendly councils will at all times command our respectful consideration.

Resolved, unanimously, That the President of this Convention likewise convey to the Governor of Virginia, our high appreciation of the able and conciliatory manner in which Mr. Leigh has conducted his mission, during which he has afforded the most gratifying satisfaction to all parties, in sustaining, towards us, the kind and fraternal relations of his own State.

On motion of Mr. Barnwell, the Convention then adjourned until Monday at 10 o'clock.

ISAAC W. HAYNE,

Clerk of the Convention.

MONDAY, March 18, 1833.

The Convention met, pursuant to adjournment, at 10 o'clock, A. M. The proceedings were opened by a prayer from the Rev. Mr. Tradewell, and the Journal of yesterday read. The amendments of Mr. Wilson, as to that part of the Ordinance relating to the oath of allegiance, were then taken up for consideration, and supported in a speech, by the mover. After which, on motion of Mr. Barnwell, a recess was taken until 4 o'clock, P. M.

Four o'clock, P. M.

The Convention re-assembled, and Mr. Wilson's amendments were again taken up. On his motion the Ayes and Noes were taken, and found to be as follows:

AYES—R. Anderson, Arnold, Boone, Bradwell, J. G. Brown, F. Burt, Barton, Black, Cordes, Felder, P. G. Gourdin, Goodwyn, Gailliard, Hatton, King, Long, Lancaster, McCord, W. C. Pinckney, Rowe, J. G. Spann, J. Spann, W. Smith, Scott, Singleton, Ulmer, Wilson, Walker, Williams, Whitefield.—30.

NOES—Robert Y. Hayne, President, B. Adams, J. Adams, Ayer, J. Anderson, Baker, Ball, Bee, Barnwell, Blewett, Butler, John G. Brown, Bauskett, A. Burt, Brockman, Bowie, Belin, Cohen, T. H. Colcock, C. J. Colcock, Capers, Clifton, Caughman, Counts, Crooke, Chambers, Campbell, Cureton, Chesnut, Cannon, Clinton, Coggeshall, Dubose, Dawson, J. Douglas, G. Douglas, Elmore, Earle, R. Ervin, W. Evans, J. P. Evans, Fuller, T. L. Gourdin, Griffin, Glenn, Gibson, Gregg, Gause, Gill, J. Hamilton, Jr., Heyward, Harrison, Harllee, Huguenin, l'On, Jeter, Johnston, James, Jacobs, Keith, Key, Levy, Lowry, Lacoste, Lawton, Logan, Littlejohn, Magrath, Maner, Murray, Mills, McCall, Means, Mays, McDuffie, Moore, J. L. Miller, S. D. Miller, J. B. Miller, Nowell, O'Neale, O'Bannon, P. Phillips, J. W. Phillips, Parker, Porcher, Palmer, Perry, T. Pinckney, C. C. Pinckney, Rivers, Rogers, Ray, Simons, Shand, J. M. Smith, G. H. Smith, S. Smith, R. B. Smith, Stringfellow, Symmes, Sims, Shannon, Stevens, Sistrunk, Turnbull, Tyler, Tidyman, Vaught, Woodward, Williamson, Wardlaw, Whatley, Watt, Waties, Wilkins, Ware, Warren, Young.—118.

Chancellor Johnston then moved to strike out that part of the Ordinance, as reported, relating to the requisition of an oath of allegiance, and to insert the following, to wit:

" *We do further Ordain and Declare,* That the allegiance of the citizens of this State, while they continue such, is due to the said State ; and that obedience only, and not allegiance, is due by them to any other power or authority, to whom a control over them has been, or may be delegated by the State : and the General Assembly of the said State is hereby empowered, from time to time, when they may deem it proper, to provide for the administration to the citizens and officers of the State, or such of the said officers as they may think fit, of suitable oaths or affirmations, binding them to the observance of such allegiance, and abjuring all other allegiance ; and, also, to define what shall amount to a violation of their allegiance, and to provide the proper punishment for such violation."

Judge Colcock proposed the following amendment to that amendment :

" *Resolved,* That it is expedient to refer the subject of an oath of allegiance, to the Legislature, with a recommendation that a Bill be introduced to make it a Constitutional provision, in the mode pointed out by that instrument ; which would afford the people an opportunity of expressing their opinions on the subject."

The vote having been taken on this, it was rejected.

The question then recurring on Chancellor Johnston's amendment, the Ayes and Noes were called for, and found to be as follows, to wit :

Ayes—Robert Y. Hayne, President, B. Adams, Ayer, J. Anderson, Baker, Ball, Bee, Boone, Barnwell, Blewett, John G. Brown, Bauskett, A. Burt, Bowie, Belin, Cohen, Cordes, T. H. Colcock, C. J. Colcock, Capers, Caughman, Counts, Chambers, Campbell, Coggeshall, Dubose, Dawson, J. Douglas, G. Douglas, Elmore, Earle, Fuller, Griffin, Glenn, J. Hamilton, Jr., Heyward, Harrison, Hatton, Harllee, Huguenin, I'On, Jeter, Johnston, Jacobs, Keith, Legare, Lawton, Long, Logan, Littlejohn, Magrath, Maner, Murray, Mills, McCall, Means, Mays, McDuffie, Moore, J. L. Miller, Nowell, O'Bannon, Parker, Porcher, Palmer, C. C. Pinckney, T. Pinckney, Quash, Rivers, Rogers, Ray, J. G. Spann, Simons, Shand, J. M. Smith, G. H. Smith, W. Smith, R. B. Smith, Stringfellow, Sims, Stevens, Turnbull, Tyler, Ulmer, Vaught, Vanderhorst, Williams, Wardlaw, Whatley, Watt, Young—90.

Noes—J. Adams, R. Anderson, Arnold, Bradwell, Butler, J. G. Brown, F. Burt, Barton, Brockman, Black, Clifton, Crooke, Cureton, Chesnut, Cannon, Clinton, R. Ervin, W. Evans, J. P. Evans, Felder, T. L. Gourdin, P. G. Gourdin, Goodwyn, Gailliard, Gibson, Gregg, Gause, Gill, James, Key, King, Levy, Lowry, Lacoste, Lancaster, S. D. Miller, J. B. Miller, McCord, O'Neale, P. Phillips, J. W. Phillips, Perry, W. C. Pinckney, Rowe, J. Spann, W. Smith, Scott, Symmes, Shannon, Singleton, Sistrunk, Tidyman, Wilson, Walker, Woodward, Williamson, Whitefield, Waties, Wilkins, Ware, Warren.—60.

The amendment was consequently adopted.

The Hon. S. D. Miller moved to strike out all that part of the Ordinance, after the words " the enforcement thereof," including Chancellor Johnston's amendment. The Ayes and Noes were again called for, and were as follows, to wit :

Ayes—J. Adams, R. Anderson, Arnold, Baker, Bee, Boone, Bradwell, Blewett, John G. Brown, F. Burt, Barton, Brockman, T. H. Colcock, C. J. Colcock, Clifton, Counts, Crooke, Cureton, Chesnut, Cannon, Clinton, J. Douglas, Earle, R. Ervin, J. P. Evans, Felder, Fuller, T. L. Gourdin, P. G. Gourdin, Gailliard, Griffin, Gibson, Gause, Gill, Harrison, Jeter, Johnston, James, Keith, Levy, Lowry, Lacoste, Lawton, Littlejohn, Lancaster, Means, J. L. Miller, S. D. Miller, J. B. Miller, Nowell, O'Neale, P. Phillips, Palmer, Perry, Rowe, Ray, J. G. Spann, J. Spann, W. Smith, Stringfellow, Shannon, Singleton, Sistrunk, Tyler, Tidyman, Ulmer, Wilson, Walker, Wardlaw, Whatley, Wilkins, Ware, Warren.—73.

Noes—Robert Y. Hayne, President, B. Adams, Ayer, J. Anderson, Ball, Barnwell, Butler, J. G. Brown, Bauskett, A. Burt, Bowie, Black, Belin, Cohen, Cordes, Capers, Caughman, Chambers, Cambell, Coggeshall, Dubose, Dawson, G. Douglas, Elmore, W. Evans, Goodwyn, Glenn, Gregg, J. Hamilton, Jr., Heyward, Hatton, Harllee, Huguenin, I'On, Jacobs, Key, King, Legare, Long, Logan, Magrath, Maner, Murray, Mills, McCall, Mays, McDuffie, Moore, McCord, O'Bannon, J. W. Phillips, Parker, Porcher, C. C. Pinckney, W. C. Pinckney, T. Pinckney, Quash, Rivers, Rogers, Simons, Shand, J. M. Smith, G. H. Smith, S. Smith, R. B. Smith, Scott, Symmes, Sims, Stevens,

Turnbull, Vaught, Vanderhorst, Williams, Woodward, Williamson, Whitefield, Watt, Waties, Young.—79.

The Ayes and Noes were now called for, upon the question of the adoption of the Ordinance as amended, and being taken, were found to be as follows, to wit:

AYES—Robert Y. Hayne, President, B. Adams, J. Adams, Ayer, J. Anderson, R. Anderson, Arnold, Baker, Ball, Bee, Boone, Barnwell, Bradwell, Blewett, Butler, John G. Brown, J. G. Brown, Bauskett, A. Burt, F. Burt, Barton, Bowie, Black, Belin, Cohen, Cordes, T. H. Colcock, C. J. Colcock, Capers, Clifton, Caughman, Counts, Chambers, Campbell, Coggeshall, Dubose, Dawson, J. Douglas, G. Douglas, Elmore, Earle, W. Evans, Felder, Fuller, T. L. Gourdin, P. G. Gourdin, Goodwyn, Gailliard, Griffin, Glenn, Gregg, J. Hamilton, Jr., Heyward, Harrison, Hatton, Harllee, Huguenin, I'On, Jeter, Johnston, James, Jacobs, Keith, Key, King, Lacoste, Legare, Lawton, Long, Logan, Littlejohn, Lancaster, Magrath, Maner, Murray, Mills, McCall, Means, Mays, McDuffie, Moore, J. L. Miller, S. D. Miller, J. B. Miller, McCord, Nowell, O'Bannon, J. W. Phillips, Parker, Porcher, Palmer, C. C. Pinckney, W. C. Pinckney, T. Pinckney, Quash, Rivers, Rowe, Rogers, Ray, J. G. Spann, J. Spann, Simons, Shand, J. M. Smith, G. H. Smith, W. Smith, S. Smith, R. B. Smith, Stringfellow, Scott, Symmes, Sims, Singleton, Stevens, Turnbull, Tyler, Tidyman, Ulmer, Vaught, Vanderhorst, Walker, Williams, Woodward, Williamson, Wardlaw, Whatley, Whitefield, Watt, Waties, Ware, Warren, Young.—132.

NOES—Brockman, Crooke, Cureton, Chesnut, Cannon, Clinton, R. Ervin, J. P. Evans, Gause, Gill, Levy, Lowry, O'Neale, P. Phillips, Perry, Shannon, Sistrunk, Wilson, Wilkins.—19.

The following letter from Judge Richardson, was then read; to wit:

"March 18, 1833.

" GENTLEMEN:

" According to my individual understanding of the end and object of the high trust confided to me, by the People, who made me a Delegate to the State Convention of South Carolina, they have been virtually fulfilled, by the present adjustment of the Tariff, our proceedings thereupon, and the answer to the Virginia Commission. I beg leave, therefore, with deep regard for the confidence which has been reposed, to resign my seat.

With the highest consideration and

respect, your obedient servant,

J. S. RICHARDSON.

To the President and Members of the General Convention of the State of South Carolina."

This letter was ordered to lie on the table.

The Report accompanying the Ordinance just adopted, was read, and on motion of Mr. Edwin J. Scott, amended, by striking out from the sentence preceding the last, the words after the word " State." The Report as amended was then adopted by the Convention.

It was moved to take up the Resolutions introduced on Thursday last by Gen. Hamilton and R. Barnwell Smith, Esq., but the vote being taken, it was agreed not to consider them.

The Hon. J. L. Wilson, from the Engrossing Committee, reported the Ordinance nullifying the Force Bill, as engrossed. It was then ratified, in the presence of the Convention, by the signatures of the President and Clerk.

The Report and Ordinance, as adopted by the Convention, are as follows, to wit:

REPORT.

The Committee, to whom was referred the Act of the Congress of the United States, entitled " An Act further to provide for the collection of duties on imports," beg leave to

REPORT:

That they have, so far as time would allow, considered the Act with such attention as the importance of the matters contained in it would seem to require. At the present moment, when a question, which has long divided and perplexed the country, has been adjusted, on terms calculated to quiet agitation and restore harmony, it would have been matter of peculiar gratification, to be able to indulge, without restraint, the feelings which such adjustment was calculated to excite. But your Committee regret to say, that at the moment of returning peace, the most serious and alarming cause of dissatisfaction has been afforded by the Act under consideration. Your Committee do most solemnly believe that the principles sought to be established by the Act, are calculated, when carried into practice, to destroy our Constitutional frame of Government, to subvert the public liberty, and to bring about the utter ruin and debasement of the Southern States of this Confederacy.

The general purpose of the whole Act, though not expressed in the terms of it, is perfectly well known to have been to counteract and render inefficacious an Act of this State, adopted in her sovereign capacity, for the protection of her reserved rights. Believing, as we most fully do, that the power attempted to be exercised by the State, is among the reserved powers of the States, and that it may be exercised consistently with the Constitution of the United States, an opinion formed by the good people of this State, upon the fullest and most careful consideration, and expressed through their Delegates in Convention, your Committee must on that ground alone, have been convinced that the purpose of counteracting that Act, and the means by which it is sought to be counteracted, are unauthorized by the Constitution. We think that this will become more apparent by attending to the leading provisions of the Act of Congress.

The Act gives the President of the United States, for a limited time, an almost unlimited power of control over the commerce of the whole United States; though certainly the power was only contemplated to be exercised against that of South Carolina.

It exempts property in the hands of the officer of the Revenue, alleged to be detained for enforcing the payment of duties, from liability to the process of the State Courts.

It exempts a class of persons residing within the State—officers of the United States, and persons employed by them, or acting under their direction, or any other person, professing to act in execution of the Revenue Laws—from all responsibility to the State laws or State tribunals, for any crime or wrong, when it is alleged that the act was done in execution of the Revenue Laws or under color thereof.

It gives to the same class of persons, the right to seek redress for any alleged injury whatever, either to person or property, however foreign to the proper subjects of the jurisdiction, in the Courts of the United States ; provided the injury be received in consequence of any act done in execution of the Revenue Laws.

It directly supposes all the Courts of the State to be inferior and subordinate to those of the United States, and provides for rendering them so, by directing to them the writ of *certiorari* superseding their jurisdiction.

It affects to limit and control the jurisdiction of the Courts of the State ; providing for the removal of causes from their cognizance ; declaring their judgments void, and providing for the discharge of persons confined under their process.

It tyrannically provides for rendering persons liable to punishment for acts done by them in execution of the laws of the State and the process of its Courts, to which they are bound to yield obedience, and which they are compelled, under the highest sanctions, to enforce.

It not only provides for the punishment of persons thus acting, by the civil tribunals, but authorizes the employment of military force, under color of executing the laws of the United States, to resist the execution of the laws of the State ; superseding, with the quick execution of the sword, the slower process of Courts.

The Act authorizes the confinement of persons in unusual places—which can only mean on board ships—in which persons from the most remote parts of the State may be confined.

The Committee believe that all these positions are distinctly sustained by the Act in question. By the Constitution of the United States, the power to regulate commerce, is given to Congress. It is an important portion of the Legislative power, and, as Legislative power, is incapable of delegation. Congress has, however, in effect, delegated to the President the power to abolish, at his discretion, any port of the United States, or interrupt or destroy its commerce. This may easily be effected, under the authority to remove the Custom-house to any port or harbor within the Collection District, by fixing it at inconvenient or inaccessible places. To say nothing of the unusual and tremendous character of this power, which New York or Philadelphia might perhaps apprehend, if there were any expectation of its being exercised with respect to them, and the enormous abuse to which it is liable, does the Constitution contemplate or authorize, the delegation of this discretion to an individual ? If it were exercised, it would be a plain violation of that part of the Constitution which directs that, in regulations of commerce, no preference shall be given to the ports of one State over those of another. The same inequality is occasioned by directing the payment of Cash Duties. It is vain to say that this has been rendered necessary by the Act of the State, and without it, the collection of revenue would be impracticable. Whatever latitude may be allowed in the selection of means necessary and proper to carry into effect the granted powers of Congress, we believe no one has yet imagined, that a plain provision of the Constitution may be violated, as a means of carrying into effect a power granted by another provision. Although we may concede the power of Congress, for sufficient cause and in good faith, to abolish one port of entry and establish another, yet we, of course, cannot concede that it may delegate this power ; or, that the sovereign Act of the State, for the vindication of her reserved rights, constitutes sufficient cause, or that this act has been done in good faith.

The provisions of the Act, that all property in the hands of any officer or other person, detained under any Revenue Law, shall be subject only to the orders and decrees of the Courts of the United States, plainly enact, that it shall not be subject to any process, order or decree of the Courts of the State. We have heretofore been accustomed to regard our Superior Courts as having jurisdiction over all persons and all property within the limits of the State. This jurisdiction is, of course, superseded, whenever any other Court of concurrent jurisdiction has possession or custody of any cause or any property. But that a ministerial, executive officer, or that property in his hands, should be exempted from the jurisdiction and authority of State

Courts, we believe to be unprecedented in our legislation, and without any shadow of Constitutional authority.

One of the most extraordinary and exceptionable provisions of the Act, appears to be that authorizing the removal, previous to trial, of suits or prosecutions from the State Courts, upon affidavit made, and a certificate of the opinion of some counsellor or attorney to the same effect, that the suit or prosecution was for, or on account of any act done under the Revenue Laws of the United States, or under color thereof, or for, or on account of any right, authority or title, set up or claimed by any officer or other person, under any such law of the United States. If there be any violation of the law of the State—if there be a wrong done to person or property within the limits of the State—have not the Courts of the State jurisdiction of that matter? By what authority does the Congress of the United States limit that jurisdiction? What shadow of Constitutional provision is there to sanction this flagrant usurpation? True, such a violation of the law of the State may, sometimes, be justified, as being done in execution of a Constitutional law of the United States; but this is a matter of defence, to be tried as every other defence is to be tried, and can have no effect in ousting the jurisdiction, or in giving the Courts of the United States original jurisdiction of offences against the State laws. So any person is authorized to bring suit in the Courts of the United States, for any injury to person or property, for, or on account of, any act done in execution of the Revenue Laws. The Constitution gives to the Courts of the United States, jurisdiction of all cases in law and equity arising under the Constitution and laws of the United States. An assault on the person or trespass to property, is a violation of the laws of the State. Can it make a difference, that a violation of the State law was provoked by an act done under color of executing the law of the United States? The protection of persons and property has, heretofore, been supposed the province of the States. In assuming to itself this new function, the Federal Government indicates most clearly its tendency to engross all power, and control all State authority.

It is plain likewise from the various provisions of the Act, that such suits are intended to be allowed against persons acting in execution of the process of the State Courts. Judgments of those Courts are declared to be void, and persons and property exempted from their jurisdiction.

It is not only our law but part of the law of the civilized world, that the judgment of a Court of competent jurisdiction is valid, until it be reversed by a competent authority. The judgment of a Superior Court of general jurisdiction can never be void for want of jurisdiction. When there are Courts of concurrent jurisdiction, that which obtains possession of the cause is entitled to retain it; its process must be respected, and all other jurisdiction is excluded. It is true that the judgments of Courts of limited jurisdiction (and such are the Courts of the United States, and so they themselves have determined) are void, if the jurisdiction be transcended. This distinction would seem to determine whether sovereignty is to be attributed to the State or to the Federal authority. Hitherto, it has never occurred to any one to doubt that an officer, acting in execution of the process of a Court of general jurisdiction, and all persons acting under his direction, are exempted from all responsibility for that Act. He is bound under the highest sanction to execute that process; and shall he be punished for performing his duty?

If this Act were submitted to, the entire administration of the criminal justice of the State might be interrupted; and it is not too much to say, that the State Governments would be rendered impracticable. The worst criminal—one stained with the guilt of murder—upon making an affidavit, which no such criminal would hesitate to make, and procuring a certificate, which any criminal might easily procure, would be able to elude the criminal justice of the State. His cause must be removed to the Federal Court; and when, upon his trial, it shall appear that his act was not done in execution of the law of the United States, your Committee do not perceive what other consequence can follow, than that he must be acquitted and go with impunity.

Having taken this view of the provisions of the Act in question, the Committee would submit to the solemn consideration and determination of this Convention, whether they do not effect an entire change in the character of our Constitution, and will not, when carried into practice, abolish every vestige of liberty, and render this an absolute Consolidated Government, without limitation of powers. It has been truly said, that if these things may be done, the most solemn acts of the highest authorities of the State may be regarded as the unauthorized proceedings of individuals ; the Courts of justice may be shut up ; the Legislature dispersed, as a lawless mob ; and we, ourselves, representing, as we vainly believe, the sovereignty of the State, called to answer for what we have said and done on this floor, at the bar of a Circuit Court of the United States. Is this an exaggerated picture ? Let us examine it a little more closely. If these provisions may be made to enforce the execution of the Revenue Laws of the United States, they may be made to enforce any other Act which Congress shall think proper to pass. No matter how oppressive, how clearly unconstitutional, there is no power in the constituted authorities of the State to resist it. If one class of cases may be removed from the jurisdiction of the State Courts, any other class, subject only to the discretion of Congress, may be likewise removed. If the process of the Courts be void, and the officer executing it, and those acting under his direction, responsible civilly, or punishable criminally, the Judge who directed the process must be answerable in like manner. He was equally without authority, and having commanded the act, is a partaker of the guilt. The Legislature who commanded the act of the Judge, and the Convention of the people in obedience to whose mandate every thing was done, must have the same participation. If the sheriff, and his posse, obstructing the execution of the Revenue laws, may constitute that unlawful combination and assemblage, on being notified of which, the President is authorized to use the military force of the United States to disperse them, then the Courts, the Legislature, or the Convention, in obedience to whose authority alone the Sheriff acts, and who are the efficient causes of the obstruction, are assemblages of similar character, and may be dispersed by military force. The whole purpose of the act is to confound the acts of the constituted authorities of the State, however solemn and well considered, with the lawless and irregular acts of individuals or mobs. The certain effect of it must be, to restrain the States from the exercise of any other authority than such as Congress, or the sectional majority represented in Congress, shall think fit to permit them to exercise ; and to ensure the enforcement of every law which that majority may think proper to enact. It involves the cruelty and absurdity of making the community responsible to hostile force for its acts as a community, and the individuals of the community, punishable for their acts in obedience to the laws of their Government; an obedience from which they 'cannot exempt themselves, unless they absolve themselves from their allegiance, by self-banishment.

That the object of many of the politicians who supported this bill—the politicians of that majority in whose hands all power will be—is to establish a Consolidated Government, is now hardly at all disguised. The chimera of a Government partly consolidated, partly federative, is now scarcely contended for. The same class of politicians have always had in view the same object. It was attempted to be effected in the Convention which framed the Constitution of the United States. The attempt was there foiled. After the formation of the Government, those who affected Consolidation, assumed the term of " Federal," and denied that the opinions held by them, led to that result. The possession of power, however, developed their views, and the first marked indication of their disposition to engross the powers of the States, and meddle with their internal concerns, was afforded by the alien and sedition laws. This attempt was so strongly rebuked by public opinion, which led to the change of administration in 1800, that the hopes of consolidation seemed abandoned forever. They remained dormant, until revived by the agitations springing out of our late protecting system. It was perceived that nothing less strong than a consolidated Government could sustain that system of iniquity. Gradually, we have been told, that the States have parted with a portion of their sovereignty; then, that they were never sovereign; until at length, availing themselves of the excitement of a particular crisis, and passion for power, and the influence of an individual, the act before us has been passed, sweeping away every vestige of State Sovereignty and Reserved Rights, or causing them to be held at the mercy of the majority; compared to which, the alien and sedition laws sink into measures harmless and insignificant.

And what is it to the Southern States, to be subjected to a consolidated Government? These States constitute a minority, and are likely to do so forever. They differ in institutions and modes of industry, from the States of the majority, and have different, and in some degree, incompatible interests. It is to be governed, not with reference to their own interests or according to their own habits and feelings, but with reference to the interests, and according to the prejudices of their rulers, the majority. It has been truly said that the protecting system constitutes but a small part of our controversy with the Federal Government. Unless we can obtain the recognition of some effectual Constitutional check on the usurpation of power, which can only be derived from the sovereignty of the States, and their right to interpose for the preservation of their reserved powers, we shall experience oppression more cruel and revolting than this.

While there remains within the States any spirit of liberty, prompting them to repel Federal usurpations, one of the most obvious means to break that spirit and reduce the States to subjection, will be that which has been attempted by the act before us. It will be to create or to sustain, by the patronage of Government or other means, a party within the State devoted to Federal power, exempted from responsibility to the State authorities, and having power to harass and degrade the State authorities, by means of the tribunals of the United States. Thus will be created a Government within a Government, with all the consequences, which experience informs us, are likely to arise from that state of things, and such as did arise from the independent ecclesiastical jurisdictions within the Governments of Europe. The Federal Government will interfere with every department of the State Governments; it will influence elections; it will raise up and put down parties, as they shall be more servile to its will. Pretexts for interference will never be wanting. Already has it been said, that ours is no longer a Republican Government, because the State, in vindicating its sovereignty, has refused to entrust with any portion of its authority, those who deny or refuse to recognize that sovereignty. Other classes of individuals might be found, within the State, whom it might suit the majority to suppose disfranchised, in derogation of true republican principles, and to require their interference and protection. This interference will be practiced at first with moderation, and with some apparent respect for the rights of the States. Gradually, as the power of the Government shall be established, and the Southern States become weakened and less capable of resistance, the shew of moderation will be thrown off. Thus the peace of those States will be embroiled ; their prosperity interrupted, their character degraded ; until in the natural progress of things, your Committee think it not too strong to say, that they will be more miserable, more utterly enslaved, more thoroughly debased, than any provinces that have ever been rendered subject by the sword.

In alluding to the oath, which the State has heretofore thought proper to exact of its citizens, and to one somewhat similar, which the Committee propose to recommend, they think proper to disclaim, as they do most solemnly disclaim, on behalf of themselves and the Convention, that this or any other measure which the Convention has adopted, has been adopted upon mere party views, to secure party ascendancy, or gratify party resentment. They appeal to God, that their only object has been to vindicate their just rights and liberties, and the common liberties of the whole South. This object they have pursued in singleness of purpose ; though exposed to much obloquy—threatened with much danger, and discountenanced by those from whom they had a right to expect support. They have never sought to endanger this Union ; but to perpetuate it by rendering it compatible with, and a security for liberty.

The firmness of the State seems, at length, in some degree, to have triumphed. But let it be recollected that the moment of triumph is commonly one of danger. Let it be kept in mind, that this is not a contest ended, but a contest not more than begun, and not to be determined, till this act shall cease to disgrace the statute book. Let this contest be carried on firmly, steadily, without passion and without faultering. If the vigilance of the State should relax ; if it should cease to raise up barriers against the head of usurpation, which threatens to overwhelm us, the torrent will break loose, and sweep our liberties along with it. Let every man consider this his own peculiar business. If liberty be saved, every thing is saved : If liberty be lost, every thing is lost.

As the provisions of the act have reference only to certain acts of the people and Legislature of this State, which have been superseded by the late modification of the Tariff, it could not have been contemplated that it should have any immediate operation. And your Committee doubted whether, regarding it as merely a menace, they should recommend any action upon it, or only that the sentiments of the Convention should be expressed, in regard to the principles it contains. But most of its provisions are made permanent, and may be put in practice on some future occasion. The Committee cannot doubt that it expresses the true principles of many of those who voted for it, and who will seek occasion to reduce them to practice. As a precedent, it is most dangerous. The vote on the very act, shows how little is to be expected from a majority. It is incumbent on South Carolina, unsupported as she is, to take care that no federal authority, unauthorized by our federal compact, shall be exercised within the limits of the State. For the purpose of providing that the act shall never have operation or effect, within the limits of the State, the Committee beg leave to report the following Ordinance.

AN ORDINANCE,

To Nullify an Act of the Congress of the United States, entitled " An Act further to provide for the Collection of Duties on Imports," commonly called the Force Bill.

We, the People of the State of South Carolina, in Convention assembled, do Declare and Ordain, That the Act of the Congress of the United States, entitled " An Act further to provide for the collection of duties on imports," approved the 2d day of March, 1833, is unauthorized by the Constitution of the United States, subversive of that Constitution, and destructive of public liberty ; and that the same is, and shall be deemed null and void, within the limits of this State ; and it shall be the duty of the Legislature, at such time as they may deem expedient, to adopt such measures and pass such acts as may be necessary to prevent the enforcement thereof, and to inflict proper penalties on any person who shall do any act in execution or enforcement of the same within the limits of this State.

We do further Ordain and Declare, That the allegiance of the citizens of this State, while they continue such. is due to the said State : and that obedience only, and not allegiance, is due by them to any other power or authority, to whom a control over them has been, or may be delegated by the State; and the General Assembly of the said State is hereby empowered from time to time, when they may deem it proper, to provide for the administration to the citizens and officers of the State, or such of the said officers as they may think fit, of suitable oaths or affirmations, binding them to the observance of such allegiance, and abjuring all other allegiance; and, also, to define what shall amount to a violation of their allegiance, and to provide the proper punishment for such violation.

Done in Convention, at Columbia, the eighteenth day of March, in the year of our Lord, one thousand eight hundred and thirty-three, and in the fifty-seventh year of the Sovereignty and Independence of the United States of America.

ROBERT Y. HAYNE, Del-
egate from the Parishes of *President of the Convention.*
St. Philip and St. Michael,

ISAAC W. HAYNE, *Clerk.*

Gen. Hamilton then introduced the following Resolutions, which were adopted, to wit:

" *Resolved,* That the Clerk do order to be printed, by the printer of this Convention, to be appended to the copies now on hand of the proceedings of the former session of the Convention, five hundred copies of the Journal, Ordinances, and Reports of the present session; a copy of each to be distributed to each Member of the Convention and Legislature—also, separately, three thousand copies of the Ordinances and Reports of the present session, to be distributed to the people of this State; and it be made the duty of the Clerk to attend to the distribution of the same."

" *Resolved,* That the President of this Convention do transmit to the President of the United States, and to the Governors of the several States, copies of the Reports and Ordinances of this Convention, adopted at its present session."

It was now moved by Gen. Hamilton, that the Convention should resolve itself into a Committee of the whole; which being agreed to, Mr. Turnbull was called to the chair. Col. Samuel Warren then introduced the following Resolution, which was adopted unanimously, and ordered to be so entered on the Journal, to wit:

" *Resolved, unanimously,* That the thanks of this Covention be presented to his Excellency, Robert Y. Hayne, for the dignity, ability, and impartiality, with which he has presided over its deliberations."

The Committee rose and Reported to the Convention. On motion of Mr. Turnbull, it was

" *Resolved,* That the Convention do now adjourn, *sine die,* and that it be dissolved."

After a prayer from the Rev. Mr. Ray, the President pronounced the Convention dissolved.

RESOLVES

OF THE

LEGISLATURE

OF

ILLINOIS.

RESOLVES.

WHEREAS, the President of the United States, in his proclamation of the 10th instant, has exhibited a just view of the origin of our free constitution, and of the powers confided by that sacred instrument to the States and the General Government; and whereas, by the said proclamation, the assumed power of a State to annul a law of Congress is conclusively shown to be "incompatible with the existence of the Union, contradicted expressly by the letter of the constitution, unauthorized by its spirit, inconsistent with every principle on which it was founded, and destructive of the great object for which it was formed;" and whereas, the particular application of this assumed power to the alleged grievances of South Carolina is most ably and unanswerably refuted, and the dangerous and treasonable doctrine of the right of secession, combated by the clearest reasoning, is denounced in a spirit of devoted attachment to the Union; and whereas, also, the Executive has expressed a confident reliance on the undivided support of the nation, in his "determination to execute the laws, to preserve the Union by all constitutional means, and to arrest, if possible, by moderate but firm measures, the necessity of a recourse to force:" therefore

Resolved by the people of the State of Illinois, represented in the General Assembly, That we highly approve the sentiments contained in the said proclamation, and the avowed purpose of repelling the unconstitutional and dangerous designs announced in the "disorganizing edict" of the South Carolina Convention.

Resolved, That, whilst we admire the firmness that would resist " the mad project of disunion," we cordially approve the spirit of moderation which deprecates " any offensive act on the part of the United States."

Resolved, That " disunion by armed force is treason," and should be treated as such by the constituted authorities of the nation.

Resolved, That, whilst we deplore the spirit of disaffection manifested by our South Carolina brethren, and should hail with unmingled satisfaction their return to the first great principles of our Union, we hold it to be the duty of every citizen of the United States, without distinction of sect or party, to rally to the support of the great charter of American freedom.

Resolved, That, should the pacific invitation and solemn warning of our illustrious President fail to recall the disaffected to their duty—should the anti-republican doctrine of nullification be persisted in, and treason rear its polluted form within the bosom of our prosperous, patriotic, and peaceful Republic, we do hereby instruct our Senators in Congress, and request our Representative, to unite in the most speedy and vigorous measures on the part of the General Government for the preservation of the peace, integrity, and honor of the Union. And we do hereby solemnly pledge the faith of our State in support of the administration of the laws and constitution of our beloved country.

Resolved, That a copy of the foregoing resolutions be transmitted to the President of the United States, to the heads of the several departments at Washington, and to our Senators and Representative in Congress.

I certify the foregoing preamble and resolutions were unanimously adopted by the House of Representatives.

DAVID PRICKETT,
Clerk of the House of Representatives.

ALEXANDER M. JENKINS,
Speaker of the House of Representatives.

I certify the foregoing preamble and resolutions were unanimously adopted by the Senate.

JESSE B. THOMAS, Jr.
Secretary of the Senate.

ZADOC CASEY,
Speaker of the Senate.